Peter Reading
December 1972
95p
C3

CASEBOOK SERIES

Shakespeare: *Measure for Measure*

D0413053

Casebook Series

GENERAL EDITOR: A. E. Dyson

Shakespeare

Measure for Measure

A CASEBOOK

EDITED BY

C. K. STEAD

MACMILLAN

Selection and editorial matter © C. K. Stead 1971

All rights reserved. No part of this publication
may be reproduced or transmitted, in any form or
by any means, without permission.

First published 1971 by
THE MACMILLAN PRESS LTD
London and Basingstoke
Associated companies in Toronto
Dublin Melbourne Johannesburg and Madras

SBN 333 07160 3 (hard cover)

Printed in Great Britain by
RICHARD CLAY (THE CHAUCER PRESS), LTD
Bungay, Suffolk

The Papermac edition of this book is sold subject to the condition
that it shall not, by way of trade or otherwise, be lent, re-sold,
hired out, or otherwise circulated without the publisher's prior
consent in any form of binding or cover other than that in which
it is published and without a similar condition including this
condition being imposed on the subsequent purchaser.

CONTENTS

ACKNOWLEDGEMENTS

Richard David, 'Measure for Measure on the Modern Stage', from 'Shakespeare's Comedies and the Modern Stage', in Shakespeare Survey, IV (1951) (Cambridge University Press); Harold Hobson, 'Recent Productions of Measure for Measure', Introduction to the Folio Society Measure for Measure (Folio Society Ltd); W. W. Robson, 'All Difficulties are but Easy...?' [here entitled 'Shakespeare and his Modern Editors'], from The Cambridge Quarterly, 1 i (1965–6) (The Cambridge Quarterly and Mr W. W. Robson); G. Wilson Knight, 'Measure for Measure and the Gospels', from The Wheel of Fire (Methuen & Co. Ltd); W. W. Lawrence, extracts from 'Measure for Measure' [here entitled 'Real Life and Artifice'], from Shakespeare's Problem Comedies (the Publishers have been unable to trace the copyright-holder for this item, but will be pleased to make the necessary arrangements at the first opportunity); L. C. Knights, 'The Ambiguity of Measure for Measure', from Scrutiny, x (1942) (Cambridge University Press); Clifford Leech, 'The "Meaning" of Measure for Measure', from Shakespeare Survey, III (1950) (Cambridge University Press); E. M. W. Tillyard, 'Measure for Measure' [here entitled 'Realism and Folk-lore'] from Shakespear's Problem Plays (Chatto & Windus Ltd, Mrs Veronica Sankaran and The University of Toronto Press); William Empson, 'Sense in Measure for Measure', from The Structure of Complex Words (Chatto & Windus Ltd and New Directions, New York); David L. Stevenson, extract from 'Design and Structure in Measure for Measure: A New Appraisal', from English Literary History, XXIII iv (1956) (© Johns Hopkins Press); Ernest Schanzer, 'Justice and King James in Measure for Measure', from 'Measure for Measure', in The

Problem Plays of Shakespeare (Routledge & Kegan Paul Ltd and Schocken Books).

The editor records with gratitude the helpful comments and advice he has received, in preparing this volume, from his colleagues Sydney Musgrove and MacDonald P. Jackson.

GENERAL EDITOR'S PREFACE

Each of this series of Casebooks concerns either one well-known and influential work of literature or two or three closely linked works. The main section consists of critical readings, mostly modern, brought together from journals and books. A selection of reviews and comments by the author's contemporaries is also included, and sometimes comments from the author himself. The Editor's Introduction charts the reputation of the work from its first appearance until the present time.

The critical forum is a place of vigorous conflict and disagreement, but there is nothing in this to cause dismay. What is attested is the complexity of human experience and the richness of literature, not any chaos or relativity of taste. A critic is better seen, no doubt, as an explorer than as an 'authority', but explorers ought to be, and usually are, well equipped. The effect of good criticism is to convince us of what C. S. Lewis called 'the enormous extension of our being which we owe to authors'. A Casebook will be justified only if it helps to promote the same end.

A single volume can represent no more than a small selection of critical opinions. Some critics have been excluded for reasons of space, and it is hoped that readers will follow up the further suggestions in the Select Bibliography. Other contributions have been severed from their original context, to which some readers may wish to return. Indeed, if they take a hint from the critics represented here, they certainly will.

A. E. DYSON

INTRODUCTION

The Accounts Book of the Revels Office records that a play called *Meſur for Meſur* by one 'Shaxberd' was performed on St Stephen's night 1604 by His Majesty's Players at Whitehall. It seems King James attended. The play's story, a traditional one deriving in part from real life, had come to Shakespeare from at least two earlier writers: George Whetstone, and the Italian Geraldi Cinthio. Cinthio had told the story first in his collection *Hecatommithi* (1565) and had later made a play of it, *Epitia* (published 1583). Whetstone had first used it as the plot of his two-part play *Promos and Cassandra* (1578) and had retold it as fiction in his *Heptameron of Civil Discourses* (1582). Though earlier forms of the story tell of a husband condemned to death and of a wife suing for his pardon, Cinthio's, Whestone's and Shakespeare's versions have in common that the man condemned is the brother of the girl who pleads for his life. In each case it is the deputy of the ruler of the state who corruptly offers to spare the condemned man if the sister will yield to him. But in Shakespeare's version alone the sister refuses, the real ruler (who has only pretended to absent himself) proposing the substitution of another woman in the deputy's bed, and, in his disguise as a friar, steering events towards a happy conclusion. It is clear that Shakespeare was reshaping the second-hand material to suit a pattern and purpose of his own.

It is widely supposed that Shakespeare introduced elements into the play that might be of special interest to King James. And since we know how well the play can be made to work on the stage we may assume that the King enjoyed his entertainment on the night after Christmas, 1604. The play has been performed many times since, and though it has gone out of fashion for periods it has never been considered a failure on the

stage. But if playgoers have enjoyed it, many critics
have not; or at least the critics have not been able to
agree about its merits. J. M. Nosworthy, editor of the
New Penguin edition of the play, describes it as 'Probably the most complex and even the most contradictory of Shakespeare's works'; and he adds, 'there exists
no single agreed formulation of what the play actually
does or how well it does it'.

The critical argument about *Measure for Measure*,
then, is a particularly vigorous and complicated one;
and a part of the purpose of this introduction will be
to sketch its historical outlines so that each point of
view represented in this book will more clearly be seen
in relation to the whole debate. But such a presentation must itself be governed in some degree by a point
of view. No editor with a mind of his own can be expected to enter that arena of conflict and return without having formulated to his own satisfaction opinions
about what has taken place there. Such is the present
editor's case. By entering the arena he becomes, un-
avoidably, a participant. His purpose is not, of course,
to usurp the place of the critics, of all shades of
opinion, he has brought together. But if there is to be
an introduction at all (and readers may choose to
ignore it) he must be allowed his own preferences and
discriminations.

Dryden, Johnson and Coleridge are three formidable
names in the history of English criticism, and from the
three together we can derive scarcely a good word for
Measure for Measure. In his essay 'Dramatic Poetry of
the Last Age' Dryden dismisses it (along with several
other Shakespearean plays) as 'grounded on impossi-
bilities, or at least so meanly written, that the comedy
neither caused your mirth, nor the serious part your
concernment'. Dr Johnson says 'the light or comick
part is very natural and pleasing, but the grave scenes,
if a few passages be excepted, have more labour than
elegance'. He complains because Angelo goes unpunished and believes 'every reader feels some indignation'

at this. Indignation was certainly Coleridge's response.
He found the play 'the only painful part' of Shakespeare's works. The comedy is 'disgusting', the tragic
parts 'horrible', and the pardon and marriage of
Angelo 'baffles the strong indignant claim of Justice'.

The nineteenth century is the first in which we find
a large number of critics writing about the play. Their
opinions about its merits differ widely, but they have
in common certain assumptions and responses which
reflect a society in some ways more remote from the
society that produced *Measure for Measure* than is our
own. In the first place, though an Elizabethan and a
Victorian might well be able to agree on what constituted immorality, there was a great difference in their
tolerance to the representation of it in works of literature; so that the frankness, and what might very nearly
be called the *neutrality*, of Shakespeare's representation of it in *Measure for Measure*, constituted a problem for the nineteenth century as it scarcely does for
the mid-twentieth. Further, the critic of the last century lived in the great age of the novel. He approached
plays as books to be read, thinking always in terms of
character rather than in terms of poetic or dramatic
design. These facts must be kept in mind when we are
considering the criticism of *Measure for Measure* that
belongs to what will be called here 'the nineteenth-
century tradition' (though included under that head-
ing will be critics like Walter Raleigh, E. K. Chambers
and Arthur Quiller-Couch, whose writings on the subject appeared in the early years of the twentieth).

For the critic in this tradition there was no problem
about Angelo until his escape in the final act. Everyone
disliked him, but that was as it should be since he was,
after all, the villain. The problems arose, rather, with
Isabella and the Duke, characters who, it was felt,
were meant to be admirable but who were not – or
whose behaviour was in some degree 'irregular'.

Almost every critic in this tradition complains about
the Duke. Schlegel, Hazlitt, Swinburne (by implication), Mrs Jameson, E. K. Chambers and Quiller-Couch

– all find his concealment, his secrecy, his deliberate
and unnecessary complication of affairs, unpalatable
and morally contradictory. And the feeling was increased by a distaste for the Duke's most important
piece of trickery (for which Shakespeare and not the
sources was inexplicably responsible): his substitution
of Mariana for Isabella in Angelo's bed.

On the subject of Isabella's character opinion was
more divided. There were, inevitably, a number of
critical Angelos who simply fell in love with her virginity. Schlegel described her as 'an angel of light'.
Dowden wrote of her 'pure zeal', her 'rectitude of will',
her 'virgin sanctity', 'saintliness' and 'holiness'. Mrs
Jameson wrote of 'moral grandeur', 'saintly grace' and
'vestal dignity and purity'.

On the other hand there were those who found
Isabella's unwillingness to exchange her virginity for
her brother's life difficult to accept. Coleridge found
her 'unamiable'. Hazlitt (to Mrs Jameson's great distress) was not 'greatly enamoured of Isabella's rigid
chastity'. Quiller-Couch found something 'rancid' in it.
Walter Raleigh and E. K. Chambers were at least cool
to the idea that she represented a moral ideal.

Of the critics in this tradition Schlegel, Pater and
Raleigh were alone in not finding the play in some
degree 'painful' or 'unpleasant', a fact to be explained,
perhaps, by their ability to accept the low life as the
play presents it and not draw back from it in horror.
And perhaps as a consequence of this, all three found a
quality that no one before them had remarked upon.
Schlegel was the first to emphasise the theme of forgiveness which has been stressed in this century by G.
Wilson Knight. 'The true significance of the whole,'
Schlegel says, 'is the triumph of mercy over strict justice.' Raleigh follows him, approving because the play
'condemns no one, high or low', and finding Shakespeare's 'greatness' in this 'wonderful sympathy'.

Pater's conclusions are similar. He is the most
modern of these critics, approaching the play not in
terms of character but as a total design. His interest is

poetic form. But by means of that aesthetic interest is discovered, paradoxically, what might be called a higher, or broader, ethic. The very tolerance of the poetic imagination, its openness to all forms of life, becomes in effect an ethic of charity; and where so many critics had found *Measure for Measure* contradictory or painful, Pater believed he saw in it 'an epitome of Shakespeare's moral judgements'.

Much of the modern debate about the play must be seen as a succession of attempts to resolve the problems raised by critics of the preceding century; and these resolutions focus especially upon the character of the Duke – inevitably, since he controls the action and yet remains, despite his great authority, shadowy as a character.

Two of the most significant modern studies of the play appeared within a year of one another – G. Wilson Knight's in 1930, W. W. Lawrence's in 1931. Each might be said to have answered the nineteenth-century critics' objections to the character of the Duke, but in opposite and apparently contradictory ways.

W. W. Lawrence's answer to the problem of the Duke's behaviour was to say that it belongs to stage convention and must be accepted as such. Duke Vincentio is a *stage* Duke, unashamedly manipulated and manipulating to bring about the comic resolution. It is no use complaining that his actions are implausible, morally contradictory or unnecessarily complicated. The complications might be unnecessary in terms of real life; but *Measure for Measure* is not real life – it is a play. Without the Duke's actions there could be no resolution; and since his actions are all directed to that end, his inconsistencies have a special licence. This description of the Duke's function was to receive general support some years later from E. E. Stoll in his book *From Shakespeare to Joyce*.

G. Wilson Knight's approach, on the other hand, was to ignore the contradictions and arbitrariness of the Duke's behaviour, and by ignoring them to imply

either that they did not exist or at least that they were
of no consequence. The play, Wilson Knight argued, is
a parable which has to be seen in terms of the Gospels.
The Duke, the central figure, is the prophet of an
'enlightened ethic' – that of universal forgiveness and
mercy. He assumes 'proportions evidently Divine'. He is
'compared to the Supreme Power'. His 'ethical attitude' is 'exactly correspondent' with that of Jesus.

Lawrence had swept away those nineteenth-century
objections to the play by conventionalising the Duke;
Wilson Knight dismissed them by theologising him.
But were the two arguments as contradictory as they
seemed? Can the Duke not be Divine Providence *and* a
'stage Duke'?

Undoubtedly in general terms he can be both. These
critics were both saying in effect that the play gives the
Duke a special dispensation by which he is permitted
to act however he pleases, on the understanding that
whatever he does will be for the best, and that however
he may complicate matters, the end will be fortunate.
The convention of comedy requires this kind of certainty. It is a world in which the one safe assumption
must be that, however dark the passages, at the end
there will be light, happiness and marriage. And if one
figure in a comedy – a Duke Vincentio, or a Prospero –
should manipulate events towards the expected happy
conclusion, that figure will have about him an air of
special power.

Lawrence had argued that the Duke is 'a stage
Duke'; and E. E. Stoll agreed. 'Unreasonable, implausible, sensational and stagey,' Stoll called him. But Stoll
did not omit to mention that he is also 'a power'. He is
a power precisely because of this special licence the
convention allows him to do as he pleases and yet remain, by definition, a force for good.

In general terms, then, Wilson Knight's and Lawrence's views need not conflict. But at this point the
particular emphasis we give to the Duke's guiding role
becomes all-important. Wilson Knight's argument requires not only that we see the Duke as a power but

that we see him as the embodiment of an 'ethical attitude'. It is here that problems arise; for surely, seeing
the Duke in this way we must be allowed to inspect his
actions closely; and inspecting them closely we will
find ourselves confronted precisely by all those questions which troubled the critics of the preceding century. Why does this prophet of mercy tell Juliet that
her contracted husband, the father of the child in her
womb, is to die 'tomorrow', when in fact he has no
intention of allowing the execution to occur? Why
does he load more pain on the already suffering Isabella by letting her believe Claudio has been executed? Why does he sententiously urge Juliet to repent
of her 'mutual entertainment' with Claudio, and then
urge Mariana into Angelo's bed (assuring her it is 'no
sin') – when the contract of *neither* pair has been
blessed by the church? Why does he labour to convince
the suffering Claudio that there is no escape from
death? Why does he manipulate events to bring about
the marriage of the virtuous Mariana to a man who has
attempted (in effect) both rape and murder?

Accepting Lawrence's view we can give to every one
of these questions, and to others like them, one of two
general answers: either 'convention' or 'dramatic
necessity'. But if, as Wilson Knight requires, we are to
look to the Duke, as to Jesus, for a consistent ethic; if
the play is a parable and hangs upon his actions; then
these questions inevitably arise to challenge us. And
though we may think of plausible answers to this or
that among them, our answers will never be plausible
in unison; they will jangle together like notes out of
tune, contradicting one another.

Yet Wilson Knight was not alone in his view of the
play. He was supported ten years later by F. R. Leavis,
whose article was written specifically to contradict a
critic (L. C. Knights) who had approached the play in
the same spirit as Wilson Knight, looking for its ethical design, and who had concluded that it was 'ambiguous'.

* Permission to reprint it in this volume was refused.

The play, Leavis insisted, was not ambiguous, and Wilson Knight had written 'the only adequate account' of it. The Duke is 'a kind of Providence directing the action from above'. 'His attitude ... *is* meant to be ours – his total attitude, which is the total attitude of the play.' The moral of the play is that guilt is universal and hence that mercy must have primacy over strict justice.

It is unlikely any critic would deny that this very proper weighing of mercy over justice is one – and one of the most important – of the many and various ethical propositions thrown up in the course of the action. Indeed it could hardly have been otherwise, since the proposition is inherent in the story Shakespeare had chosen to tell. But that the play is designed to promote this moral truism is much more difficult to accept. Once again it is an argument that directs us to look for ethical rather than artistic consistency, and consequently leaves us with a host of unanswered questions. Was Angelo, for example, right or wrong to attempt to stamp out 'the trade'? If he was wrong, was he wrong only because he was not himself pure, or would it have been wrong under any circumstances? Should the prostitutes and panders have been tolerated and merely subjected to moral harangues of the kind the Duke, disguised as a friar, delivers upon them? Are those harangues seriously meant, or are they only an aspect of the disguise? Was the Duke right in his original intention to clean up the city? Or was this not his intention at all, but only a concealment of his real objective, to catch out the 'seemer' Angelo? If Claudio has 'committed a serious offence' (as Leavis insists) how should it have been dealt with? And what of Angelo? He attempts rape and murder, yet he gets off with rather less suffering than has been imposed on Claudio. Does the 'new ethic' of which the Duke is supposed to be prophet imply that theological forgiveness must overrule even the practical application of the law? Must we see ethical considerations, and not the convention of the comic romance ending, governing even the pardon and marriage of Angelo?

It is noticeable that to sustain his view Leavis is forced to blur the distinctions between degrees of guilt. Early in his essay he argues that Claudio's offence is 'serious'. In the last few pages he insists 'the point of the play depends upon Angelo's not being a certified criminal-type, capable of wickedness that marks him off from you and me'. *Leavis's* point certainly depends upon it; but whether Leavis's point is the point of the play is something we must each be permitted to determine for ourselves.

'If we don't see ourselves in Angelo,' Leavis continues, 'we have taken the play very imperfectly.' This forceful assertion (and the closer one looks at it the more it will assume the aspect of a steamroller) must be carefully considered. Just previously in his essay Leavis has quoted for the second time Isabella's lines from Act II scene ii:

> Go to your bosom,
> Knock there and ask your heart what it doth know
> That's like my brother's fault. If it confess
> A natural guiltiness such as his is
> Let it not sound a thought upon your tongue
> Against my brother's life.

— and earlier Leavis has said this is 'the moral' of the play. It has, he says, 'a wider application than that which is immediately intended by the speaker'. It refers not merely to Claudio's sin (we can easily identify with *that*) but to all sin — even Angelo's.

But is Angelo's 'a *natural* guiltiness'? His desiring Isabella, of course, is entirely natural. But since he cannot accept it as natural his discovery of it destroys his conception of himself as a saint, and drives him to extremes of viciousness. It will be as well to remind ourselves of what he does. First, he presents a virgin novice with the alternative of defilement or the death of her brother. He points out that his reputation for virtue will protect him if she attempts to denounce him. He further threatens to have the brother tortured to death. Finally, when he believes he has had his way with the virgin, he still orders the execution of the brother. Such actions are entirely credible in the character as he is presented (and Angelo is the most penetrating and original of Shakespeare's character-creations in this play); but there is no point in pretending they are commonplace.

What does it mean, then, to say we must 'see ourselves in Angelo'? We can pity him, certainly. We can recognise that no man is blameless, and that we have, in so far as this is true, some general ground in common with him. But we do not all err as Angelo errs. The quality and the degree of his guilt, springing from a nature uncommonly warped, is what defines him as a character. Not all men – or more correctly, *few* men – put in Angelo's position would act as he acts; because most would accept the inclination which Angelo is shocked to discover in himself. It never occurs to Angelo that he might simply woo Isabella. He must rape her, because his puritanism defines that perfectly natural inclination as mortal sin. He has already condemned a man to death for acting on it. Now he condemns himself to the role of devil incarnate.

In short, the closer one looks at Leavis's insistence that we must 'see ourselves in Angelo', the more it is likely to seem a piety which evades rather than meets the problem of defining how, and in what degree, we identify with a 'bad' character on the stage. And in terms of the psychology of a theatre audience (which was Shakespeare's professional concern) it is nearer the truth to say we 'see ourselves' in Claudio and Isabella – in the victims of Angelo's tyranny; and that our wish – the wish that carries our interest forward through the story – is to see this tyranny removed. That is way the Duke must be permitted to impose suffering on characters whom the terms of the drama define as innocent: because by this means the conclusion is made to be more eagerly anticipated, and more enjoyable when it arrives. An old-fashioned shorthand would call Angelo the villain, and it is not an unserviceable shorthand. Indeed, if one objects to the heavy moral emphasis given to the play by critics like Leavis and Wilson Knight it is likely to be because such an emphasis, however worthy its moral propositions, subverts that unquestioning acceptance of, and response to, the 'story', on which a large part of the play's effect in the theatre depends. And it is to this kind of response that Lawrence's approach, on the other hand, gives the necessary recognition.

The primacy of mercy over strict justice is asserted, then, at various points in the play. It is an ethical formulation acceptable to us and (we may suppose) to Shakespeare. But that *Measure for Measure* was written to illustrate this (or any other) moral truism is a narrowing view against which we may find the play itself rising in protest. If such were the purpose of the play, and if we were to take Shakespeare's collected works as our gospel, we might reasonably ask why Angelo is permitted to live while Othello must die; or why Angelo is forgiven and Macbeth condemned. The answers to such questions must relate, not to ethics at all but to the conventions in which these characters have their being. Angelo survives because he exists in a comic world; Macbeth and Othello die because they belong to the world of tragedy.

And yet it is at precisely this point that Wilson Knight and his followers may seem to have their strongest point; for they have something better than mere convention to appeal to in order to explain why Angelo is spared. He is spared because this is the practical application of what they see as the play's ethic of forgiveness and mercy. What, on the other hand, has Lawrence to say on this point? Only that 'the claims of strict justice are secondary to those of stage entertainment'; and when the reason is formulated in these terms – in terms of 'entertainment' – our feelings that the whole business is more serious than *that* are likely to be aroused. Has not Lawrence given the play away to those earlier moralists – Johnson, Coleridge, Swinburne and others – who complained precisely that our sense of justice is *flouted* by the play's conclusion? Certainly in some degree he has, except that he says Angelo's pardon is not difficult to accept if you can accept the convention. Is it, then, *mere* convention? A question which has lain in wait for us must now be faced: If we are not to take the play in the terms proposed for us by Leavis and Wilson Knight, can we take it *seriously*, or must it be diminished to the stature of those works whose sole ambition is to divert us? This is perhaps a question which lies at the heart of all Shakespeare criticism. And if the moralist tradition has predominated in our century, it may be less because its findings are entirely plausible than because to reject them seems to diminish the importance and the weight we all feel inclined to ascribe to Shakespeare's plays. For a moment, then, we must be permitted to strike out into broader territory.

Both comedy and tragedy are conventional worlds. They differ from the real world in that each is predictable. Othello, it has been suggested, must die, Angelo must live, because they are given their existences within, respectively, the tragic and the comic mode. Neither comedy nor tragedy pretends to be life quite as we know it. Rather, they act out two basic human intuitions, or two kinds of 'knowledge'. Tragedy enacts the certainty of death, and tends to associate it with the knowledge of our sinful condition. Comedy enacts that stalwart human faith in the perpetuation of self, and tends to associate it with universal forgiveness and mercy. In one we sin and we die; in the other we err and yet are forgiven. Neither is primarily concerned to teach us ethics, or to teach us (in Arnold's phrase) 'how to live'. Neither is telling us how to avoid sin, or, having sinned, how to make amends. That is the function of the pulpit, not of the stage; and the playwright who confuses these functions is not the playwright who succeeds and survives. Sin in these conventions is recognised for what it is; but it is also taken as a fact of life. Each of these forms, each enacting a basic human perception, is helping us to come to terms with our experience by universalising it. And if that is the case we need never speak of *mere* convention. The measure of a conventional play's greatness is not the quality of its moral lessons but the degree to which it arouses in us and extends our capacity to think and to feel – the degree to which, in the fullest sense, it 'brings us to life'.

It has been suggested that Lawrence's emphasis on theatrical convention answers the major nineteenth-century anxieties about Duke Vincentio – anxieties which sprang principally from treating character and situation as if they were 'real'. The objection that this reduces the weight or importance of the play has been anticipated and answered with the assertion that we must never speak of *mere* convention. There remains, however, a further problem, peculiar to *Measure for Measure* – one which may be introduced obliquely by returning for a moment to the character of Isabella.

Feeling about Isabella ran high in the nineteenth century, and the debate about her has continued into the twentieth, strict theologians defending the correctness of her decision to put her immortal soul before her brother's life, liberal humanists replying that God is not a strict theologian and that her refusal to save Claudio is heartless and selfish. No one has suggested Isabella is not a credible character. It has been a question, rather, of whether her violence with Claudio does not undermine her function in the play as a whole by alienating our sympathy. And here it seems important to make the assertion that a lingering on the printed page has not always done justice to the effect produced in the theatre, where it seems almost unavoidable that Isabella's decision will emerge, not as a reasoned choice but as a helpless flight from defilement. To yield herself willingly to Angelo is very nearly as difficult for Isabella as it is difficult for Claudio to yield himself willingly to death. In emotional terms what is being demanded of each of them is pretty equally matched.

She, like her brother, is alone, helpless, threatened and
full of fear; and such a state of mind produces blind
selfishness on either side. It is in the degree to which we
are made to feel all this that the greatness of that
archetypal sibling confrontation in Act III scene i resides. His 'Sweet sister, let me live', producing her 'O,
you beast! / O faithless coward! O dishonest wretch!'
(which should come forth, not coldly but in a storm of
tears and anguish) elicits our sympathy for *both*, in-
tensifying (as we have seen) our sense of Angelo's
tyranny, increasing our desire to see it removed and
indirectly enhancing the authority of the disguised
figure who alone can save them from it.

Seeing Isabella in this way renders the condemnation of her behaviour irrelevant – quite as irrelevant as
those somewhat suspect Victorian ecstasies about her
'virgin saintliness'. She is neither saint nor hypocrite,
but a girl overwhelmed by an appalling dilemma.

But a critic who has thought the matter through to
this point has resolved one problem only to create
another. For he has on the one hand argued that Isabella's behaviour is entirely credible according to
human psychology as real life teaches us to understand
it; while on the other he is left with a Duke whose
implausible behaviour is to be explained, not in terms
of real life at all but in those of theatrical convention.
And since Isabella's confrontations with Angelo and
with Claudio are the centre of attention in the first
half of the play, while the Duke's manoeuvrings dominate the second, we have arrived at different criteria of
judgement for the two halves, and thus lent accidental
support to those critics – E. M. W. Tillyard most
notably – who have argued that the play breaks into
two parts which do not hang together to form a coherent work of art.

Tillyard's argument is only an extension of a part of
Lawrence's that has not yet been mentioned. Lawrence
distinguishes between two kinds of material in the
play: first, the source story of the corrupt justice de-
manding a woman yield to him before he will save her

husband's, or her brother's life – a story deriving from
real life, and 'real' in Shakespeare's presentation of it;
and second, the conventional material of the disguised
ruler, the substituted bed-mate and the comic resolution. Lawrence does not at any point say directly that
one kind of material is superior and the other inferior;
but he seems to imply it. The conventional material
Shakespeare added to the source story Lawrence refers
to as 'artificial elements ... exhibiting archaisms and
improbabilities'. He speaks of 'archaic plotting'. And
he seems to excuse these elements on the grounds that,
however much difficulty *we* may have with them,
Shakespeare's audience had none.

Tillyard, acknowledging his debt to Lawrence, draws
the same distinction. The conventional aspects he calls
'themes that belong to the world of fairy tale'; and he
makes it clear that he, too, finds the 'real' superior to
the merely conventional as material for drama. This in
itself is difficult to accept. The conventional is surely
not inherently superior or inferior; what matters is the
way it is used and the skill of the dramatist. But Tillyard's principal point may be a stronger one. The real
and the conventional, he argues, are not kept in balance throughout the play. For the first half 'realism
admits no folk-lore ... while all the folk-lore occurs in
the second half'. It is this point we have anticipated in
recognising that Isabella and the Duke need to be explained in different sets of terms.

Tillyard's argument is a strong one; but it would be
easier to accept in its entirety if we knew no other
Shakespeare play. The pattern Tillyard describes – a
movement from the 'real' to the artificial – is one
Shakespeare used more than once. In particular, it is
the pattern of *The Winter's Tale*, a play which has
elicited from critics almost unanimous praise. If we are
to look, then, for what it is in *Measure for Measure*
that lies behind the critics' uncertainty about its
merits, we can scarcely locate it solely in this particular
dramatic pattern. But we may be helped towards an
explanation by comparing the *use* of that pattern in

Measure for Measure with its use in *The Winter's Tale*.

The Winter's Tale moves from the horror and violence of Leontes' jealous madness to the artificialities of the statue scene, the restoration of lost love and the usual marriages of the comic resolution. Without being exact, the correspondences with *Measure for Measure* are none the less noticeable. Leontes' cruelty approximately matches Angelo's. Hermione's innocent suffering matches Isabella's and Claudio's. Paulina's manipulation of events towards a happy conclusion matches Duke Vincentio's. And the final scenes, stage-managed by Paulina in one case and by the Duke in the other, have qualities in common.

But the differences are significant. In the first place there is something artificial, or operatic, about the writing throughout *The Winter's Tale* – a quality which leaves us in no doubt that however pained we may be by events, they will, none the less, have a fortunate conclusion. Leontes, unlike Angelo, is a normal man with normal affections and attachments. He loves his wife, his son and his friends; and they and his courtiers love and remain loyal to him. His madness sweeps in as if from outside him, an arbitrary affliction, unheralded and undeserved, rather than something intrinsic to his nature. In this sense it has an artificial quality. It is an element of the plot, a premise we must accept in order that everything else may follow. This tempest breaks over the hero for no better reason than that the play requires it. Thus even the earliest scenes, 'real' as they may be in many of their details, have a story-like quality that prepares us for the conclusion. And finally – unlike *Measure for Measure* – *The Winter's Tale* spans a period of sixteen years, so that our acceptance of Leontes' repair at the end of the play is made doubly easy. The evil he does has never seemed a true expression of his character; and added to this, he has had sixteen years of Paulina to foster his remorse.

In *Measure for Measure*, on the other hand, Angelo's

corruption seems entirely real – something 'home-grown', not an affliction arbitrarily imposed by the gods, and certainly not the predictable wickedness of a pasteboard villain. It is a true expression of his character – that of a man corrupted by virtue:

> but it is I
> That, lying by the violet in the sun,
> Do as the carrion does, not as the flower,
> Corrupt with virtuous season.

And so the suffering he causes is correspondingly real. Isabella's inability to accept his proposition increases our sense of his tyranny, and the feeling is intensified as this in turn imposes further suffering on Claudio.

There is, then, in *Measure for Measure*, a greater gap to be bridged between the quality of the earlier scenes and that of the last Act than is the case in *The Winter's Tale*, and less fictional time in which to bridge it. And, more important, the talent which had to build the bridge was not as assured in its purely technical accomplishment as that employed in *The Winter's Tale*. The greatest differences in the two plays are to be found in comparing the 'bridge' – the fourth Act – in each case. In *The Winter's Tale* Shakespeare scorned all explanation of how Paulina contrived the concealment of Hermione and the preparation of the denouement; and in the fifth Act he merely reported Leontes' reunion with Polixines and Perdita. The sheep-shearing festival in Act IV is much longer than is strictly necessary for the practical purpose of introducing Perdita and Florizel; but it adds a dimension and depth to the play that would be missing if he had allowed himself to become preoccupied with explanatory matter.

In Act IV of *Measure for Measure*, on the other hand, he is almost entirely occupied, not with the addition of a further imaginative dimension but with precisely how and why events are being manipulated – and uncertain, too, so that we can detect him at work, feeling his way. He introduces Barnardine solely, one suspects, to provide the necessary 'head' as a substitute for Claudio's. He labours diligently to persuade his audience that it does not matter if Barnardine dies – that Barnardine is unfeeling and will not mind. But he fails to persuade *himself*. No execution could be lightly passed over in a play which has included Claudio's lines on death. So Barnardine survives, and Ragozine is invented only to die of a fever and provide the necessary property.

In any piece of writing, fiction or drama, there is a delicate balance to be kept between the linear narrative structure and that texture in the writing which alone can give it depth. The reader's or spectator's question 'And then? And then?' must be met; his appetite for sequential development satisfied. But where the texture is flowing richly and freely from the writer the narrative line may be very thin. *Hamlet* is a long play in which very little happens; yet its interest never wanes, because the telling of that creaky old revenge story, with its ghost and its poisoned rapier and cup, tapped in Shakespeare a vein of exuberant, anguished wit that for long periods dismisses every other appetite. Hamlet procrastinates because he has so much to say!

Narrative alone, on the other hand, will divert us for an hour or so, but that is all. *The Mousetrap*'s unending season is a measure of the appetite for plot; yet no one will dispute the play's total inconsequence.

In the first half of *Measure for Measure* narrative structure and poetic texture are kept in a rich and dynamic balance. In Act IV we have narrative and little else, and so are led to inspect the convention rather than to experience the play. Shakespeare is doing what he scorned to do later in *The Winter's Tale*: *explaining* his way towards the comic conclusion, instead of *writing* his way there; and the more prosaically and literally he explains, the more prosaically and literally we are led to question. The power of those great confrontations between Isabella and

Angelo and between Isabella and Claudio are still present in our minds. Nothing of comparable force has replaced them. And then, without the kind of imaginative transition Shakespeare achieved in *The Winter's Tale*, we are suddenly in the world of theatrical contrivance, tying and untying knots, forgiving and marrying. The juxtaposition is too sharp; the effect is of a contraction rather than of an expansion; and our feelings of dissatisfaction are likely to come to rest where the dissatisfactions of the greatest English critical minds – Johnson's and Coleridge's – rested: on Angelo. We are unlikely to express ourselves in the same terms as Johnson and Coleridge, who complain because Angelo goes unpunished. But in the mode of our own century we are giving expression to discontent at the same point – locating the same weak spot – if we say that we do not believe in the *reform* of Angelo. He is still too sharply present to us as a real man, a man corrupted by virtue, to become suddenly a conventional figure, duly repentant, and ready for one of those happy marriages which enact our continuing faith in life, in the natural processes and in the redeeming power of time.

The artificiality of the comic romance ending works partly by making us continually aware that it is artificial – engaging our imagination and our faith willingly in what we know to be unreal. But this can only happen successfully at the conclusion of a play (again *The Winter's Tale* serves as example) which has never allowed us to lose consciousness of that unreality. In *Measure for Measure* we do lose it in the early Acts. These contain some scenes that are among the greatest of their kind Shakespeare ever wrote. And the play's concluding scene is very good of *its* kind. But by the end of the play two kinds of theatrical experience have affected us, and it is difficult to see how – with only Act iv as it is to join them – the response can ever be a unified one such as a perfectly coherent work of art offers.

The objection, then, is not to the conventional

material as such. Nor is it to the pattern which moves
from something approximately 'real' to something
almost totally artificial. It is, rather, to the application
of the pattern in this particular case. Shakespeare, perhaps we may conclude, was attempting in this play
something he was to do much more successfully a few
years later.

If this is our conclusion, however, it is not one supported by several recent studies which have affirmed
that the play is an unmixed success. One significant
influence on recent attitudes was the 1950 Peter Brook
production at Stratford on Avon, with John Gielgud as
Angelo. Accounts of this production were written in
scholarly journals; and the conclusion seems to have
been that it confirmed neither the present view, that
the play is structurally imperfect, nor that of the theol-
ogisers and moralisers. Robert M. Smith (*Shakespeare
Quarterly*, 1, 1950) wrote: 'What had seemed so complex and paradoxical in plot and character emerges as
natural and sun-clear. Instead of the heavy gloom and
especially "the great moral purpose", which well-inten-
tioned moralists have vainly endeavoured to reassure us
the play possesses, we have, according to one responsive
spectator, a "merry, bawdy, and irresistible evening's
entertainment for audiences both critical and uncriti-
cal".' And Smith continued a few pages on: 'The real
test of the play's integrity as a whole is found therefore,
not in conjectural efforts to resolve inconsistencies and
discrepancies found by closet-scholars, but by two
hours' traffic with the play on the stage where, as so
often happens in productions, the problems and per-
plexities of Shakespeare disappear.'
    And Richard David writing of the same production
(in a note reprinted in this selection) concluded that
Measure for Measure 'is a play of ideas rather than of
impressions and is concerned more with lines of conduct followed out to their logical conclusions than
with the confusions and compromises of real life'.
    These views – that it is not a parable, and not a

failure, but a coherent intellectual comedy, a play of ideas – have been echoed since by two American scholars, each of whom has produced a full-length book on the play.*

Josephine Waters Bennett is mainly concerned with the play as an entertainment written especially for King James – not a new idea, but one which Miss Bennett may have succeeded in labouring to death. And her description of the general quality of the play is unlikely to find wide support:

> The play is, from beginning to end, pure comedy, based on an absurdity, like *The Mikado*, full of topical allusions to a current best-seller [King James's *Basilikon Doron*], and every situation exaggerated into patent theatricality. The great emotional scenes, first Isabella's, then Angelo's, and then Claudio's, each in a different way [,] keep the emotions in check, as they must be kept in check in a comedy, because we cannot be amused when our sympathies are deeply involved. We must feel superior to the foolish people in the play.

We have come a long way from the play Coleridge found 'the most painful of all Shakespeare's genuine works'! Apparently 'comedy' for Miss Bennett is synonymous with 'amusement' and rules out sympathy. And we may wonder (among all the things there are to wonder at) why certain scenes are described as 'great emotional scenes' if they 'keep the emotions in check'.

But broadly the same point of view has been argued much more plausibly by David L. Stevenson, first in 1956 in an article (part of which is reproduced in this selection) and then in a full book on the play (1966). Stevenson sees the play as a 'brilliant intellectual *tour*

---

* The only other full book on the play, and perhaps the best, is that by Mary Lascelles. It is not referred to in this introduction only because it defies paraphrase at every point. Its very considerable merits, and its limitations, spring from the same source: a scrupulous refusal to arrive at general conclusions.

de force', closer to Johnson's plays than other Shakespeare wrote, working rather like a poem by Donne,
engaging our intellect rather than our emotions, 'made
up of a series of intricately interrelated moral ironies
and reversals, held together by the twin themes of
mercy and justice, and resolved by a final balancing
out of paradox'. Stevenson then traces the various
ironies, reversals, parallels and paradoxes that make up
the play's structure and concludes that *Measure for
Measure* is 'a very great comedy', unencumbered by
any special theological emphasis, and (apparently) un-
flawed. In 1966 he goes a little further and describes it
as Shakespeare's greatest comedy.

The patterns Stevenson traces are no doubt there;
but whether their presence and our appreciation of
them rules out our emotional involvement in the
sufferings of Isabella and Claudio is quite another
matter. Nor does the fact that the play can be made to
work, and work well, on the stage, mean that what it
offers there is a perfectly unified experience.

Of all the many problems of detail arising out of
Measure for Measure there is one especially that seems
to call for a brief final comment, because our conclusions on it must in a significant degree affect our
view of the play as a whole. It is the problem of how
seriously we are meant to take Claudio's offence. The
present editor's belief is a simple one: that the offence
is venial, indeed scarcely more than technical; that it is
meant to be accepted as such so that Angelo's sentence
will seem more than ever a tyrannical one; that Lucio,
at his own level and in his own terms, is putting the
attitude of the *play* when he says, 'What a ruthless
thing ... for the rebellion of a codpiece to take away
the life of a man.'

It is not only the low life characters who adopt this
attitude. Escalus and the Provost (both unambiguously
'good' characters) share it, as does the shadowy Justice.
Isabella insists that Claudio's is 'a natural guiltiness'
such as exists in all. Claudio himself protests that he

has been condemned for 'a name'. And the Duke clearly has no intention of allowing the offence to be punished.

Yet F. R. Leavis is not alone in his belief that morally 'Claudio has committed a serious offence'. Two passages have seemed to lend support to this view. The first is the exchange between Lucio and Claudio in Act I scene ii:

> *Lucio.* Why, how now, Claudio? Whence comes this
> restraint?
> *Claudio.* From too much liberty, my Lucio. Liberty,
> As surfeit, is the father of much fast;
> So every scope by the immoderate use
> Turns to restraint. Our natures do pursue,
> Like rats that ravin down their proper bane,
> A thirsty evil; and when we drink, we die.

Most critics, it seems, would accept at least Leavis's view that Claudio is 'bitterly self-reproachful and self-condemnatory' here. Yet a problem exists in the fact that Claudio a moment previously has railed against the tyranny of 'the demi-god, Authority', which has caused him to be arrested; and a moment later is pointing out that Juliet 'is fast my wife' and (twice) that he has been condemned for 'a name'. It is in this apparent contradiction that L. C. Knights principally locates the play's moral 'ambiguity'.

Certainly Claudio's lines are bitter; but is the bitterness directed against himself? The context suggests that it is directed against 'the demi-god, Authority'. What seems to have been overlooked in the consideration of these lines is that it is 'Authority' itself which has permitted the 'liberty' (the statute has been in abeyance fourteen years) for which Claudio is now condemned. Surely, then, Claudio is saying something like this: 'If we are given a liberty we will, being human, exercise it. But for the same Authority to permit an action and then condemn it, is to treat us like rats, enticing us with a bait in which poison has been concealed.' And if the lines are read in this way (which makes sense of the passage as a whole) there is no warrant for seeing in them Claudio's self-disgust (or Shakespeare's sexual disgust, which has also been found there) but rather a bitter irony directed against the arbitrary exercise of judicial authority.

The other passage which has been cited is Act II scene iii, in which the Duke, in his disguise as a friar, calls on Juliet to repent. It should be noted that this is one of those points where it is dangerous to assume that the Duke says precisely what he means, since his statements are a part of his disguise. It is, however, clear enough that Juliet willingly and sincerely expresses penitence. But to say that this increases our sense of a serious moral lapse on Claudio's part is quite the reverse of its effect in the theatre. Juliet affirms that she loves Claudio and that the offence was committed 'mutually'; her demeanour and her penitence establish her virtue; and this makes a sharp and necessary distinction between her love relationship with Claudio and the sexuality of the low life characters. This is surely the scene's principal dramatic purpose; and its effect is to render Claudio's offence more than ever insignificant. Indeed, in a society which displays at one extreme the diseased libertinism of the low life characters and at the other the diseased puritanism of Angelo, Claudio's 'natural guiltiness' stands forth as a positive good.

C. K. STEAD

I have said nothing in this Introduction about William Empson's essay only because it stands slightly apart from the main lines of the argument. It seems to me in many ways the most original and the most interesting piece of critical writing on the subject of *Measure for Measure*.

PART ONE

Earlier Critics of
Measure for Measure

SAMUEL JOHNSON

There is perhaps not one of *Shakespear*'s plays more darkened than this by the peculiarities of its Authour, and the unskilfulness of its Editors, by distortions of phrase, or negligence of transcription.

ACT I SCENE i (I i 7–9)
> Then no more remains;
> But that to your sufficiency, as your worth is able,
> And let them work.

This is a passage which has exercised the sagacity of the Editors, and is now to employ mine.

Sir *Tho. Hanmer* having caught from Mr *Theobald* a hint that a line was lost, endeavours to supply it thus.

> Then no more remains,
> But that to your sufficiency you join
> A will to serve us, *as your worth is able*.

He has by this bold conjecture undoubtedly obtained a meaning, but, perhaps not, even in his own opinion, the meaning of *Shakespear*.

That the passage is more or less corrupt, I believe every reader will agree with the Editors. I am not convinced that a line is lost, as Mr *Theobald* conjectures, nor that the change of *but* to *put*, which Dr *Warburton* has admitted after some other Editor, will amend the fault. There was probably some original obscurity in the expression, which gave occasion to mistake in repetition or transcription. I therefore suspect that the Authour wrote thus,

> Then no more remains,
> But that to your sufficiencies your worth is abled,
> And let them work.

Then nothing remains more than to tell you that your Virtue is now invested with power equal to your knowledge and wisdom. Let therefore your knowledge and your virtue now work together. It may easily be conceived how *sufficiencies* was, by an inarticulate speaker, or inattentive hearer, confounded with *sufficiency as,* and how *abled,* a word very unusual, was changed into *able.* For *abled* however, an authority is not wanting. *Lear* uses it in the same sense, or nearly the same, with the Duke. As for *sufficiencies,* D. *Hamilton* in his dying speech, prays that *Charles* II *may exceed both the* virtues *and* sufficiencies *of his father.*

ACT I SCENE ii (I i 51)
    We have with a leaven'd *and prepared choice.*

Leaven'd has no sense in this place: we should read LEVEL'D *choice.* The allusion is to archery, when a man has fixed upon his object, after taking good aim. – WARBURTON.

No emendation is necessary. *Leaven'd choice* is one of *Shakespear*'s harsh metaphors. His train of ideas seems to be this. *I have proceeded to you with choice* mature, concocted, fermented, *leavened.* When Bread is *leavened,* it is left to ferment: a *leavened* choice is therefore a choice not hasty, but considerate, not declared as soon as it fell into the imagination, but suffered to work long in the mind. Thus explained it suits better with *prepared* than *levelled.*

ACT II SCENE ix (II iii 11–12)
    Who falling in the flaws *of her own youth,*
    Hath blister'd *her report.*

Who does not see that the integrity of the metaphor requires we should read FLAMES *of her own youth* – WARBURTON.

Who does not see that upon such principles there is no end of correction.

ACT III SCENE i (III i 13–15)
>   *Thou art not noble:*
> *For all th' accommodations, that thou bear'st.*
> *Are nurs'd by baseness.*

Dr *Warburton* is undoubtedly mistaken in supposing that by *baseness* is meant *self-love* here assigned as
the motive of all human actions. *Shakespear* meant
only to observe, that a minute analysis of life at once
destroys that splendour which dazzles the imagination.
Whatever grandeur can display, or luxury enjoy, is
procured by *baseness*, by offices of which the mind
shrinks from the contemplation. All the delicacies of
the table may be traced back to the shambles and the
dunghill, all magnificence of building was hewn from
the quarry, and all the pomp of ornaments, dug from
among the damps and darkness of the mine.

ACT III SCENE i (III i 16–17)
>   *The soft and tender fork*
> *Of a poor worm.*

Worm is put for any creeping thing or *serpent.*
Shakespear supposes falsely, but according to the vulgar notion, that a serpent wounds with his tongue, and
that his tongue is *forked.* He confounds reality and
fiction, a serpent's tongue is *soft* but not *forked* nor
hurtful. If it could hurt, it could not be soft. In *Mid-
summer-Night's Dream* he has the same notion.

>   *With* doubler *tongue*
> *Than thine, O serpent, never adder* stung.

ACT III SCENE i (III i 17–19)
>   *Thy best of rest is sleep,*
> *And that thou oft provok'st; yet grosly fear'st*
> *Thy death which is no more.*

Evidently from the following passage of *Cicero;*
Habes somnum imaginem Mortis, eamque quotidie

induis, & dubitas quin sensus in morte nullus sit,
cum in ejus simulacro videas esse nullum sensum.
But the Epicurean insinuation is, with great judgment, omitted in the imitation. – WARBURTON.

Here Dr *Warburton* might have found a sentiment
worthy of his animadversion. I cannot without indignation find *Shakespear* saying, that *death is only sleep*,
lengthening out his exhortation by a sentence which in
the *Friar* is impious, in the reasoner is foolish, and in
the poet trite and vulgar.

ACT III SCENE i (III i 32–41)
> *Thou hast nor youth, nor age:*
> *But as it were an after dinner's sleep,*
> *Dreaming on both.*

This is exquisitely imagined. When we are young we
busy ourselves in forming schemes for succeeding time,
and miss the gratifications that are before us; when we
are old we amuse the languour of age with the recol-
lection of youthful pleasures or performances; so that
our life, of which no part is filled with the business of
the present time, resembles our dreams after dinner,
when the events of the morning are mingled with the
designs of the evening.

ACT III SCENE i (III i 36–8)
> *When thou'rt old and rich,*
> *Thou hast neither heat, affection, limb, nor beauty*
> *To make thy riches pleasant.*

But how does beauty make *riches pleasant?* We
should read BOUNTY, which compleats the sense, and
is this; Thou hast neither the pleasure of enjoying
riches thy self, for thou wantest vigour: nor of seeing
it enjoyed by others, for thou wantest *bounty*. Where
the making the want of *bounty* as inseparable from
old age as the want of *health*, is extremely satirical
tho' not altogether just. – WARBURTON.

I am inclined to believe that neither man nor woman will have much difficulty to tell how *beauty makes riches pleasant*. Surely this emendation, though it is elegant and ingenious, is not such as that an opportunity of inserting it should be purchased by declaring ignorance of what every one knows, by confessing insensibility of what every one feels.

ACT III SCENE ii (III i 137–8)
> *Is't not a kind of incest, to take life*
> *From thine own sister's shame?*

In *Isabella's* declamation there is something harsh, and something forced and far-fetched. But her indignation cannot be thought violent when we consider her not only as a virgin but as a nun.

ACT IV SCENE viii (IV iii 4–5)
> *First here's young Mr Rash, &c.*

This enumeration of the inhabitants of the prison affords a very striking view of the practices predominant in *Shakespeare's* age. Besides those whose follies are common to all times, we have four fighting men and a traveller. It is not unlikely that the originals of these pictures were then known.

ACT IV SCENE xiii (IV v 1)
> DUKE. *These letters at fit time deliver me.*

Peter never delivers the letters, but tells his story without any credentials. The poet forgot the plot which he had formed.

ACT V SCENE vii (v i 448)
> *'Till he did look on me.*

The *Duke* has justly observed that *Isabel* is *importuned against all sense* to solicit for *Angelo*, yet here *against all sense* she solicits for him. Her argument is extraordinary.

> *A due sincerity govern'd his deeds,*
> *'Till he did look on me; since it is so,*
> *Let him not die.*

That *Angelo* had committed all the crimes charged against him, as far as he could commit them, is evident. The only *intent* which *his act did not overtake*, was the defilement of *Isabel*. Of this *Angelo* was only intentionally guilty.

Angelo's crimes were such, as must sufficiently justify punishment, whether its end be to secure the innocent from wrong, or to deter guilt by example; and I believe every reader feels some indignation when he finds him spared. From what extenuation of his crime can *Isabel*, who yet supposes her brother dead, form any plea in his favour. *Since he was good 'till he looked on me, let him not die.* I am afraid our Varlet Poet intended to inculcate, that women think ill of nothing that raises the credit of their beauty, and are ready, however virtuous, to pardon any act which they think incited by their own charms.

ACT v SCENE viii (v i 479 foll.)

It is somewhat strange, that *Isabel* is not made to express either gratitude, wonder or joy at the sight of her brother.

After the pardon of two murderers *Lucio* might be treated by the good *Duke* with less harshness; but perhaps the Poet intended to show, what is too often seen, *that men easily forgive wrongs which are not committed against themselves.*

The novel of *Cynthio Giraldi*, from which *Shakespear* is supposed to have borrowed this fable, may be read in *Shakespear illustated*, elegantly translated, with remarks which will assist the enquirer to discover how much absurdity *Shakespear* has admitted or avoided.

I cannot but suspect that some other had new modelled the novel of *Cynthio*, or written a story which in some particulars resembled it, and that *Cinthio* was

not the authour whom *Shakespeare* immediately followed. The Emperour in *Cinthio* is named *Maximine*,
the Duke, in *Shakespear*'s enumeration of the persons
of the drama, is called *Vincentio*. This appears a very
slight remark; but since the Duke has no name in the
play, nor is ever mentioned but by his title, why should
he be called *Vincentio* among the *Persons*, but because
the name was copied from the story, and placed super-
fluously at the head of the list by the mere habit of
transcription? It is therefore likely that there was then
a story of *Vincentio* Duke of *Vienna*, different from
that of *Maximine* Emperour of the *Romans*.

Of this play the light or comick part is very natural
and pleasing, but the grave scenes, if a few passages be
excepted, have more labour than elegance. The plot is
rather intricate than artful. The time of the action is
indefinite; some time, we know not how much, must
have elapsed between the recess of the *Duke* and the
imprisonment of *Claudio*; for he must have learned
the story of *Mariana* in his disguise, or he delegated his
power to a man already known to be corrupted. The
unities of action and place are sufficiently preserved.

(from *Johnson on Shakespeare,* ed. Walter Raleigh,
1908)

A. W. SCHLEGEL

In *Measure for Measure* Shakspeare was compelled, by
the nature of the subject, to make his poetry more
familiar with criminal justice than is usual for him. All
kinds of proceedings connected with the subject, all
sorts of active or passive persons, pass in review before
us: the hypocritical Lord Deputy, the compassionate
Provost, and the hard-hearted Hangman; a young man
of quality who is to suffer for the seduction of his mistress before marriage, loose wretches brought in by the
police, nay, even a hardened criminal, whom even the
preparations for his execution cannot awaken out of

his callousness. But yet, notwithstanding this agitating
truthfulness, how tender and mild is the pervading
tone of the picture! The piece takes improperly its
name from punishment; the true significance of the
whole is the triumph of mercy over strict justice; no
man being himself so free from errors as to be entitled
to deal it out to his equals. The most beautiful em-
bellishment of the composition is the character of Isabella, who, on the point of taking the veil, is yet pre-
vailed upon by sisterly affection to tread again the per-
plexing ways of the world, while, amid the general corruption, the heavenly purity of her mind is not even
stained with one unholy thought: in the humble robes
of the novice she is a very angel of light. When the cold
and stern Angelo, heretofore of unblemished reputation, whom the Duke has commissioned, during his
pretended absence, to restrain, by a rigid administration of the laws, the excesses of dissolute immorality, is
even himself tempted by the virgin charms of Isabella,
supplicating for the pardon of her brother Claudio,
condemned to death for a youthful indiscretion; when
at first, in timid and obscure language, he insinuates,
but at last impudently avouches his readiness to grant
Claudio's life to the sacrifice of her honour; when Isabella repulses his offer with a noble scorn; in her
account of the interview to her brother, when the latter
at first applauds her conduct, but at length, overcome
by the fear of death, strives to persuade her to consent
to dishonour; – in these masterly scenes, Shakspeare
has sounded the depths of the human heart. The interest here reposes altogether on the represented
action; curiosity contributes nothing to our delight, for
the Duke, in the disguise of a Monk, is always present
to watch over his dangerous representative, and to
avert every evil which could possibly be apprehended;
we look to him with confidence for a happy result. The
Duke acts the part of the Monk naturally, even to deception; he unites in his person the wisdom of the
priest and the prince. Only in his wisdom he is too
fond of round-about ways; his vanity is flattered with

acting invisibly like an earthly providence; he takes
more pleasure in overhearing his subjects than govern
ing them in the customary way of princes. As he ultimately extends a free pardon to all the guilty, we do
not see how his original purpose, in committing the
execution of the laws to other hands, of restoring their
strictness, has in any wise been accomplished. The poet
might have had this irony in view, that of the number-
less slanders of the Duke, told him by the petulant
Lucio, in ignorance of the person whom he is addressing, that at least which regarded his singularities and
whims was not wholly without foundation. It is deserv-
ing of remark, that Shakspeare, amidst the rancour of
religious parties, takes a delight in painting the condition of a monk, and always represents his influence as
beneficial. We find in him none of the black and
knavish monks, which an enthusiasm for Protestant-
ism, rather than poetical inspiration, has suggested to
some of our modern poets. Shakspeare merely gives his
monks an inclination to busy themselves in the affairs
of others, after renouncing the world for themselves;
with respect, however, to pious frauds, he does not represent them as very conscientious. Such are the parts
acted by the monk in *Romeo and Juliet*, and another
in *Much Ado About Nothing*, and even by the Duke,
whom, contrary to the wellknown proverb, the cowl
seems really to make a monk.

(from *A course of Lectures on Dramatic Art and
Literature*, 1809, trans. John Black, 1846)

S. T. COLERIDGE

This play, which is Shakespeare's throughout, is to me
the most painful – say rather, the only painful – part of
his genuine works. The comic and tragic parts equally
border on the μισητόν, the one disgusting, the
other horrible; and the pardon and marriage of
Angelo not merely baffles the strong indignant claim

of justice (for cruelty, with lust and damnable baseness, cannot be forgiven, because we cannot conceive
them as being *morally* repented of) but it is likewise
degrading to the character of woman. Beaumont and
Fletcher, who can follow Shakespeare in his errors only,
have presented a still worse because more loathsome
and contradictory instance of the same kind in [the]
Night-Walker, in the marriage of Alathe to Algripe. Of
the counterbalancing beauties of the *Measure for
Measure* I need say nothing, for I have already said
that it is Shakespeare's throughout.

[III i 130–3. Claudio to Isabella:
    The weariest and most loathed worldly life
    That age, ache, penury, and imprisonment
    Can lay on nature is a paradise
    To what we fear of death.

'This natural fear of *Claudio*, from the antipathy
we have to death, seems very little varied from that
infamous wish of *Maecenas* recorded in the 101st
Epistle of *Seneca*.

        . . .
        Vita dum superest, bene est,
        Hanc mihi, vel acuta
        Si sedeam cruce, sustine.'
                            Warburton's note.]

I cannot but think this rather an heroic resolve than
an infamous wish. It appears to me the grandest symp-
tom of an immortal spirit, even when that bedimmed
and overwhelmed spirit recked not of its own immortality – [to seek] the privilege to *be*, to be a mind, a
will.

[III ii 245–6.
        Pattern in himself to know,
        Grace to stand and virtue go;]

Worse metre indeed, but better English, were

> Grace to stand, virtue to go.

(from *Coleridge's Shakespeare Criticism*, ed. T. M.
Rayser, 1930).

Measure for Measure is the single exception to the de-
lightfulness of Shakspeare's plays. It is a hateful work,
although Shakspearian throughout. Our feelings of
justice are grossly wounded in Angelo's escape. Isabella
herself contrives to be unamiable, and Claudio is de-
testable.

(from *The Table Talk and Omniana of Samuel
Taylor Coleridge*, ed. T. Ashe (London, 1888) p. 48)

WILLIAM HAZLITT

This is a play as full of genius as it is of wisdom. Yet
there is an original sin in the nature of the subject,
which prevents us from taking a cordial interest in it.
'The height of moral argument' which the author has
maintained in the intervals of passion or blended with
the more powerful impulses of nature, is hardly sur-
passed in any of his plays. But there is in general a
want of passion; the affections are at a stand; our sympathies are repulsed and defeated in all directions.
The only passion which influences the story is that of
Angelo; and yet he seems to have a much greater passion for hypocrisy than for his mistress. Neither are we
greatly enamoured of Isabella's rigid chastity, though
she could not act otherwise than she did. We do not
feel the same confidence in the virtue that is 'sublimely
good' at another's expense, as if it had been put to
some less disinterested trial. As to the Duke, who makes
a very imposing and mysterious stage-character, he is
more absorbed in his own plots and gravity than
anxious for the welfare of the state; more tenacious of

his own character than attentive to the feelings and apprehensions of others. Claudio is the only person who feels naturally; and yet he is placed in circumstances of distress which almost preclude the wish for his deliverance. Mariana is also in love with Angelo, whom we hate. In this respect, there may be said to be a general system of cross-purposes between the feelings of the different characters and the sympathy of the reader or the audience. This principle of repugnance seems to have reached its height in the character of Master Barnardine, who not only sets at defiance the opinions of others, but has even thrown off all self-regard – 'one that apprehends death no more dreadfully but as a drunken sleep; careless, reckless, and fearless of what's past, present, and to come'. He is a fine antithesis to the morality and the hypocrisy of the other characters of the play. Barnardine is Caliban transported from Prospero's wizard island to the forests of Bohemia or the prisons of Vienna. He is the creature of bad habits as Caliban is of gross instincts. He has however a strong notion of the natural fitness of things, according to his own sensations – 'He has been drinking hard all night, and he will not be hanged that day' – and Shakespear has let him off at last. We do not understand why the philosophical German critic, Schlegel, should be so severe on those pleasant persons, Lucio, Pompey, and Master Froth, as to call them 'wretches'. They appear all mighty comfortable in their occupations, and determined to pursue them, 'as the flesh and fortune should serve'. A very good exposure of the want of self-knowledge and contempt for others, which is so common in the world, is put into the mouth of Abhorson, the jailor, when the Provost proposes to associate Pompey with him in his office – 'A bawd, sir? Fie upon him, he will discredit our mystery.' And the same answer will serve in nine instances out of ten to the same kind of remark, 'Go to, sir, you weigh equally; a feather will turn the scale.' Shakespear was in one sense the least moral of all writers; for morality (commonly so called) is made up of antipathies; and his talent consisted in sympathy with human nature, in all its shapes, degrees, depressions, and elevations. The object of the pedantic moralist is to find out the bad in everything: his was to shew that 'there is some soul of goodness in things evil'. Even Master Barnardine is not left to the mercy of what others think of him; but when he comes in, speaks for himself, and pleads his own cause, as well as if counsel had been assigned him. In one sense, Shakespear was no moralist at all: in another, he was the greatest of all moralists. He was a moralist in the same sense in which nature is one. He taught what he had learnt from her. He shewed the greatest knowledge of humanity with the greatest fellow-feeling for it.

One of the most dramatic passages in the present play is the interview between Claudio and his sister, when she comes to inform him of the conditions on which Angelo will spare his life. . . .

What adds to the dramatic beauty of this scene and the effect of Claudio's passionate attachment to life is, that it immediately follows the Duke's lecture to him, in the character of the Friar, recommending an absolute indifference to it.

(from *Characters of Shakespeare's Plays*, 1817, re-printed 1926)

WALTER PATER

In *Measure for Measure*, as in some other of his plays, Shakespeare has remodelled an earlier and somewhat rough composition to 'finer issues', suffering much to remain as it had come from the less skilful hand, and not raising the whole of his work to an equal degree of intensity. Hence perhaps some of that depth and weightiness which make this play so impressive, as with the true seal of experience, like a fragment of life itself, rough and disjointed indeed, but forced to yield in places its profounder meaning. In *Measure for*

Measure, in contrast with the flawless execution of
Romeo and Juliet, Shakespeare has spent his art in just
enough modification of the scheme of the older play to
make it exponent of this purpose, adapting its terrible
essential incidents, so that Coleridge found it the only
painful work among Shakespeare's dramas, and leaving for the reader of to-day more than the usual
number of difficult expressions; but infusing a lavish
colour and profound significance into it, so that under
his touch certain select portions of it rise far above the
level of all but his own best poetry, and working out of
it a morality so characteristic that the play might well
pass for the central expression of his moral judgments.
It remains a comedy, as indeed is congruous with the
bland, half-humorous equity which informs the whole
composition, sinking from the heights of sorrow and
terror into the rough scheme of the earlier piece; yet it
is hardly less full of what is really tragic in man's existence than if Claudio had indeed 'stooped to death'.
Even the humorous concluding scenes have traits of
special grace, retaining in less emphatic passages a
stray line or word of power, as it seems, so that we
watch to the end for the traces where the nobler hand
has glanced along, leaving its vestiges, as if accidentally
or wastefully, in the rising of the style.

   The interest of *Measure for Measure*, therefore, is
partly that of an old story told over again. We measure
with curiosity that variety of resources which has enabled Shakespeare to refashion the original material
with a higher motive; adding to the intricacy of the
piece, yet so modifying its structure as to give the whole
almost the unity of a single scene; lending, by the light
of a philosophy which dwells much on what is complex
and subtle in our nature, a true human propriety to its
strange and unexpected turns of feeling and character,
to incidents so difficult as the fall of Angelo, and the
subsequent reconciliation of Isabella, so that she
pleads successfully for his life. It was from Whetstone, a
contemporary English writer, that Shakespeare derived

the outline of Cinthio's 'rare history' of *Promos and Cassandra*, one of that numerous class of Italian stories, like Boccaccio's *Tancred of Salerno*, in which the mere energy of southern passion has everything its own way, and which, though they may repel many a northern reader by a certain crudity in their colouring, seem to have been full of fascination for the Elizabethan age. This story, as it appears in Whetstone's endless comedy, is almost as rough as the roughest episode of actual criminal life. But the play seems never to have been acted, and some time after its publication Whetstone himself turned the thing into a tale, included in his *Heptameron of Civil Discourses*, where it still figures as a genuine piece, with touches of undesigned poetry, a quaint field-flower here and there of diction or sentiment, the whole strung up to an effective brevity, and with the fragrance of that admirable age of literature all about it. Here, then, there is something of the original Italian colour: in this narrative Shakespeare may well have caught the first glimpse of a composition with nobler proportions; and some artless sketch from his own hand, perhaps, putting together his first impressions, insinuated itself between Whetstone's work and the play as we actually read it. Out of these insignificant sources Shakespeare's play rises, full of solemn expression, and with a profoundly designed beauty, the new body of a higher, though sometimes remote and difficult poetry, escaping from the imperfect relics of the old story, yet not wholly transformed, and even as it stands but the preparation only, we might think, of a still more imposing design. For once we have in it a real example of that sort of writing which is sometimes described as *suggestive*, and which by the help of certain subtly calculated hints only, brings into distinct shape the reader's own half-developed imaginings. Often the quality is attributed to writing merely vague and unrealised, but in *Measure for Measure*, quite certainly, Shakespeare has directed the attention of sympathetic readers along certain channels of meditation beyond the immediate scope of his work.

Measure for Measure, therefore, by the quality of these higher designs, woven by his strange magic on a texture of poorer quality, is hardly less indicative than *Hamlet* even, of Shakespeare's reason, of his power of moral interpretation. It deals, not like *Hamlet* with the problems which beset one of exceptional temperament, but with mere human nature. It brings before us a group of persons, attractive, full of desire, vessels of the genial, seed-bearing powers of nature, a gaudy existence flowering out over the old court and city of Vienna, a spectacle of the fulness and pride of life which to some may seem to touch the verge of wantonness. Behind this group of people, behind their various action, Shakespeare inspires in us the sense of a strong tyranny of nature and circumstance. Then what shall there be on this side of it – on our side, the spectators' side, of this painted screen, with its puppets who are really glad or sorry all the time? What philosophy of life, what sort of equity?

Stimulated to read more carefully by Shakespeare's own profounder touches, the reader will note the vivid reality, the subtle interchange of light and shade, the strongly contrasted characters of this group of persons, passing across the stage so quickly. The slightest of them is at least not ill-natured: the meanest of them can put forth a plea for existence – *Truly, sir, I am a poor fellow that would live!* – they are never sure of themselves, even in the strong tower of a cold unimpressible nature: they are capable of many friendships and of a true dignity in danger, giving each other a sympathetic, if transitory, regret – one sorry that another 'should be foolishly lost at a game of tick-tack'. Words which seem to exhaust man's deepest sentiment concerning death and life are put on the lips of a gilded, witless youth; and the saintly Isabella feels fire creep along her, kindling her tongue to eloquence at the suggestion of shame. In places the shadow deepens: death intrudes itself on the scene, as among

other things 'a great disguise', blanching the features
of youth and spoiling its goodly hair, touching the fine
Claudio even with its disgraceful associations. As in
Orcagna's fresco at Pisa, it comes capriciously, giving
many and long reprieves to Barnardine, who has been
waiting for it nine years in prison, taking another
thence by fever, another by mistake of judgment, em-
bracing others in the midst of their music and song.
The little mirror of existence, which reflects to each for
a moment the stage on which he plays, is broken at last
by a capricious accident; while all alike, in their yearning for untasted enjoyment, are really discounting
their days, grasping so hastily and accepting so inex-
actly the precious pieces. The Duke's quaint but excellent moralising at the beginning of the third act
does but express, like the chorus of a Greek play, the
spirit of the passing incidents. To him in Shakespeare's
play, to a few here and there in the actual world, this
strange practical paradox of our life, so unwise in its
eager haste, reveals itself in all its clearness.

The Duke disguised as a friar, with his curious
moralising on life and death, and Isabella in her first
mood of renunciation, a thing 'ensky'd and sainted',
come with the quiet of the cloister as a relief to this lust
and pride of life: like some grey monastic picture
hung on the wall of a gaudy room, their presence cools
the heated air of the piece. For a moment we are within the placid conventual walls, whither they fancy at
first that the Duke has come as a man crossed in love,
with Friar Thomas and Friar Peter, calling each other
by their homely, English names, or at the nunnery
among the novices, with their little limited privileges,
where

> If you speak you must not show your face,
> Or if you show your face you must not speak.

Not less precious for this relief in the general structure
of the piece, than for its own peculiar graces is the
episode of Mariana, a creature wholly of Shakespeare's

invention, told, by way of interlude, in subdued prose. The moated grange, with its dejected mistress, its long, listless, discontented days, where we hear only the voice of a boy broken off suddenly in the midst of one of the loveliest songs of Shakespeare, or of Shakespeare's school,* is the pleasantest of many glimpses we get here of pleasant places – the field without the town, Angelo's garden-house, the consecrated fountain. Indirectly it has suggested two of the most perfect compositions among the poetry of our own generation. Again it is a picture within a picture, but with fainter lines and a greyer atmosphere: we have here the same passions, the same wrongs, the same continuance of affection, the same crying out upon death, as in the nearer and larger piece, though softened, and reduced to the mood of a more dreamy scene.

Of Angelo we may feel at first sight inclined to say only *guarda e passa!* or to ask whether he is indeed psychologically possible. In the old story, he figures as an embodiment of pure and unmodified evil, like 'Hyliogabalus of Rome or Denis of Sicyll'. But the embodiment of pure evil is no proper subject of art, and Shakespeare, in the spirit of a philosophy which dwells much on the complications of outward circumstance with men's inclinations, turns into a subtle study in casuistry this incident of the austere judge fallen suddenly into utmost corruption by a momentary contact with supreme purity. But the main interest in *Measure for Measure* is not, as in *Promos and Cassandra*, in the relation of Isabella and Angelo, but rather in the relation of Claudio and Isabella.

Greek tragedy in some of its noblest products has taken for its theme the love of a sister, a sentiment unimpassioned indeed, purifying by the very spectacle of its passionlessness, but capable of a fierce and almost animal strength if informed for a moment by pity and regret. At first Isabella comes upon the scene as a tranquillising influence in it. But Shakespeare, in the development of the action, brings quite different and un-

* Fletcher in the *Bloody Brother*, gives the rest of it.

expected qualities out of her. It is his characteristic
poetry to expose this cold, chastened personality, respected even by the worldly Lucio as 'something
ensky'd and sainted, and almost as immortal spirit', to
two sharp, shameful trials, and wring out of her a fiery,
revealing eloquence. Thrown into the terrible dilemma of the piece, called upon to sacrifice that cloistral whiteness to sisterly affection, become in a moment
the ground of strong, contending passions, she develops
a new character and shows herself suddenly of kindred
with those strangely conceived women, like Webster's
Vittoria, who unite to a seductive sweetness something
of a dangerous and tigerlike changefulness of feeling.
The swift, vindictive anger leaps, like a white flame,
into this white spirit, and, stripped in a moment of all
convention, she stands before us clear, detached,
columnar, among the tender frailties of the piece. Cassandra, the original of Isabella in Whetstone's tale,
with the purpose of the Roman Lucretia in her mind,
yields gracefully enough to the conditions of her
brother's safety; and to the lighter reader of Shakespeare there may seem something harshly conceived, or
psychologically impossible even, in the suddenness of
the change wrought in her, as Claudio welcomes for a
moment the chance of life through her compliance
with Angelo's will, and he may have a sense here of
flagging skill, as in words less finely handled than in
the preceding scene. The play, though still not without
traces of nobler handiwork, sinks down, as we know, at
last into almost homely comedy, and it might be supposed that just here the grander manner deserted it.
But the skill with which Isabella plays upon Claudio's
well-recognised sense of honour, and endeavours by
means of that to insure him beforehand from the
acceptance of life on baser terms, indicates no coming
laxity of hand just in this place. It was rather that
there rose in Shakespeare's conception, as there may for
the reader, as there certainly would in any good acting
of the part, something of that terror, the seeking for
which is one of the notes of romanticism in Shake-

speare and his circle. The stream of ardent natural
affection, poured as sudden hatred upon the youth
condemned to die, adds an additional note of expression to the horror of the prison where so much of the
scene takes place. It is not here only that Shakespeare
has conceived of such extreme anger and pity as putting a sort of genius into simple women, so that their
'lips drop eloquence', and their intuitions interpret
that which is often too hard or fine for manlier reason;
and it is Isabella with her grand imaginative diction,
and that poetry laid upon the 'prone and speechless
dialect' there is in mere youth itself, who gives utterance to the equity, the finer judgments of the piece on
men and things.

From behind this group with its subtle lights and
shades, its poetry, its impressive contrasts, Shakespeare,
as I said, conveys to us a strong sense of the tyranny of
nature and circumstance over human action. The most
powerful expressions of this side of experience might
be found here. The bloodless, impassible temperament
does but wait for its opportunity, for the almost accidental coherence of time with place, and place with
wishing, to annul its long and patient discipline, and
become in a moment the very opposite of that which
under ordinary conditions it seemed to be, even to itself. The mere resolute self-assertion of the blood
brings to others special temptations, temptations
which, as defects or over-growths, lie in the very qualities which make them otherwise imposing or attractive;
the very advantage of men's gifts of intellect or sentiment being dependent on a balance in their use so
delicate that men hardly maintain it always. Something also must be conceded to influences merely
physical, to the complexion of the heavens, the skyey
influences, shifting as the stars shift; as something also
to the mere caprice of men exercised over each other in
the dispensations of social or political order, to the
chance which makes the life or death of Claudio dependent on Angelo's will.

The many veins of thought which render the poetry

of this play so weighty and impressive unite in the image of Claudio, a flowerlike young man, whom, prompted by a few hints from Shakespeare, the imagination easily clothes with all the bravery of youth, as he crosses the stage before us on his way to death, coming so hastily to the end of his pilgrimage. Set in the horrible blackness of the prison, with its various forms of unsightly death, this flower seems the braver. Fallen by 'prompture of the blood', the victim of a suddenly revived law against the common fault of youth like his, he finds his life forfeited as if by the chance of a lottery. With that instinctive clinging to life, which breaks through the subtlest casuistries of monk or sage apologising for an early death, he welcomes for a moment the chance of life through his sister's shame, though he revolts hardly less from the notion of perpetual imprisonment so repulsive to the buoyant energy of youth. Familiarised, by the words alike of friends and the indifferent, to the thought of death, he becomes gentle and subdued indeed, yet more perhaps through pride than real resignation, and would go down to darkness at last hard and unblinded. Called upon suddenly to encounter his fate, looking with keen and resolute profile straight before him, he gives utterance to some of the central truths of human feeling, the sincere, concentrated expression of the recoiling flesh. Thoughts as profound and poetical as Hamlet's arise in him; and but for the accidental arrest of sentence he would descend into the dust, a mere gilded, idle flower of youth indeed, but with what are perhaps the most eloquent of all Shakespeare's words upon his lips.

As Shakespeare in *Measure for Measure* has refashioned, after a nobler pattern, materials already at hand, so that the relics of other men's poetry are incorporated into his perfect work, so traces of the old 'morality', that early form of dramatic composition which had for its function the inculcating of some moral theme, survive in it also, and give it a peculiar ethical interest. This ethical interest, though it can escape no attentive reader, yet, in accordance with that artistic law which demands the predominance of form everywhere over the mere matter or subject handled, is not to be wholly separated from the special circumstances, necessities, embarrassments, of these particular dramatic persons. The old 'moralities' exemplified most often some rough-and-ready lesson. Here the very intricacy and subtlety of the moral world itself, the difficulty of seizing the true relations of so complex a material, the difficulty of just judgment, of judgment that shall not be unjust, are the lessons conveyed. Even in Whetstone's old story this peculiar vein of moralising comes to the surface: even there, we notice the tendency to dwell on mixed motives, the contending issues of action, the presence of virtues and vices alike in unexpected places, on 'the hard choice of two evils', on the 'imprisoning' of men's 'real intents'. *Measure for Measure* is full of expressions drawn from a profound experience of these casuistries, and that ethical interest becomes predominant in it: it is no longer *Promos and Cassandra*, but *Measure for Measure*, its new name expressly suggesting the subject of *poetical justice*. The action of the play, like the action of life itself for the keener observer, develops in us the conception of this poetical justice, and the yearning to realise it, the true justice of which Angelo knows nothing, because it lies for the most part beyond the limits of any acknowledged law. The idea of justice involves the idea of rights. But at bottom rights are equivalent to that which really is, to facts; and the recognition of his rights therefore, the justice he requires of our hands, or our thoughts, is the recognition of that which the person, in his inmost nature, really is; and as sympathy alone can discover that which really is in matters of feeling and thought, true justice is in its essence a finer knowledge through love.

> 'Tis very pregnant:
> The jewel that we find we stoop and take it,
> Because we see it; but what we do not see
> We tread upon, and never think of it.

It is for this finer justice, a justice based on a more delicate appreciation of the true conditions of men and things, a true respect of persons in our estimate of actions, that the people in *Measure for Measure* cry out as they pass before us; and as the poetry of this play is full of the peculiarities of Shakespeare's poetry, so in its ethics it is an epitome of Shakespeare's moral judgments. They are the moral judgments of an observer, of one who sits as a spectator, and knows how the threads in the design before him hold together under the surface: they are the judgments of the humourist also, who follows with a half-amused but always pitiful sympathy, the various ways of human disposition, and sees less distance than ordinary men between what are called respectively great and little things. It is not always that poetry can be the exponent of morality; but it is this aspect of morals which it represents most naturally, for this true justice is dependent on just those finer appreciations which poetry cultivates in us the power of making, those peculiar valuations of action and its effect which poetry actually requires.

(from *Appreciations,* 1889)

EDWARD DOWDEN

When *Measure for Measure* was written Shakspere was evidently bidding farewell to mirth; its significance is grave and earnest; the humorous scenes would be altogether repulsive were it not that they are needed to present without disguise or extenuation the world of moral licence and corruption out of and above which rise the virginal strength and severity and beauty of Isabella. At the entrance to the dark and dangerous tragic world into which Shakspere was now about to pass stand the figures of Isabella and of Helena, – one the embodiment of conscience, the other the embodiment of will. Isabella is the only one of Shakspere's

women whose heart and eyes are fixed upon an impersonal ideal, to whom something abstract is more, in the
ardour and energy of her youth, than any human personality. Out of this Vienna in which

> Corruption boils and bubbles
> Till it o'errun the stew,

emerges this pure zeal, this rectitude of will, this virgin
sanctity. Isabella's saintliness is not of the passive,
timorous, or merely meditative kind. It is an active
pursuit of holiness through exercise and discipline. She
knows nothing of a Manichean hatred of the body; the
life runs strongly and gladly in her veins; simply her
soul is set upon things belonging to the soul, and uses
the body for its own purposes. And that the life of the
soul may be invigorated she would bring every unruly
thought into captivity, 'having in a readiness to revenge all disobedience'.

> *Isab*. And have you nuns no farther privileges?
> *Tran*. Are these not large enough?
> *Isab*. Yes, truly. I speak not as desiring more;
>   But rather wishing a more strict restraint
>   Upon the sisterhood.

This severity of Isabella proceeds from no real turning away on her part from the joys and hopes of
womanhood; her brother, her schoolfellow Julia, the
memory of her father, are precious to her; her severity
is only a portion of the vital energy of her heart; living
actively she must live purely; and to her the cloister is
looked upon as the place where her energy can spend
itself in stern efforts towards ideal objects. Bodily
suffering is bodily suffering to Isabella, whose 'cheek-
roses' proclaim her physical health and vigour; but
bodily suffering is swallowed up in the joy of quick-
ened spiritual existence: —

> Were I under the terms of death
> The impression of keen whips I'd wear as rubies,

And strip myself to death, as to a bed
That longing have been sick for ere I'd yield
My body up to shame.

And as she had strength to accept pain and death for
herself rather than dishonour, so she can resolutely
accept pain and death for those who are dearest to her.
When Claudio falters back dismayed from the immediate prospect of the grave, Isabella utters her pite-
ous 'Alas, alas!' to perceive the tenderness and timor-
ousness of his spirit; but when he faintly invites her to
yield herself to shame for his sake, she severs herself
with indignation, not from her brother, not from
Claudio, but from this disgrace of manhood in her
brother's form — this treason against fidelity of the
heart:

> O, you beast!
> O, faithless coward! O, dishonest wretch!
> Wilt thou be made a man out of my vice?
> ...
> Take my defiance!
> Die; perish!

Isabella does not return to the sisterhood of Saint
Clare. Putting aside from her the dress of religion, and
the strict conventual rule, she accepts her place as
Duchess of Vienna. In this there is no dropping away,
through love of pleasure or through supineness, from
her ideal; it is entirely meet and right. She has learned
that in the world may be found a discipline more strict,
more awful than the discipline of the convent; she has
learned that the world has need of her; her life is still a
consecrated life; the vital energy of her heart can exert
and augment itself through glad and faithful wife-
hood, and through noble station more fully than in
seclusion. To preside over this polluted and feculent
Vienna is the office and charge of Isabella, 'a thing
ensky'd and sainted':

> Spirits are not finely touched
> But to fine issues; nor Nature never lends
> The smallest scruple of her excellence,
> But, like a thrifty goddess, she determines
> Herself the glory of a creditor,—
> Both thanks and use.

(from *Shakspere – His Mind and Art,* 1875)

A. C. SWINBURNE

The relative disfavour in which the play of *Measure for Measure* has doubtless been at all times generally held is not in my opinion simply explicable on the theory which of late years has been so powerfully and plausibly advanced and advocated on the highest poetic or judicial authority in France or in the world, that in the land of many-coloured cant and many-coated hypocrisy the type of Angelo is something too much a prototype or an autotype of the huge national vice of England. This comment is in itself as surely just and true as it is incisive and direct: but it will not cover by any manner of means the whole question. The strong and radical objection distinctly brought forward against this play, and strenuously supported by the wisest and the warmest devotee among all the worshippers of Shakespeare, is not exactly this, that the Puritan Angelo is exposed: it is that the Puritan Angelo is unpunished. In the very words of Coleridge, it is that by his pardon and his marriage 'the strong indignant claim of justice' is 'baffled'. The expression is absolutely correct and apt: justice is not merely evaded or ignored or even defied: she is both in the older and the newer sense of the word directly and deliberately baffled; buffeted, outraged, insulted, struck in the face. We are left hungry and thirsty after having been made to thirst and hunger for some wholesome single grain at least of righteous and too long retarded retribution: we are tricked out of our dole, defeated of our due, lured and led on to look for some equitable and satisfying upshot, defrauded and derided and sent empty away.

That this play is in its very inmost essence a tragedy, and that no sleight of hand or force of hand could give it even a tolerable show of coherence or consistency when clipped and docked of its proper and rightful end, the mere tone of style prevalent throughout all its better parts to the absolute exclusion of any other would of itself most amply suffice to show. Almost all that is here worthy of Shakespeare at any time is worthy of Shakespeare at his highest: and of this every touch, every line, every incident, every syllable, belongs to pure and simple tragedy. The evasion of a tragic end by the invention and intromission of Mariana has deserved and received high praise for its ingenuity: but ingenious evasion of a natural and proper end is usually the distinctive quality which denotes a workman of a very much lower school than the school of Shakespeare. In short and in fact, the whole elaborate machinery by which the complete and completely unsatisfactory result of the whole plot is attained is so thoroughly worthy of such a contriver as 'the old fantastical duke of dark corners' as to be in a moral sense, if I dare say what I think, very far from thoroughly worthy of the wisest and mightiest mind that ever was informed with the spirit of genius of creative poetry.

(from *A Study of Shakespeare,* 1879)

PART TWO

Some Recent Comments on Production and Editing

Richard David

MEASURE FOR MEASURE ON THE MODERN STAGE (1951)

Measure for Measure has no comparable problems. The niceties (if they may be so called) of a few passages of bawdry are unintelligible without notes, but their general drift is plain and in any case does not affect the action. There are some startling leaps of imagery and syntax, but nothing to nonplus an audience acquainted with *Hamlet* and *Lear*. A dozen textual confusions require straightening out. Peter Brook did not scruple to make cuts in all these, and emendations in the last, but he made them fairly and firmly. The worst sufferers were deservedly the banter of Lucio and his two gentlemen, and the long-winded prose in which the Duke expounds his plot to Isabella – at worst reviser's stuff, at best an experiment, superseded by Shakespeare's later work, in contriving a measured prose to link scenes of highly-wrought verse. There was less excuse for the drastic compression of the last scene (no apology by the Duke for the circuitousness of his proceedings, no Barnardine); the aim here was clearly to remove anything that might dull either the climax and point of the play, or the Duke's nobility. In this it was no longer the minor difficulties of his text that the producer was tackling but, with equal hardihood, his main problem – what *is* to be the total effect of the play?

The simplicity of the text of *Measure for Measure*, as compared with that of *Love's Labour's Lost*, is a function of its more serious mood. It is a play of ideas rather than of impressions and is concerned more with lines of conduct followed out to their logical conclusions than with the confusions and compromises of real life. There is still controversy as to how far these ideas form a coherent argument, and *Shakespeare Survey* had already given space to notable pleadings on either side. The one maintains that *Measure for Measure* is Shakespeare's considered opinion on the apparent conflict in Renaissance theory between the Christian duty of the Ruler to secure Justice, and that of the individual to be merciful. The other finds in the purpose and character of Isabella and the Duke as many dislocations as in the time-scheme, and holds that Shakespeare, here more even than usual, was concerned only to contrive a series of fine dramatic moments, heightening the effect of each as best might be, without regard to the philosophic or psychological coherence of the whole. A modern producer is apparently faced with the alternative of abandoning any totality of effect for the sake of the incidental beauties, or of clouding these by the imposition of a 'programme' that will be bewildering to his audience.

Peter Brook's solution of the conundrum was symbolized in the setting that he himself devised for the play. This was a double range of lofty arches, receding from the centre of the stage on either side to the wings upstage. These arches might remain open to the sky in those scenes where some air and freshness is required – the convent at night where Isabella hears from Lucio of her brother's plight, Mariana's moated grange, and the street scene in which all odds are finally made even; or, in a moment, their spaces could be blanked out, with grey flats for the shabby decorum of the courtroom, with grilles for the prison cells. Downstage, at either side, stood a heavy postern gate, also permanently set, serving as focus for the subsidiary scenes to which the full stage would have given undue emphasis, or those, such as the visiting of the imprisoned Claudio, which gain by a cramped setting. The single permanent set gave coherence to the whole; its continuous shadowy presence held together the brilliant series of closet-scenes played on a smaller section of the stage, that glorious succession of duets, Lucio–Isabella, Isabella–Angelo, Claudio–Duke, Isabella–Claudio, in

which Shakespeare conceived the action. These were
given all the more definition, and urgency, by the
apparently confined space in which they were played,
although their scope was restricted more by lighting
than by any material barrier, and at any moment the
whole span of the stage might spring to life and remind
us of our bearings in the play. The occasions for such a
broadening of effect are not many, but the producer
made the most of them. To the progress of Claudio and
Juliet to prison, with all corrupt Vienna surging and
clamouring about them, and to the final marshalling of
all the characters for judgement, he added a third full-
stage scene, in which the prisoners, processing through
the central hall of the prison, brought its holes and
corners for a moment into relation with each other.
Shakespeare's text gives only the slimmest pretext for
this, in Pompey's enumeration of the old customers
whom he has met again in his new employment; but
the expansion – in both senses – came happily as a
central point of relief in a chain of scenes each requir-
ing a confined attention.

The great duets largely play themselves. It is they
that make the play memorable, and such tense and
moving writing is found elsewhere in Shakespeare only
in the great tragedies. There is of course the notorious
danger that to a modern audience Isabella may appear
unbearably self-centred and priggish. Isabella knows,
and a Jacobean audience took for granted, that there
can be no compromise with evil, that, though the only
road to right may appear to lie through wrong, the
taking of it can do no one any good. Claudio acknow-
ledges it, when not blinded by his panic, for he finally
begs his sister's pardon for suggesting otherwise; and
we know it, too. But we are shy of being dogmatic
about it in the manner of the Jacobeans; though we
may admit Isabella's reasons we find it hard to swallow
her matter-of-fact schematization of them – 'More than
our brother is our chastity.'

The producer and Barbara Jefford together saved
our faces. Miss Jefford's was a young Isabella, a novice

indeed, with no mature *savoir-faire* with which to meet her predicament, but only the burning conviction that two blacks cannot make a white. When she came to the perilous words she turned, from speaking full to the audience, to hide her face passionately against the wall behind her, as if herself ashamed that her intellect could find no more adequate expression of her heart's certainty. In the same way her tirade against her brother, when he begs her to save his life at any cost, was made to appear as much anger with her own failure as a witness to truth, her own inability to communicate it to others. It was indeed skilful, and a good illustration of one kind of 'translation', to substitute the pathos of the inarticulate for an affronting insensitivity, and convert what is often an offence to modern playgoers into the very engine to enforce their sympathy. Altogether it was a moving performance, that found its perfect foil in the suppressed and twisted nobility of John Gielgud's Angelo. With such interpreters the producer could risk the boldest effects. The climax of the play was breath-taking. Mariana has passionately implored Isabella to kneel to the Duke for Angelo's pardon; the Duke has warned her that to do so would be 'against all sense' – 'He dies for Claudio.' The pause that followed must have been among the longest in theatre history. Then hesitantly, still silent, Isabella moved across the stage and knelt before the Duke. Her words came quiet and level, and as their full import of mercy reached Angelo, a sob broke from him. It was perfectly calculated and perfectly timed; and the whole perilous manoeuvre had been triumphantly brought off.

Yet it is not Isabella, still less Angelo, that is the crux of the producer's problem, but the Duke. If the play is to mean anything, if it is to be more than a series of disjointed magnificences, we must accept the Duke's machinations as all to good purpose, and himself as entirely wise and just. Peter Brook presented Vincentio rather as Friar turned Duke than as Duke turned Friar, and maintained throughout the impressiveness of his appearance at the cost of rendering his disguise completely unconvincing. He had found in Harry Andrews a Duke whose commanding presence could dominate the play, as the half-seen arches the stage, and whose charm of manner could convince us of his integrity and wisdom. If his speaking could have been more measured, more confident, more natural ease and less careful manipulation, we might have had the Vincentio of a generation.

It remains (since *Measure for Measure* is still a comedy) to say something about the comics. In refreshing defiance of tradition, Pompey, Elbow, and Abhorson were left to make their proper effect as natural English 'characters', instead of being reduced, as in most productions of the play, to circus clowns and fantastics. Peter Brook has not always escaped censure for that overemphasis on 'business' which I have already denounced as the fatal Siren of modern producers. Here, where so much depended on control, the supporting elements in the play were not allowed to get much out of hand. The Viennese mob was extremely loud and energetic, but then the outrageousness of his manners (a motif echoed in the Brueghelesque grotesquery of Brook's costumes) is an essential contrast to the nobility of the play's main themes. Pompey was assiduous in distributing advertisements of Mistress Overdone's establishment to all with whom he came in contact, a 'turn' for which the cue can only be wrung from the text with difficulty; but it is in character, and was carefully confined to those moments when no 'necessary question of the play was then to be considered'. It was permissible, too, having provided a pit from which an admirable Barnardine emerged with his true effect, to use it for a tumultuous 'exeunt omnes' at the end of the scene. The only real excrescence was some buffoonery with Pompey's fetters that for a moment put the Duke's dignity in jeopardy. This must be forgiven a producer of such restraint elsewhere that he could keep the crowd in the background of his prison scenes silent and motionless through almost an entire act; could dispense with music, save a tolling bell and the herald's trumpet; and at the close could allow his couples merely to walk, 'hand in hand, with wandering steps and slow', in silence from the stage – and to what great effects!

SOURCE: *Shakespeare Survey*, IV, 1951.

Harold Hobson

RECENT PRODUCTIONS OF
MEASURE FOR MEASURE (1964)

The Stratford on Avon *Measure for Measure* in the 1962 season continued a tradition recently established when, just before the outbreak of the 1939–45 war, George Robey played Falstaff. In the late 'forties Stratford brought another famous star of musical comedy and the halls, Jay Laurier, to give breadth and a sort of vulgar humanity to some of Shakespeare's more clownish parts. In *Measure for Measure* Norah Blaney, who had appeared in some of the most celebrated musicals of the 'twenties, such as *Oh, Kay,* was engaged to provide a very juicy performance as Mistress Overdone. This, however, as it turned out, was only a small point of antiquarian interest. What made John Blatchley's production memorable was something quite different from the introduction into Shakespeare of players formerly famous in the world of song and dance shows. The striking thing about it was its exaltation of the Duke.

There was, it is true, no ducal splendour about John Bury's setting, which was impressive, but very simple. At the back of the stage there was an enormous wall of what looked like grey rough stone. There was a rough stage surface of a similar texture, across which ran a wide wooden platform diagonally. This facilitated the swift movement of the Duke. It enabled him to pass rapidly from point to point, to dart hither and thither, to be (almost) omnipresent. This swiftness, this speed, this ubiquity, were established against the darkness and gloom of Vienna under his notorious deputy, Angelo. And throughout the evening this deputy – it is a vital fact of the production – remained a deputy only: nothing more.

From his first appearance this Angelo was a man who was cowardly afraid of his soul: he had no worldly authority, no joy in the glorious pageantry of ducal existence, in the possessions of wealth, or of power over the lives and deaths of men and women. He was played by Marius Goring, an actor who began his career at the Old Vic with a fine, rhetorical and romantic panache. He was an Old Vic Romeo in *his* twenties and the age's thirties. Behind this early picturesque glow, however, was a mind keenly interested in historical developments. There are few players who have studied as deeply as Mr Goring the sordid history and the appalling terrors of our times. This knowledge has marked Mr Goring. As an actor he is as accomplished as ever, but his old frank welcoming of rich emotions has disappeared. He is an expert now in the neurotic, the morbid, and the brilliantly unbalanced.

All this was evident in his Angelo. Mr Goring played Angelo with unseeing, staring eyes. His face was blanched. Wherever he was, on the platform of justice, or in the secrecy of his candle-lit and concupiscent chamber, he stood frozen in fear. He was ever in the midst of appalled silences. It was impossible to believe that anybody, the weak, dark, poetic Claudio of Ian Holm, or the strangely bouncing Isabella of Judi Dench, rosy from the fleshpots of the world, could be at his mercy.

Long before he felt the least temptation towards Isabella he was plainly at the mercy of a being more terrible than himself. From the beginning his nerve had gone. Neither he, nor Miss Dench's robust Isabella, more fitted to the breezy pastures of East Anglia than to the cold seclusion of a convent, dominated the play. They were both dwarfed by the alarming phenomenon of the meddling Duke. For the first time in my experience the Duke, and not Angelo or Isabella, was the principal figure in the play.

This man, played by Tom Fleming with eager authority, zestfully disguising himself as a monk, teaching Isabella how to trap Angelo into bed with another

woman, popping up in prison to decide whose head is
to be chopped off today, ranking as blasphemy any
joke made at his expense, punishing sin, rewarding
virtue, playing cruelly with his creatures till his moment comes to dispense final judgement, grew larger
and larger as the play progressed. At the end he was
everywhere, on the magistrates' bench, in gaol, in robes
of state, under the monk's cowl, all-interfering and
omnipotent.

It was thus that Mr Blatchley brought the audience
to consider the problems and paradoxes of religion.
Who is this Duke? Is he indeed a man, or a god? He
has in his area of activity all power. He can bring
about his aims by a wave of the arm. Why, then, does
he not give the immediate signal that would end all
ills? Why does he choose to accomplish his desires by
means so unnecessarily tortuous, so unnecessarily tor-
turing? Why does he achieve the happiness of his
people only through their pain, when pain could be
dismissed by one straight word from his lips? Through
Mr Blatchley's direct and unequivocal vision Shakespeare posed a problem which has vexed all theologies
that accept the reality of evil: how can the continuance of this evil be reconciled with the universal and
irresistible goodness of God?

Shakespeare himself gave his answer in another
play. It was a bitter answer. The gods, he says, enjoy
our torture. It is not an answer we are bound to accept.
In philosophy, whatever may be the case in literature,
Shakespeare abides our question as much as most, and
more than Berkeley.

It is easy to see why Mr Blatchley did not adopt the
conventional approach to *Measure for Measure*. The
change which has taken place during the twentieth
century in our ideas about morality has made this one
of the most difficult, the least obviously and superfici-
ally viable, of all Shakespeare's major works. It is
founded upon an extraordinary reverence for chastity.
It regards physical purity as the greatest of virtues. It
accords to virginity a mystical importance. In terms of

human happiness I am not by any means sure that it is
not wise to do so. But wise or not, it has a view of
chastity which few people anywhere hold today, and
practically no one in the theatre. I do not think that it
is too much to say that no living actress could make
acceptable as the central feature of the play Isabella's
single-minded preoccupation with her bodily integrity.

If chastity cannot any longer be relied on to furnish
the play's *raison d'être*, what about the thing against
which chastity is a protection, namely, sex? It was sex
that Peter Brook's production of the play emphasized,
also at Stratford, a few years ago. There was a hot flow
of lubricity in Mr Brook's presentation which undoubtedly gave to the play a powerful vitality. Isabella' impossible purity was subordinated to brothels
and bawds. But this is the kind of interpretation that
cannot be done twice. It is not a thing that wears. John
Blatchley perceived this. He began the production,
true enough, in a puddle of sex. In his interpretation
the act of sex rode the imagination of Isabella as
powerfully as it did that of Angelo, or of Lucio, or of
Pompey the bawd, who talks about it all the time. But
Mr Blatchley saw that these were horses that would not
a second time run to the end. Whereas normally Pompey and his companions in all classes of society are life-
sized people whose problems and preoccupations are
intended to horrify, to perturb, and to melt the hearts
of the audience, at Stratford in 1962 they gradually
diminished into nasty-minded children, dwarfed by
the frightening Duke. In these difficult circumstances
Mr Blatchley chose a quite new interpretation: an
interpretation that brought up the question of government and of evil still continuing despite the existence
of incontrovertible moral power.

I dwell in some detail on the circumstances and attitude of the 1962 production at Stratford because it is
the beautifully characterized costumes designed by
Alix Stone which are illustrated in this volume. But
there is also another reason. The advent of Peter Hall
at Stratford, and the subsequent invasion of London at

the Aldwych Theatre by the Royal Shakespeare Company is a major development in the history of the British drama, and especially in the interpretation of Shakespeare. Mr Hall has brought about a new attitude towards the production of Shakespeare in this country, and this attitude is brilliantly illustrated by the *Measure for Measure* which was presented under his auspices.

Britain, of course, has always had a great tradition of Shakespearean acting. It has been a tradition built up by stars. There is no reason to suppose that Shakespeare himself would resent this. He did much of his work – much of his finest work – to the measure of a particular star of his own time, Burbage. After Burbage we have had Garrick and Edmund Kean and Irving and, in our own age, John Gielgud and Laurence Olivier. The old tradition of Shakespearean playing – the old tradition at its best, a tradition that paid enormous and intelligent tribute to the proper speaking of the verse – still held sway when I first began to visit the London theatre. It yielded some magnificent things. In the 'thirties there was a production of *Twelfth Night* in London – it was called the black and white production, because the scenery and costumes were in those colours only – in which Cecil Ramage spoke with such nobility and repose the lines beginning 'Mark it, Cesario, it is old and plain, the spinsters and the knitters in the sun Do use to chant it' that I went to see it over and over again. Or, to be absolutely exact, I went over and over again to hear Mr Ramage speak those particular lines. The feeling of peace which they gave, the balm, the surcease to all anxiety and strife was something I shall carry with me all my life.

A little before this I saw Gielgud's Richard II. Here was not peace, but a sword: no calm, but an almost intolerable tension. This was the performance of a man stretched to the very limit of his nerves, yet preserving in his agony a luscious enjoyment of his own misery expressed in lambent and selfindulgent verse of

unsurpassable loveliness. Gielgud standing aloft on the
battlements of a lonely castle and speaking through
clenched teeth to the rebellious Bolingbroke, 'We are
amazed; and thus long have we stood To watch the
fearful bending of thy knee,' all his majesty outraged,
yet finding a masochistic enjoyment in so magnificently
marking the depth of his humiliation, is a memory that
cannot be forgotten. Shakespearean playing before
Peter Hall was full of such superb achievements.

It is now the fashion to view such matters with misgiving. We have come back to the Macaulay view that
the mind of Shakespeare is our triumph, not a dozen
lines of rhetoric. We no longer believe Shaw when he
argues that Shakespeare is a master musician, but a
poor thinker. We now rate the thought above the
music. Only we are not absolutely certain what the
thought is. We go behind the lines in order to see what
the lines mean. The development of modern psychology is such that we are quite ready to believe that
Shakespeare, for all his unrivalled mastery of words,
was often saying things of which he himself was quite
unaware. It is thus that we find that the most admired,
the most popular, and the most accomplished Shakespearean productions of our times are remarkable, not
for the performance of the principal character, not for
the general beauty of the treatment of the verse, but
for an interpretation of the meaning of the play which
would have astonished our predecessors. We have a
King Lear from Peter Brook which shows that Lear was
a tiresome old man, against whom Goneril and Regan
had many legitimate causes of complaint: he petu-
lantly knocked over tables which had been set for a
dinner, a habit which no hostess could be expected to
endure. We have from Peter Hall himself a *Twelfth
Night* in which the grief-stricken Olivia is a comic
character; and we have from Mr Blatchley the *Measure
for Measure* of which I have been speaking.

I do not believe it is possible to say that the one
method of Shakespearean approach is better than the
other. The pre-Hall method is a thing of dazzling, iso-

lated, sensuous effects; the Hall method achieves an integrated, intellectual and emotional interpretation that is all of a piece. One sends a shiver, many shivers, down the spine; the other feeds and stimulates the mind. One is outside time; the other speaks directly, through Shakespeare, to the fears and feelings of the contemporary world. The Royal Shakespeare Company makes Shakespeare relevant to the problems of our age. The best productions that preceded the Royal Shakespeare revolution made us for a moment forget our problems, and so perhaps increased our strength to deal with them. All this is a matter for argument. My own feeling is that the older method of playing Shakespeare had had a long innings, and was becoming a little weary. It was time for it to retire to the pavilion after knocking up a very large score, and for a new batsman to emerge. But he, too, will tire in his time, and there will be need either of a successor or of a restoration. But at present the Royal Shakespeare approach to Shakespeare, of which *Measure for Measure* is a very sound example, is hitting hard all round the wicket.

SOURCE: Introduction to the Folio Society *Measure for Measure*, 1964.

W. W. Robson

SHAKESPEARE AND HIS MODERN EDITORS (1965)

That new 'Ardens' should supersede old 'Ardens' has come to seem, to those interested in such matters, as inevitable a process as the changing seasons. There are still some more to come, so that this may not be a particularly appropriate moment to ask whether the changes are all for the better, whether modern methods of editing Shakespeare are an unqualified improvement on the old. Yet there may be this excuse for taking the opportunity to make a few general remarks; that the latest edition to the series is *Measure for Measure*, a play which I cannot believe will ever cease to be relevant to the deepest concerns of civilized men; since it is the vivid imagining in art, by the greatest English mind known to us, of the consequences in one particular case of an attempt to impose morality by legislation. Being as such permanently topical (if the phrase may pass) it may be allowed to provide the occasion for raising the general question about the series that I have referred to. I emphasize the generality of the question; Dr Lever's work seems to me in no way inferior, of its kind, to some other editions in the series, and it deserves, as it will get, a 'professional' review in a learned journal. What I am questioning is, not his competence within the framework of the assumptions about editing which he has taken over, but those assumptions themselves.

One thing to be immediately noticed about the new edition is that it contains much more that is not by Shakespeare than the old one. That is, the reader is expected to take in, along with *Measure for Measure*, much more in the way of academic wrappings, impedimenta, and the small change of Elizabethan scholarship. There is evidently no expectation, then, of any other public for this edition than university lecturers, sixth-form teachers, undergraduates, and so on. It does not cater for – and so, perhaps in a small way, helps to diminish – a class of readers whom one *could* imagine using older editions; readers not particularly 'literary', or 'academic', or 'theatrical' in their interests, who still read Shakespeare for pleasure and disinterested profit. Such readers could still dig out of Dr Lever's work what they want: a good text, and glossing of the difficult words or phrases (not only the obviously obsolete ones, but the *faux amis*, the ones that have changed in meaning). Dr Lever's conservatism as an editor is the good thing about this edition. He sensibly disposes of unnecessary and far-fetched theories such as Dover Wilson's (that the play must have undergone successive revisions). And so, being free from this sort of *parti pris,* he is able to deal convincingly with the textual anomalies (and find less of them) and explain most of the peculiarities of the Folio text as consistent with the view that it is based on Shakespeare's uncorrected manuscript. This sort of 'backroom' work helps our (perhaps to-day largely imaginary) common reader. Also Dr Lever's notes are rarely as irrelevant, and never as absurd, as many of his predecessor's. The common reader is helped by some of these. What else does he need? I think what he also needs, and what would probably interest him more than all the textual discussion or explicatory footnotes, would be some indication of what the really distinguished critics of Shakespeare (this would be a very short list, where *Measure for Measure* is concerned) have thought about the play, over the centuries. Knowledge of the small fry an editor can keep to himself; the best insights are the one thing needful. It is hereabouts that Dr Lever is so unsatisfactory – and his unsatisfactoriness is so representative – that a more extensive comment seems justified.

There can be few of the plays of Shakespeare about which recent opinion has changed so radically as about

Measure for Measure. It is true that some writers, such
as the late A. P. Rossiter, have held to the old tradition
that it is unwholesome, cynical, or morally equivocal;
but on the whole that tradition has been displaced.
Nor is it now common to find the later scenes of the
play, in which the Duke is prominent, dismissed as
theatrical sleight of hand, a mere arbitrary winding-up
having no vital relationship with what has gone before.
In this respect, as in others, the editorial introduction
is a reliable index of present-day attitudes.

Unfortunately this introduction also reveals less
pleasant aspects of the familiar academic process of
assimilating critical insights. Far-reaching changes in
taste and appreciation, and consequently in the analysis and judgment of particular plays of Shakespeare,
are no doubt due to various and complex causes. But
as we look back at the process whereby modern
opinion, here represented by Dr Lever, has come to
find *Measure for Measure* artistically sound and
morally coherent, we must suppose that the work of
original critics has played some part. And to this work
Dr Lever's introduction does not do justice. His brief
reference (p. lvii) to Wilson Knight gives no indication
of the remarkable pioneering quality or the lasting
impact of chapter iv of *The Wheel of Fire.* Indeed, his
way of referring to this essay is misleading, and misleading in the same direction as other parts of the introduction; for in speaking of Knight's view as something merely 'outlined', which later interpreters
'schematically developed', he appears to have missed its
true value, which lies, not in offering an abstract
scheme, but a new stimulus, a suggestion, a prompting.
But for Knight's word 'parable' his successors substituted 'allegory'. Now it is true that some of the Parables in the Synoptic Gospels were interpreted as alleg-
ories, not only by the Fathers but even by the Evan-
gelists themselves; but the consensus of informed
opinion today is that this was not their original character. At any rate, the elaborate allegory of Christ's
Atonement which Knight's successors imposed on

Measure to Measure is open to many of the objections that still later critics, including Dr Lever, have brought against it. The result has been to bring attempts at interpretation of the play to an impasse – is it *either* an allegory *or* a drama of men and women? – and so to threaten to renew the confusion from which Knight's original essay seemed to offer a means of release.

What is really deplorable is Dr Lever's omission of any reference to the essay of F. R. Leavis reprinted in *The Common Pursuit*. The explanation for this cannot be that the editor is deferring to some tabu on the mention of anything that appeared in *Scrutiny*, for in the notes (p. 15) he refers to the article of 1942 by L. C. Knights which actually called forth Leavis's defence of the play. Dr Lever may not agree that that defence is one of the most distinguished pieces of Shakespeare criticism written in this century. But it is hard to see how anyone knowing of an argument so challenging and comprehensive, yet economical, could prefer to send students to any of the marginal or minor contributions which Dr Lever rounds up. And Dr Lever's list of these is very exhaustive.

Dr Lever's introduction itself is a good specimen of the mandarin style of much modern academic discussion of Shakespeare: —

> The *ad hominem* call for Angelo to acknowledge his own 'natural guiltiness' is all too plainly *a femina* and inadvertently suggestive.
>
> For Escalus, justice dissolves in the amoralism of nature; for Angelo it is impaled on the absolutes of the spirit.

Points are being made here: but do we want to encourage students to think that this is the best way to write?

Dr Lever's style provokes me to ask: what is the most important qualification for editing Shakespeare? To judge from the manner in which modern editions are often reviewed in scholarly journals, it is a capacity to

handle present-day bibliographical machinery, to learn
what a Hinman or a Bowers has to teach. Historical
and linguistic competence are also much recom-
mended. And no one will deny they are necessary. But
rarely is it suggested that an editor should be a critic,
in the broadest sense of the word. Yet an editor's
ability in criticism, in that sense, determines his use, or
misuse, of his scholarship; determines not only his in-
troductory interpretation, but matters of text, what he
annotates, how he annotates it; his whole way of pre-
senting the play in book form.

Now a truly probing critique of *Measure for Measure* would have to ask, and make us ask ourselves, what
is *essential* in the play? and what is relatively inert?
Or, if it is all essential, to show us that. But who can
feel that *all* the topics Dr Lever claims are treated by
Shakespeare in this play are vividly present to any conceivable playgoer or reader? Yet this closely-woven,
well-informed historical discussion has the effect of im-
plying that everything it mentions is equally important, equally 'there'. This leads to the illusory conviction that we *now* are clear about everything. My own
reaction, when I come to such a typical assertion as
'True virtue, like true authority, rests in the Duke' (p.
lxxxi), is to feel that it makes the play sound easy. Why
then were so many people, at least from Coleridge on-
wards, worried by it?

Some of Dr Lever's more distinctive contributions to
the discussion of the play concern the Duke, and the
problems of authority – problems for the man and
ruler – that are dramatized in him. Dr Lever argues for
this as an important Renaissance topic; how important
is it in the play? It seems to me that if the material Dr
Lever dwells on is important in the play, *Measure for
Measure* is seriously faulty. The essay of Leavis I mentioned helps us to see Shakespeare's handling of the
Duke as a bold use of frank contrivance and theatre-
convention which does not demand, in regard to the
other characters, any suspension of our reasonable ex-
pectations of credibility or an induced anaesthesia of

our normal moral sense. But, if Dr Lever's introduction is relevant, the play seems both to demand, and to refuse to gratify, an interest in the Duke as man and ruler. On the other hand, if we accept the kind of reading favoured by Leavis, we are left with apparently extraneous matter on our hands. Of course I do not suggest that such difficulties cannot be dealt with, or that Dr Lever's work cannot be used to help us to deal with them; only that his treatment of them is insufficiently critical, and so does not bring them into focus.

But now a misgiving might arise. Let us imagine the ideal edition of *Measure for Measure* – or of any other great play – in which the editor-critic, having responded fully to the experience of the play, and got it into perspective, produces something memorable, first-rate and first-hand as criticism; suppose him also to have been able and willing to master all the necessary specialisms. Would we want so distinguished a critique bound up with the play? The better it was, the more pernicious its influence might be; students might read it instead of the play. On the other hand, if the introduction is to be colourless, why bother with it? I am not sure if the misgiving is soundly based. Distinguished criticism *must* send us to the play; it offers nothing that can be 'mugged up'. In any case, the question is somewhat unreal: what likelihood is there of getting anything so rare as first-rate criticism from an editor? A more practical request is for something brief and modest.

Short criticisms can also be sharper. Certainly what Dr Lever gives us is in obvious ways an improvement on the old Arden edition, with its moral horror at the play, and the 'morbid pessimism' it insisted on seeing there. Yet it strikes me that while the old editor (Hart) may only have been voicing the conventionality of his day, his naïve dismay, which makes his introduction a period piece, does also suggest that he had been more gripped and disturbed by the play than the present editor. Dr Lever brings much wider reading in the

moralists of Shakespeare's age to his discussion of the
great themes of the play. But one wonders if any of his
remarks on these will stick in the mind as does Johnson's indignation at the impiety of the Friar's speech
'Be absolute for death. . . .' Surely when Dr Lever remarks of that speech that it 'might seem to be a statement of "doctrine" by Holy Church in the guise of a
friar' – though he goes on to comment on things in it
which are not Christian – he is failing to focus attention on one of the strangest things in this strange play.
Isabella had reminded Angelo that

> . . . all the souls that were forfeit once,
> And He that might the vantage best have took
> Found out the remedy.

Yet the Friar, supposedly preparing Claudio for his reconciliation with God, makes no reference to Christ's
atoning sacrifice. Is not this quite as surprising whether
or not *Measure for Measure* is 'Catholic', as Coghill
thought, or 'Protestant', as Dr Lever thinks?

Most of the contents of Dr Lever's introduction and
notes are what one expects to find in a modern
scholarly edition of Shakespeare. How much of all this
scholarship is useful? Dr Lever is not always persuasive
that much of it is. Thus, working towards his own
interpretation of the *genre* of *Measure for Measure*, he
expounds Guarini's recipe for tragicomedy, suggesting
that this was 'in the air' at the (presumable) time of
composition of Shakespeare's play. But, as he then goes
on to show that Shakespeare's play does not really
answer to Guarini's account, we are left wondering
what was the point of bringing in Guarini. This raises
a general question: while it is certainly an editor's
duty to acquaint himself with such background
material, does it have to be unloaded on the reader?
New irrelevance, by very reason of its being subtler
and more persuasively introduced than the Victorian
editor's, may be more of a nuisance. Likewise I do not
much care for his painstaking discussion – convention-

ally acceptable as it may be – of possible sources and
analogues for the interlocking stories on which Shakespeare built the play. The student, if not the ordinary
reader, needs directing to *Promos and Cassandra*, but is
it too drastic to suggest that he needs little else? At any
rate, I would have preferred, as more plainly relevant
than this *Quellenforschung*, a fuller discussion of *All's
Well*, that other play of Shakespeare's which presents
comparable difficulties, whatever we may think of its
relative scale or value.

Skill and labour have obviously gone to the making
of this new edition. The introduction, if used with
care, yields some possibly useful background material,
as do the appendices. But otherwise the really surprising thing – the ironical thing, surely – is that, after all
this fuss about 'modern methods' and scientific bibliography and so on, the text printed by Dr Lever differs
very little – to the unprofessional eye, at any rate –
from Hart's.

SOURCE: *Cambridge Quarterly*, I i (1965–6).

PART THREE

Modern Studies of
Measure for Measure

G. Wilson Knight

MEASURE FOR MEASURE AND THE GOSPELS (1930)

In *Measure for Measure* we have a careful dramatic pattern, a studied explication of a central theme: the moral nature of man in relation to the crudity of man's justice, especially in the matter of sexual vice. There is, too, a clear relation existing between the play and the Gospels, for the play's theme is this:

> Judge not, that ye be not judged.
> For with what judgement ye judge, ye shall be judged: and with what measure ye mete, it shall be measured to you again. (Matthew vii 1)

The ethical standards of the Gospels are rooted in the thought of *Measure for Measure*. Therefore, in this analysis, we shall, while fixing attention primarily on the play, yet inevitably find a reference to the New Testament continually helpful, and sometimes essential.

Measure for Measure is a carefully constructed work. Not until we view it as a deliberate artistic pattern of certain pivot ideas determining the play's action throughout shall we understand its peculiar nature. Though there is consummate psychological insight here and at least one person of most vivid and poignant human interest, we must first have regard to the central theme, and only second look for exact verisimilitude to ordinary processes of behaviour. We must be careful not to let our human interest in any one person distort our single vision of the whole pattern. The play tends towards allegory or symbolism. The poet elects to risk a certain stiffness, or arbitrariness, in the directing of his plot rather than fail to express dramatically, with variety and precision, the full content of his basic thought. Any stiffness in the matter of human probability is, however, more than balanced by its extreme fecundity and compacted significance of dramatic symbolism. The persons of the play tend to illustrate certain human qualities chosen with careful reference to the main theme. Thus Isabella stands for sainted purity, Angelo for Pharisaical righteousness, the Duke for a psychologically sound and enlightened ethic. Lucio represents indecent wit, Pompey and Mistress Overdone professional immorality. Barnadine is hard-headed, criminal insensitiveness. Each person illumines some facet of the central theme: man's moral nature. The play's attention is confined chiefly to sexual ethics: which in isolation is naturally the most pregnant of analysis and the most universal of all themes. No other subject provides so clear a contrast between human consciousness and human instinct; so rigid a distinction between the civilized and the natural qualities of man; so amazing, yet so slight, a boundary set in the public mind between the foully bestial and the ideally divine in humanity. The atmosphere, purpose, and meaning of the play are throughout ethical. The Duke, lord of this play in the exact sense that Prospero is lord of *The Tempest*, is the prophet of an enlightened ethic. He controls the action from start to finish, he allots, as it were, praise and blame, he is lit at moments with divine suggestion comparable with his almost divine power of fore-knowledge, and control, and wisdom. There is an enigmatic, other-worldly, mystery suffusing his figure and the meaning of his acts: their result, however, in each case justifies their initiation – wherein we see the allegorical nature of the play, since the plot is so arranged that each person receives his deserts in the light of the Duke's – which is really the Gospel – ethic.

The poetic atmosphere is one of religion and critical morality. The religious colouring is orthodox, as in *Hamlet*. Isabella is a novice among 'the votarists of St Clare' (I iv 6): the Duke disguises himself as a Friar,

exercising the divine privileges of his office towards
Juliet, Barnadine, Claudio, Pompey. We hear of 'the
consecrated fount a league below the city' (IV iii 102).
The thought of death's eternal damnation, which is
prominent in *Hamlet*, recurs in Claudio's speech:

> Ay, but to die and go we know not where;
> To lie in cold obstruction and to rot;
> This sensible warm motion to become
> A kneaded clod; and the delighted spirit
> To bathe in fiery floods, or to reside
> In thrilling region of thick-ribbed ice;
> To be imprison'd in the viewless winds,
> And blown with restless violence round about
> The pendant world; or to be worse than worst
> Of those that lawless and uncertain thoughts
> Imagine howling: 'tis too horrible!
> The weariest and most loathed worldly life
> That age, ache, penury, and imprisonment
> Can lay on nature is a paradise
> To what we fear in death.   (III i 118)

So powerful can orthodox eschatology be in *Measure
for Measure*: it is not, as I shall show, all-powerful.
Nor is the play primarily a play of death-philosophy:
its theme is rather that of the Gospel ethic. And there
is no more beautiful passage in all Shakespeare on the
Christian redemption than Isabella's lines to Angelo:

> Alas! Alas!
> Why, all the souls that were, were forfeit once;
> And He, that might the vantage best have took,
> Found out the remedy: How would you be,
> If he which is the top of judgment, should
> But judge you as you are? O, think on that;
> And mercy then will breathe within your lips,
> Like a man new made.   (II ii 72)

This is the natural sequence to Isabella's earlier
lines:

> Well, believe this,
> No ceremony that to great ones 'longs,
> Not the king's crown, nor the deputed sword,
> The marshal's truncheon, nor the judge's robe,
> Become them with one half so good a grace
> As mercy does.   (II ii 58)

These thoughts are a repetition of those in Portia's famous 'mercy' speech. There they come as a sudden, gleaming, almost irrelevant beam of the ethical imagination. But here they are not irrelevant: they are intrinsic with the thought of the whole play, the pivot of its movement. In *The Merchant of Venice* the Gospel reference is explicit:

> . . . We do pray for mercy;
> And that same prayer doth teach us all to render
> The deeds of mercy.   (IV 1 200)

And the central idea of *Measure for Measure* is this:

> And forgive us our debts as we forgive our debtors.

Thus 'justice' is a mockery: man, himself a sinner, cannot presume to judge. That is the lesson driven home in *Measure for Measure*. Now the atmosphere of Christianity pervading the play merges into the purely ethical suggestion implicit in the inter-criticism of all the persons. Though Christian ethic be the central theme, there is a wider setting of varied ethical thought, voiced by each person in turn, high or low. The Duke, Angelo, and Isabella are clearly obsessed with such ideas and criticize freely in their different fashions. So also Elbow and the officers bring in Froth and Pompey, accusing them. Abhorson is severely critical of Pompey:

> A bawd? Fie upon him! He will discredit our mystery.   (IV ii 29)

Lucio traduces the Duke's character, Mistress Overdone informs against Lucio. Barnardine is universally
despised. All, that is, react to each other in an essentially ethical mode: which mode is the peculiar and
particular vision of this play. Even music is brought to
the bar of the ethical judgement:

> . . . music oft hath such a charm
> To make bad good, and good provoke to harm.
>
> (IV i 14)

Such is the dominating atmosphere of this play. Out of
it grow the main themes, the problem and the lesson of
Measure for Measure. There is thus a pervading atmosphere of orthodoxy and ethical criticism, in which is
centred the mysterious holiness, the profound death-
philosophy, the enlightened human insight and Christian ethic of the protagonist, the Duke of Vienna.

The satire of the play is directed primarily against
self-conscious, self-protected righteousness. The Duke
starts the action by resigning his power to Angelo. He
addresses Angelo, outspoken in praise of his virtues,
Thus:

> Angelo,
> There is a kind of character in thy life,
> That to the observer doth thy history
> Fully unfold. Thyself and thy belongings
> Are not thine own so proper, as to waste
> Thyself upon thy virtue, they on thee.
> Heaven doth with us as we with torches do;
> Not light them for themselves; for if our virtues
> Did not go forth of us, 'twere all alike
> As if we had them not. Spirits are not finely touch'd,
> But to fine issues, nor Nature never lends
> The smallest scruple of her excellence,
> But, like a thrifty goddess, she determines
> Herself the glory of a creditor,
> Both thanks and use.
>
> (I i 27)

The thought is similar to that of the Sermon on the
Mount:

> Ye are the light of the world. A city that is set on an
> hill cannot be hid.
> Neither do men light a candle, and put it under a
> bushel, but on a candlestick; and it giveth light unto
> all that are in the house.   (Matthew v 14)

Not only does the Duke's 'torch'-metaphor clearly recall this passage, but his development of it is vividly
paralleled by other of Jesus' words. The Duke compares
'Nature' to 'a creditor', lending qualities and demand-
ing both 'thanks and use'. Compare:

> For the kingdom of heaven is as a man travelling
> into a far country, who called his own servants, and
> delivered unto them his goods.
> And unto one he gave five talents, to another two,
> and to another one; to every man according to his
> several ability; and straightway took his journey.
>   (Matthew xxv 14)

The sequel needs no quotation. Now, though Angelo
modestly refuses the honour, the Duke insists, forcing
it on him. Later in conversation with Friar Thomas,
himself disguised as a Friar now, he gives us reason for
his strange act:

> We have statutes and most biting laws,
> The needful bits and curbs to headstrong steeds,
> Which for this nineteen years we have let slip;
> Even like an o'ergrown lion in a cave,
> That goes not out to prey. Now, as fond fathers,
> Having bound up the threatening twigs of birch,
> Only to stick it in their children's sight
> For terror, not to use, in time the rod
> Becomes more mock'd than fear'd; so our decrees,
> Dead to infliction, to themselves are dead;
> And liberty plucks justice by the nose;

> The baby beats the nurse, and quite athwart
> Goes all decorum. (I iii 19)

Therefore he has given Angelo power and command to 'strike home'. Himself he will not exact justice, since he has already, by his laxity, as good as bade the people sin by his 'permissive pass': the people could not readily understand such a change in himself – with a new governor it would be different. But these are not his only reasons. He ends:

> More reasons for this action
> At our more leisure shall I render you;
> Only, this one: Lord Angelo is precise;
> Stands at a guard with envy; scarce confesses
> That his blood flows, or that his appetite
> Is more to bread than stone: hence shall we see
> If power change purpose, what our seemers be.
> (I iii 48)

The rest of the play slowly unfolds the rich content of the Duke's plan, and the secret, too, of his lax rule. Escalus tells us that the Duke was

> One that, above all other strifes, contended espec-
> ially to know himself. (III ii 247)

But he has studied others, besides himself. He prides himself on his knowledge:

> There is written in your brow, provost, honesty and
> constancy: if I read it not truly, my ancient skill
> beguiles me.... (IV ii 162)

Herein are the causes of his leniency. His government has been inefficient, not through an inherent weakness or laxity in him, but rather because meditation and self-analysis, together with profound study of human nature, have shown him that all passions and sins of other men have reflected images in his own soul. He is

no weakling: he has been 'a scholar, a statesman, and a
soldier' (III ii 154). But to such a philosopher government and justice may begin to appear a mockery, and
become abhorrent. His judicial method has been original: all criminals were either executed promptly or
else freely released (IV ii 137). Nowhere is the peculiar
modernity of the Duke in point of advanced psychology more vividly apparent. It seems, too, if we are to
judge by his treatment of Barnardine (IV iii 84), that he
could not tolerate an execution without the criminal's
own approval! The case of Barnardine troubles him
intensely:

> A creature unprepared, unmeet for death;
> And to transport him in the mind he is
> Were damnable.   (IV iii 71)

The Duke's sense of human responsibility is delightful
throughout: he is like a kindly father, and all the rest
are his children. Thus he now performs the experiment
of handing the reins of government to a man of ascetic
purity, who has an hitherto invulnerable faith in the
rightness and justice of his own ideals – a man of spotless reputation and self-conscious integrity, who will
have no fears as to the 'justice' of enforcing precise
obedience. The scheme is a plot, or trap: a scientific
experiment to see if extreme ascetic righteousness can
stand the test of power.

The Duke, disguised as the friar, moves through the
play, a dark figure, directing, watching, moralizing on
the actions of the other persons. As the play progresses
and his plot on Angelo works he assumes an ever-in-
creasing mysterious dignity, his original purpose seems
to become more and more profound in human insight,
the action marches with measured pace to its
appointed and logical end. We have ceased altogether
to think of the Duke as merely a studious and un-
practical governor, incapable of office. Rather he holds,
within the dramatic universe, the dignity and power of
a Prospero, to whom he is strangely similar. With both,

their plot and plan is the plot and plan of the play:
they make and forge the play, and thus are automatically to be equated in a unique sense with the poet
himself — since both are symbols of the poet's control-
ling, purposeful, combined movement of the chessmen
of the drama. Like Prospero, the Duke tends to assume
proportions evidently divine. Once he is actually compared to the Supreme Power:

> O my dread lord,
> I should be guiltier than my guiltiness,
> To think I can be undiscernible,
> When I perceive your grace, like power divine,
> Hath look'd upon my passes. (v i 371)

So speaks Angelo at the end. We are prepared for it
long before. In the rhymed octosyllabic couplets of the
Duke's soliloquy in III ii there is a distinct note of
supernatural authority, forecasting the rhymed mystic
utterances of divine beings in the Final Plays. He has
been talking with Escalus and the Provost, and dismisses them with the words:

> Peace be with you!

They leave him and he soliloquizes:

> He who the sword of heaven will bear
> Should be as holy as severe;
> Pattern in himself to know
> Grace to stand and virtue go;
> More nor less to other paying
> Than by self-offences weighing.
> Shame to him whose cruel striking
> Kills for faults of his own liking!
> Twice treble shame on Angelo,
> To weed my vice and let his grow!
> O what may man within him hide,
> Though angel on the outward side!

How may likeness made in crimes,
Making practice on the times,
To draw with idle spiders' strings
Most ponderous and substantial things!
Craft against vice I must apply:
With Angelo to-night shall lie
His old betrothed but despised;
So disguise shall, by the disguised,
Pay with falsehood false exacting,
And perform an old contracting.   (III ii 275)

This fine soliloquy gives us the Duke's philosophy: the
philosophy that prompted his original plan. And it is
important to notice the mystical, prophetic tone of the
speech. The Duke, like Jesus, is the prophet of a new
order of ethics. This aspect of the Duke as teacher and
prophet is also illustrated by his cryptic utterance to
Escalus just before this soliloquy:

Escalus. Good even, good father.
Duke. Bliss and goodness on you.
Escalus. Of whence are you?
Duke. Not of this country, though my chance is now
    To use it for my time: I am a brother
    Of gracious order, late come from the See
    In special business from his holiness.
Escalus. What news abroad i' the world?
Duke. None, but that there is so great a fever on
    goodness, that the dissolution of it must cure it:
    novelty is only in request; and it is as dangerous
    to be aged in any kind of course, as it is virtuous
    to be constant in any undertaking. There is scarce
    truth enough alive to make societies secure; but
    security enough to make fellowships accurst: much
    upon this riddle runs the wisdom of the world.
    This news is old enough, yet it is every day's news.
    I pray you, sir, of what disposition was the Duke?
Escalus. One that, above all other strifes, contended
    especially to know himself.   (III ii 226)

This remarkable speech, with its deliberate, incisive, cryptic sentences, has a profound quality and purpose which reaches the very heart of the play. It deserves exact attention. Its expanded paraphrase runs thus:

> No news, but that goodness is suffering such a disease that a complete dissolution of it (goodness) is needed to cure it. That is, our whole system of conventional ethics should be destroyed and rebuilt. A change (novelty) never gets beyond request, that is, is never actually put in practice. And it is as dangerous to continue indefinitely a worn-out system or order of government, as it is praiseworthy to be constant in any individual undertaking. There is scarcely enough knowledge of human nature current in the world to make societies safe; but ignorant self-confidence (i.e. in matters of justice) enough to make human intercourse within a society a miserable thing. This riddle holds the key to the wisdom of the world (probably, both the false wisdom of the unenlightened, and the true wisdom of great teachers). This news is old enough, and yet the need for its understanding sees daily proof.

I paraphrase freely, admittedly interpreting difficulties in the light of the recurring philosophy of this play on the blindness of men's moral judgements, and especially in the light of the Duke's personal moral attitude as read from his other words and actions. This speech holds the poetry of ethics. Its content, too, is very close to the Gospel teaching: the insistence on the blindness of the world, its habitual disregard of the truth exposed by prophet and teacher:

> And this is the condemnation, that light is come into the world, and men loved darkness rather than light, because their deeds were evil.   (John iii 19)

The same almost divine suggestion rings in many of the Duke's measured prose utterances. There are his supremely beautiful words to Escalus (IV ii 219):

> Look, the unfolding star calls up the shepherd. Put
> not yourself into amazement how these things
> should be: all difficulties are but easy when they are
> known.

The first lovely sentence – a unique beauty of Shakespearian prose, in a style peculiar to this play – derives
part of its appeal from New Testament associations:
and the second sentence holds the mystic assurance of
Matthew x 26:

> ... for there is nothing covered, that shall not be
> revealed: and hid, that shall not be known.

The Duke exercises the authority of a teacher throughout his disguise as a friar. He speaks authoritatively on
repentance to Juliet:

> *Duke.*   ... but lest you do repent,
>   As that the sin hath brought you to this shame,
>   Which sorrow is always towards ourselves, not
>   heaven,
>   Showing we would not spare heaven as we love
>   it,
>   But as we stand in fear, —
> *Juliet.* I do repent me as it is an evil,
>   And take the shame with joy.
> *Duke.* There rest. ...   (II iii 29)

After rebuking Pompey the bawd very sternly but not
unkindly, he concludes:

> Go mend, go mend   (III ii 28)

His attitude is that of Jesus to the woman taken in
adultery:

Neither do I condemn thee: go, and sin no more.
(John viii 11)

Both are more kindly disposed towards honest impurity than light and frivolous scandal-mongers, such as
Lucio, or Pharisaic self-righteousness, such as Angelo's.

The Duke's ethical attitude is exactly correspondent
with Jesus': the play must be read in the light of the
Gospel teaching, if its full significance is to be apparent. So he, like Jesus, moves among men suffering grief
at their sins and deriving joy from an unexpected
flower of simple goodness in the deserts of impurity
and hardness. He finds softness of heart where he least
expects it – in the Provost of the prison:

> *Duke.* This is a gentle provost: seldom when   -
>   The steeled gaoler is the friend of men. (IV ii 89)

So too, Jesus finds in the centurion,

> a man under authority, having soldiers under me...
> (Matthew viii 9)

a simple faith where he least expects it:

> ... I say unto you, I have not found so great faith, no,
> not in Israel.

The two incidents are very similar in quality. Now, in
that he represents a perfected ethical philosophy
joined to supreme authority, the Duke is, within the
dramatic universe, automatically comparable with
Divinity; or we may suggest that he progresses by successive modes – from worldly power, through the pro-
phecy and moralizing of the middle scenes, to the
supreme judgement at the end, where he exactly reflects the universal judgement as suggested by many
Gospel passages. There is the same apparent injustice,
the same tolerance and mercy. The Duke is, in fact a

symbol of the same kind as the Father in the Parable of the Prodigal Son (Luke xv) or the Lord in that of the Unmerciful Servant (Matthew xviii). The simplest way to focus correctly the quality and unity of *Measure for Measure* is to read it on the analogy of Jesus' parables.

Though his ethical philosophy is so closely related to the Gospel teaching, yet the Duke's thoughts on death are devoid of any explicit belief in immortality. He addresses Claudio, who is to die, and his words at first appear vague, agnostic: but a deeper acquaintance renders their profundity and truth. Claudio fears death. The Duke comforts him by concentrating not on death, but life. In a series of pregnant sentences he asserts the negative nature of any single life-joy. First, life is slave to death and may fail at any chance moment; however much you run from death, yet you cannot but run still towards it; nobility in man is inextricably twined with 'baseness' (this is, indeed, the moral of *Measure for Measure*), and courage is ever subject to fear; sleep is man's 'best rest', yet he fears death which is but sleep; man is not a single independent unit, he has no solitary self to lose, but rather is compounded of universal 'dust'; he is always discontent, striving for what he has not, forgetful of that which he succeeds in winning; man is a changing, wavering substance; his riches he wearily carries till death unloads him; he is tortured by disease and old age. The catalogue is strong in unremittent condemnation of life:

> Thou hast not youth nor age,
> But, as it were, an after-dinner's sleep,
> Dreaming on both; for all thy blessed youth
> Becomes as aged, and doth beg the alms
> Of palsied eld; and when thou art old and rich,
> Thou hast neither heat, affection, limb, nor beauty,
> To make thy riches pleasant. What's yet in this
> That bears the name of life? Yet in this life
> Lie hid moe thousand deaths: yet death we fear,
> That makes these odds all even. (III i 32)

Life is therefore a sequence of unrealities, strung together in a time-succession. Everything it can give is in
turn killed. Regarded thus, it is unreal, a delusion, a
living death. The thought is profound. True, the Duke
has concentrated especially on temporal aspect of life's
appearances, regarding only the shell of life and neg-
lecting the inner vital principle of joy and hope; he has
left deeper things untouched. He neglects Love and all
immediate transcendent intuitions. But since it is only
this temporal aspect of decayed appearances which
death is known to end, since it is only the closing of
this very time-succession which Claudio fears, it is
enough to prove this succession valueless. Claudio is
thus comforted. The death of such a life is indeed not
death, but rather itself a kind of life:

> I humbly thank you.
> To sue to live, I find I seek to die;
> And seeking death, find life: let it come on.
>   (III i 41)

Now he will 'encounter darkness as a bride', like
Antony (III i 84). The Duke's death-philosophy is thus
the philosophy of the great tragedies to follow – of
Timon, of *Antony and Cleopatra*. So, too, his ethic is
the ethic of *Lear*. In this problem play we find the
profound thought of the supreme tragedies already
emergent and given careful and exact form: the Duke
in this respect being analogous to Agamemnon in *Troilus and Cressida*. Both his ethical and his death thinking are profoundly modern. But Claudio soon reverts
to the crude time-thinking (and fine poetry) of his
famous death-speech, in which he regards the after-
life in terms of orthodox eschatology, thinking of it as a
temporal process, like Hamlet:

> Ay, but to die, and go we know not where. . . .
>   (III i 118)

In the Shakespearian mode of progressive thought it is

essential first to feel 'death's' reality strongly as the
ender of what we call 'life': only then do we begin to
feel the tremendous pressure of an immortality not
known in terms of time. We then begin to attach a
different meaning to the words 'life' and 'death'. The
thought of this scene thus wavers between the old and
the new death-philosophy

The Duke's plot pivots on the testing of Angelo.
Angelo is a man of spotless reputation, generally respected. Escalus says

> If any in Vienna be of worth
> To undergo such ample grace and honour,
> It is Lord Angelo.   (I i 23)

Angelo, hearing the Duke's praise, and his proposed
trust, modestly declines, as though he recognizes that
his virtue is too purely idealistic for the rough practice
of state affairs:

> Now, good my lord,
> Let there be some more test made of my metal,
> Before so noble and so great a figure
> Be stamp'd upon it.   (I i 48)

Angelo is not a conscious hypocrite: rather a man
whose chief faults are self-deception and pride in his
own righteousness — an unused and delicate instrument quite useless under the test of active trial. This
he half-recognizes, and would first refuse the proffered
honour. The Duke insists: Angelo's fall is thus entirely
the Duke's responsibility. So this man of ascetic life is
forced into authority. He is

> a man whose blood
> Is very snow broth; one who never feels
> The wanton stings and motions of the sense,
> But doth rebate and blunt his natural edge
> With profits of the mind, study and fast.
>   (I iv 57)

Angelo, indeed, does not know himself: no one receives
so great a shock as he himself when temptation over-
throws his virtue. He is no hypocrite. He cannot however, be acquitted of pharisaical pride: his reputation
means much to him, he 'stands at a guard with envy' (I
iii 51). He 'takes pride' in his 'gravity' (II iv 10). Now,
when he is first faced with the problem of Claudio's
guilt of adultery – and commanded, we must presume,
by the Duke's sealed orders to execute stern punishment wholesale, for this is the Duke's ostensible purpose – Angelo pursues his course without any sense of
wrongdoing. Escalus hints that surely all men know
sexual desire – how then is Angelo's procedure just?
Escalus thus adopts the Duke's ethical point of view,
exactly:

> Let but your honour know
> (Whom I believe to be most strait in virtue),
> That, in the working of your own affections,
> Had time cohered with place, or place with wishing,
> Or that the resolute acting of your blood,
> Could have attain'd the effect of your own purpose,
> Whether you had not, some time in your life,
> Err'd in this point, which now you censure him,
> And pull'd the law upon you.   (II i 8)

Which reflects the Gospel message:

> Ye have heard that it was said by them of old time,
> Thou shalt not commit adultery:
>   But I say unto you, that whosoever looketh on a
> woman to lust after her hath committed adultery
> with her already in his heart.   (Matthew v 27)

Angelo's reply, however, is sound sense:

> 'Tis one thing to be tempted, Escalus,
>   Another thing to fall.   (II i 17)

Isabella later uses the same argument as Escalus:

>   ... Go to your bosom;
> Knock there, and ask your heart what it doth
>   know
> That's like my brother's fault: if it confess
> A natural guiltiness, such as is his,
> Let it not sound a thought upon your tongue
> Against my brother's life.   (II ii 136)

We are reminded of Jesus' words to the Scribes and Pharisees concerning the woman 'taken in adultery':

> He that is without sin among you, let him first cast
>   a stone at her.   (John viii 7)

Angelo is, however, sincere: terribly sincere. He feels no personal responsibility, since he is certain that he does right. We believe him when he tells Isabella:

> It is the law, not I, condemn your brother:
> Were he my kinsman, brother, or my son,
> It should be thus with him.   (II ii 80)

To execute justice, he says, is kindness, not cruelty, in the long run. Angelo's arguments are rationally conclusive. A thing irrational breaks them, however: his passion for Isabella. Her purity, her idealism, her sanctity enslave him – she who speaks to him of

>   true prayers
> That shall be up at heaven and enter there
> Ere sun-rise, prayers from preserved souls,
> From fasting maids whose minds are dedicate
> To nothing temporal.   (II ii 151)

Angelo is swiftly enwrapped in desire. He is finely shown as falling a prey to his own love of purity and asceticism:

>   What is't I dream on?
> O cunning enemy, that, to catch a saint,
> With saints dost bait thy hook!   (II ii 179)

He 'sins in loving virtue'; no strumpet could ever
allure him; Isabella subdues him utterly – now he who
built so strongly on a rational righteousness, understands for the first time the sweet unreason of love:

> Ever till now,
> When men were fond, I smiled and wonder'd how.
> (II ii 186)

Angelo struggles hard: he prays to Heaven, but his
thoughts 'anchor' on Isabel (II iv 4). His gravity and
learning – all are suddenly as nothing. He admits to
himself that he has taken 'pride' in his well-known
austerity: adding 'let no man hear me' – a pathetic
touch which casts a revealing light both on his shallow
ethic and his honest desire at this moment to understand himself. The violent struggle is short. He sur-
renders – his ideals all toppled over like ninepins.

> Blood, thou art blood:
> Let's write good angel on the devil's horn,
> 'Tis not the devil's crest. (II iv 15)

Angelo is now quite adrift: all his old contacts are
irrevocably severed. Sexual desire has long been ana-
thema to him, so his warped idealism forbids any
healthy love. Good and evil change places in his mind,
since this passion is immediately recognized as good,
yet, by every one of his stock judgements, condemned
as evil. The devil becomes a 'good angel'. And this
wholesale reversion leaves Angelo in sorry plight now:
he has no moral values left. Since sex has been synonymous with foulness in his mind, this new love, reft
from the start of moral sanction in a man who 'scarce
confesses that his blood flows', becomes swiftly a de-
vouring and curbless lust:

> I have begun,
> And now I give my sensual race the rein.
> (II iv 159)

So he addresses Isabella. He imposes the vile condition
of Claudio's life. All this is profoundly true: he is at a
loss with this new reality – embarrassed as it were, incapable of pursing a normal course of love. In proportion as his moral reason formerly denied his instincts,
so now his instincts assert themselves in utter callousness of his moral reason. He swiftly becomes an utter
scoundrel. He threatens to have Claudio tortured. Next,
thinking to have had his way with Isabella, he is so
conscience-striken and tortured by fear that he madly
resolves not to keep faith with her: he orders Claudio's instant execution. For, in proportion as he is
nauseated at his own crimes, he is terror-struck at exposure. He is mad with fear: his story exactly pursues
the Macbeth rhythm.

> This deed unshapes me quite, makes me pregnant
> And dull to all proceedings. A deflower'd maid!
> And by an eminent body that enforced
> The law against it! But that her tender shame
> Will not proclaim against her maiden loss,
> How might she tongue me! Yet reason dares her no;
> For my authority bears so credent bulk,
> That no particular scandal once can touch
> But it confounds the breather. He should have lived,
> Save that his riotous youth, with dangerous sense,
> Might in the times to come have ta'en revenge,
> By so receiving a dishonour'd life
> With ransome of such shame. Would yet he had lived!
> Alack, when once our grace we have forgot,
> Nothing goes right: we would, and we would not.
>
> (IV iv 23)

This is the reward of self-deception, of Pharisaical
pride, of an idealism not harmonized with instinct – of
trying, to use the Duke's pregnant phrase:

> To draw with idle spiders' string
> Most ponderous and substantial things.
>
> (III ii 289)

Angelo has not been overcome with evil. He has been
ensnared by good – by his own love of sanctity, exquisitely symbolized in his love of Isabella: the hook is
baited with a saint, and the saint is caught. The cause
of his fall is this and this only. The coin of his moral
purity, which flashed so brilliantly, when tested does
not ring true. Angelo is the symbol of a false intel-
lectualized ethic divorced from the deeper springs of
human instinct.

The varied close-inwoven themes of *Measure for
Measure* are finally knit in the exquisite final act. To
that point the action – reflected image always of the
Ducal plot – marches.

> By cold gradation and well-balanced form.
> (IV iii 104)

The last act of judgement is heralded by trumpet
calls:

> Twice have the trumpets sounded;
> The generous and gravest citizens
> Have hent the gates, and very near upon
> The duke is entering.   (IV vi 12)

So all are, as it were, summoned to the final judgement.
Now Angelo, Isabella, Lucio – all are understood most
clearly in the light of this scene. The last act is the key
to the play's meaning, and all difficulties are here resolved. I will observe the judgement measured to each,
noting retrospectively the especial significance in the
play of Lucio and Isabella.

Lucio is a typical loose-minded, vulgar wit. He is the
product of a society that has gone too far in condemnation of human sexual desires. He keeps up a running
comment on sexual matters. His very existence is a
condemnation of the society which makes him a possibility. Not that there is anything of premeditated
villainy in him: he is merely superficial, enjoying the
unnatural ban on sex which civilization imposes, because that very ban adds point and spice to sexual

gratification. He is, however, sincerely concerned about
Claudio, and urges Isabella to plead for him. He can
be serious – for a while. He can speak sound sense, too,
in the full flow of his vulgar wit:

> Yes, in good sooth, the vice is of a great kindred; it is
> well allied: but it is impossible to extirp it quite,
> friar, till eating and drinking be put down. They say
> this Angelo was not made by man and woman after
> this downright way of creation: is it true, think you?
>   (III ii 108)

This goes to the root of our problem here. Pompey has
voiced the same thought (II i 236–57). This is, indeed,
what the Duke has known too well: what Angelo and
Isabella do not know. Thus Pompey and Lucio here at
least tell downright facts – Angelo and Isabella pursue
impossible and valueless ideals. Only the Duke holds
the balance exact throughout. Lucio's running wit,
however, pays no consistent regard to truth. To him
the Duke's leniency was a sign of hidden immorality:

> Ere he would have hanged a man for getting a
> hundred bastards, he would have paid for the nurs-
> ing of a thousand: he had some feeling of the sport;
> he knew the service, and that instructed him to
> mercy.   (III ii 124)

He traduces the Duke's character wholesale. He does
not pause to consider the truth of his words. Again,
there is no intent to harm – merely a careless, shallow,
truthless wit-philosophy which enjoys its own sex-chat-
ter. The type is common. Lucio is refined and vulgar,
and the more vulgar because of his refinement. Whereas Pompey, because of his natural coarseness, is less
vulgar. Lucio can only exist in a society of smug propriety and self-deception: for his mind's life is entirely
parasitical on those insincerities. His false – because
fantastic and shallow – pursuit of sex, is the result of a

false, fantastic denial of sex in his world. Like so much in *Measure for Measure* he is eminently modern. Now Lucio is the one person the Duke finds it all but impossible to forgive.

> I find an apt remission in myself;
> And yet here's one in place I cannot pardon.
> (v i 503)

All the rest have been serious in their faults. Lucio's condemnation is his triviality, his insincerity, his profligate idleness, his thoughtless detraction of others' characters:

> You, sirrah, that knew me for a fool, a coward,
> One all of luxury, an ass, a madman;
> Wherein have I so deserved of you,
> That you extol me thus?   (v i 505)

Lucio's treatment at the close is eminently, and fittingly, undignified. He is threatened thus: first he is to marry the mother of his child, about whose wrong he formerly boasted; then to be whipped and hanged. Lucio deserves some credit, however: he preserves his nature and answers with his characteristic wit. He cannot be serious. The Duke, his sense of humour touched, retracts the sentence:

> *Duke.* Upon mine honour, thou shalt marry her.
>   Thy slanders I forgive; and therewithal
>   Remit thy other forfeits. Take him to prison;
>   And see our pleasure herein executed.
> *Lucio.* Marrying a punk, my lord, is pressing to
>   death, whipping, and hanging.
> *Duke.* Slandering a prince deserves it.   (v i 524)

Idleness, triviality, thoughtlessness receive the Duke's strongest condemnation. The thought is this:

> But I say unto you, That every idle word that men
> shall speak, they shall give account thereof in the
> day of judgement.   (Matthew xii 36)

Exactly what happens to Lucio. His wit is often illuminating, often amusing, sometimes rather disgusting.
He is never wicked, is sometimes almost lovable – but
he is terribly dangerous.

Isabella is the opposite extreme. She is more saintly
than Angelo. And her saintliness goes deeper, is more
potent than his. When we first meet her, she is about to
enter the secluded life of a nun. She welcomes such a
life. She even wishes.

>   a more strict restraint
> Upon the sisterhood, the votarists of Saint Clare.
>   (I iv 4)

Even Lucio respects her. She calls forth something
deeper than his usual wit:

> I would not – though 'tis my familiar sin
> With maids to seem the lapwing and to jest,
> Tongue far from heart – play with all virgins so:
> I hold you as a thing ensky'd and sainted,
> By your renouncement as immortal spirit
> And to be talk'd with in sincerity,
> As with a saint.   (I iv 31)

Which contains a fine and exact statement of his shallow behaviour, his habitual wit for wit's sake. Lucio is
throughout a loyal friend to Claudio: truer to his
cause, in fact, than Isabella. A pointed contrast. He
urged her to help. She shows a distressing lack of
warmth. It is Lucio that talks of 'your poor brother'.
She is cold.

> *Lucio.*   Assay the power you have.
> *Isabella.* My power? Alas I doubt —
> *Lucio.*   Our doubts are traitors

And make us lose the good we oft might win,
By fearing to attempt.   (I iv 76)

Isabella's self-centred saintliness is thrown here into
strong contrast with Lucio's manly anxiety for his
friend. So, contrasted with Isabella's ice-cold sanctity, there are the beautiful lines with which Lucio
introduces the matter to her:

Your brother and his love have embraced:
As those that feed grow full, as blossoming time
That from the seedness the bare fallow brings
To teeming foison, ever so her plentous womb
Expresseth his full tilth and husbandry.

                                    (I iv 40)

Compare the pregnant beauty of this with the chastity
of Isabella's recent lisping line:

Upon the sisterhood, the votarists of Saint Clare.
                                    (I iv 5)

Isabella lacks human feeling. She starts her suit to
Angelo poorly enough – she is luke-warm.

There is a vice that most I do abhor,
And most desire should meet the blow of justice;
For which I would not plead but that I must;
For which I must not plead, but that I am
At war 'twixt will and will not.   (II ii 29)

Lucio has to urge her on continually. We begin to feel
that Isabella has no real affection for Claudio; has
stifled all human love in the pursuit of sanctity. When
Angelo at last proposes his dishonourable condition
she quickly comes to her decision:

Then, Isabel, live chaste and, brother, die.
More than our brother is our chastity.
                                    (II iv 184)

When Shakespeare chooses to load his dice like this –
which is seldom indeed – he does it mercilessly. The
Shakespearian satire here strikes once, and deep: there
is no need to point it further. But now we know our
Isabel. We are not surprised that she behaves to
Claudio, who hints for her sacrifice, like a fiend:

> Take my defiance!
> Die, Perish! Might but my bending down
> Reprieve thee from thy fate, it should proceed —
> I'll pray a thousand prayers for thy death,
> No word to save thee.   (III i 143)

Is her fall any less than Angelo's? Deeper, I think.
With whom is Isabel angry? Not only with her brother.
She has feared this choice – terribly: 'O, I do fear thee,
Claudio', she said (III i 74). Ever since Angelo's suggestion she has been afraid. Now Claudio has forced the
responsibility of choice on her. She cannot sacrifice
herself. Her sex inhibitions have been horribly shown
her as they are, naked. She has been stung – lanced on
a sore spot of her soul. She knows now that it is not all
saintliness, she sees her own soul and sees it as something small, frightened, despicable, too frail to dream
of such a sacrifice. Though she does not admit it, she is
infuriated, not with Claudio, but herself. 'Saints'
should not speak like this. Again, the comment of this
play is terribly illuminating. It is significant that she
readily involves Mariana in illicit love: it is always her
own, and only her own, chastity that assumes, in her
heart, universal importance. Isabella, however, was no
hypocrite, any more than Angelo. She is a spirit of
purity, grace, maiden charm: but all these virtues the
action of the play turns remorselessly against herself.
In a way, it is not her fault. Chastity is hardly a sin –
but neither, as the play emphasizes, is it the whole of
virtue. And she, like the rest, has to find a new wisdom.
Mariana in the last act prays for Angelo's life. Confronted by that warm, potent, forgiving, human love,

Isabella herself suddenly shows a softening, a sweet
humanity. Asked to intercede, she does so – she, who
was at the start slow to intercede for a brother's life,
now implores the Duke to save Angelo, her wronger:

> I partly think
> A due sincerity govern'd his deeds,
> Till he did look on me.   (v i 450)

There is a suggestion that Angelo's strong passion has
itself moved her, thawing her ice-cold pride. This is the
moment of her trial: the Duke is watching her keenly,
to see if she has learnt her lesson – nor does he give her
any help, but deliberately puts obstacles in her way.
But she stands the test: she bows to a love greater than
her own saintliness. Isabella, like Angelo, has progressed far during the play's action: from sanctity to
humanity.

Angelo, at the beginning of this final scene, remains
firm in denial of the accusations levelled against him.
Not till the Duke's disguise as a Friar is made known
and he understands that deception is no longer possible, does he show outward repentance. We know,
however, that his inward thoughts must have been terrible enough – his earlier agonized soliloquies put this
beyond doubt. Now, his failings exposed, he seems to
welcome punishment:

> Immediate sentence then and sequent death
> Is all the grace I beg.   (v i 378)

Escalus expresses sorrow and surprise at his actions. He
answers:

> I am sorry that such sorrow I procure:
> And so deep sticks it in my penitent heart
> That I crave death more willingly than mercy;
> 'Tis my deserving and I do entreat it.   (v i 479)

To Angelo, exposure seems to come as a relief: the

horror of self-deception is at an end. For the first time
in his life he is both quite honest with himself and with
the world. So he takes Mariana as his wife. This is just:
he threw her over because he thought she was not good
enough for him,

> Partly for that her promised proportions
> Came short of composition, but in chief
> For that her reputation was disvalued.
> In levity. (v i 219)

He aimed too high when he cast his eyes on the sainted
Isabel: now, knowing himself, he will find his true level
in the love of Mariana. He has become human. The
union is symbolical. Just as his supposed love-contact
with Isabel was a delusion, when Mariana, his true
mate, was taking her place, so Angelo throughout has
deluded himself. Now his acceptance of Mariana sym-
bolizes his new self-knowledge. So, too, Lucio is to find
his proper level in marrying Mistress Kate Keepdown,
of whose child he is the father. Horrified as he is at the
thought, he has to meet the responsibilities of his profligate behaviour. The punishment of both is this
only: to know, and to be themselves. This is both their
punishment and at the same time their highest reward
for their sufferings: self-knowledge being the supreme,
perhaps the only, good. We remember the parable of
the Pharisee and the Publican (Luke xviii).

So the Duke draws his plan to its appointed end. All,
including Barnardine, are forgiven, and left, in the
usual sense, unpunished. This is inevitable. The
Duke's original leniency has been shown by his successful plot to have been right, not wrong. Though he sees
'corruption boil and bubble' (v i 320) in Vienna, he
has found, too, that man's sainted virtue is a delusion:
'judge not that ye be not judged.' He has seen an
Angelo to fall from grace at the first breath of power's
temptation, he has seen Isabella's purity scarring, de-
facing her humanity. He has found more gentleness in
'the steeled gaoler' than in either of these. He has

found more natural honesty in Pompey the bawd than
Angelo the ascetic; more humanity in the charity of
Mistress Overdone than in Isabella condemning her
brother to death with venomed words in order to pre-
serve her own chastity. Mistress Overdone has looked
after Lucio's illegitimate child:

> ... Mistress Kate Keepdown was with child by him in
> the Duke's time; he promised her marriage; his child
> is a year and a quarter old, come Philip and Jacob: I
> have kept it myself.... (III ii 211)

Human virtue docs not flower only in high places:
nor is it the monopoly of the pure in body. In reading
Measure for Measure one feels that Pompey with his
rough humour and honest professional indecency is
the only one of the major persons, save the Duke, who
can be called 'pure in heart'. Therefore, knowing all
this, the Duke knows his tolerance to be now a moral
imperative: he sees too far into the nature of a man
to pronounce judgement according to the appearances
of human behaviour. But we are not told what will
become of Vienna. There is, however, a hint, for the
Duke is to marry Isabel, and this marriage, like the
others, may be understood symbolically. It is to be
the marriage of understanding with purity; of tolerance with moral fervour. The Duke, who alone has
no delusions as to the virtues of man, who is incapable
of executing justice on vice since he finds forgiveness
implicit in his wide and sympathetic understanding –
he alone wins the 'enskied and sainted' Isabel – more,
we are not told. And we may expect her in future
to learn from him wisdom, human tenderness, and
love:

> What's mine is yours and what is yours is mine.
> (v i 543)

Now, if we still find this universal forgiveness strange –
and many have done so – we might observe Mariana,

who loves Angelo with a warm and realistically human
love. She sees no fault in him, or none of any consequence.

> O my dear lord,
> I crave no other nor no better man.
>
> (v i 430)

She knows that

> best men are moulded out of faults,
> And, for the most, become much more the better
> For being a little bad.   (v i 444)

The incident is profoundly true. Love asks no questions, sees no evil, transfiguring the just and unjust
alike. This is one of the surest and finest ethical
touches in this masterpiece of ethical drama. Its moral
of love is, too, the ultimate splendour of Jesus' teaching.

Measure for Measure is indeed based firmly on that
teaching. The lesson of the play is that of Matthew v
20:

> For I say unto you, That except your righteousness
> shall exceed the righteousness of the scribes and
> Pharisees, ye shall in no case enter into the kingdom
> of heaven.

The play must be read, not as a picture of normal
human affairs, but as a parable, like the parables of
Jesus. The plot is, in fact, an inversion of one of those
parables – that of the Unmerciful Servant (Matthew
xviii); and the universal and level forgiveness at the
end, where all alike meet pardon, is one with the forgiveness of the Parable of the Two Debtors (Luke vii).
Much has been said about the difficulties of *Measure
for Measure*. But, in truth, no play of Shakespeare
shows more thoughtful care, more deliberate purpose,
more consummate skill in structural technique, and,

finally, more penetrating ethical and psychological insight. None shows a more exquisitely inwoven pattern. And, if ever the thought at first sight seems strange, or the action unreasonable, it will be ever found to reflect the sublime strangeness and unreason of Jesus' teaching.

SOURCE: *The Wheel of Fire,* 1930

W. W. Lawrence

REAL LIFE AND ARTIFICE (1931)

The basic theme of *Measure for Measure* ... may apparently be ultimately traced to an episode in real life.... It is not only poignantly real, but intensely dramatic. It presents one of those dreadful alternatives between conflicting demands of honour and affection which have in them the very essence of tragic drama. A beautiful and innocent woman pleads with a tyrannical official for the life of her lover or brother or husband, and is given the choice between yielding her honour to save the man she loves, or refusing, and thereby knowing that his death is assured....

In Shakespeare's play this realistic basic action is combined with plot-material taken from traditional story, and exhibiting the archaisms and improbabilities characteristic of such narrative. The introduction of these artificial elements was chiefly due to Shakespeare, not to his sources. This point seems generally to have been overlooked. The extraordinary thing is that while the main situation apparently stirred Shakespeare very deeply, and while he gave to it a power such as no other writer had attained, he made it in some respects more conventional, less like real life. The result has been confusion among the commentators. They have been puzzled by the contradictions arising from the fusion of realism and artificiality, and they have failed to understand the significance of the changes made by Shakespeare....

Nothing in the play has aroused sharper dissent than the device by which the honour of Isabella is safeguarded, and nothing has been more completely misunderstood. The Duke has been blamed for suggesting it, Isabella for consenting to it, and Mariana for carrying it out....

Such a betrothal as Mariana's was held in Elizabethan days to have much the binding force of the
complete marriage ceremony, and to confer marital
rights. The Duke, before suggesting the stratagem to
Isabella, explains the situation (III i).... He also re-
assures Mariana, in highly significant terms.

> Nor, gentle daughter, fear you not at all.
> He is your husband on a pre-contract:
> To bring you thus together, 'tis no sin,
> Sith that the justice of your title to him
> Doth flourish the deceit.

Claudio's union with Juliet was of this sort, as Claudio's speech to Lucio (I ii) makes clear. They were betrothed; 'upon a true contract I got possession of Julietta's bed'. But they lacked the 'denunciation', that is
the formal declaration of the final marriage ceremony;
they were waiting for the 'propagation', the increase, of
Juliet's dower. Meanwhile a long-neglected statute for-
bidding physical union before the final ceremony of
marriage was revived by the virtuous Angelo, and
Claudio was arrested. We do not need to take this
'statute' too seriously; law in Shakespeare's plays is
queer business. The important thing to note is that the
usage in England in Shakespeare's day was that here
represented as the common custom of Vienna, before
the reform instituted by Angelo....

In the light of these considerations, Hazlitt's remark
about the virtue that is 'sublimely good at another's
expense', and Quiller-Couch's assertions that Isabella is
'a bare procuress', and that she 'is mating a pair without wedlock', collapse like pricked bubbles. We have
seen how insistent Shakespeare is upon the purity of
Isabella, how he altered the plot, making her refuse to
sacrifice her honour even for her brother's life, and
how she desires the strictest restraint in the sisterhood
which she is about to enter. The moral justification of
the Mariana ruse would be shown, if by nothing else,

by the instant readiness with which she accepts the plan and puts it into execution. . . .

We may dismiss immediately, in view of what has just been said . . . any doubts which we may cherish as to the morality of the episode. Whether it be a sacrifice of dignity on the part of a woman to entrap her lover, as Helena entrapped her husband, is another matter. But the answer is equally plain. . . . Shakespeare was utilizing, as he so often did, a bit of archaic plotting which is hard to reconcile with the naturalness of his characters. His heroines seem so real that we find it hard to accept them in artificial situations. But such situations had been deemed suitable for heroines in the earlier traditions from which Shakespeare was drawing, they were current in the story-telling of his own day, and he therefore accepted them for his own dramatic purposes. How far he was disturbed by them we cannot tell; but it would seem, from the frequency with which he employed them, that he felt far less their lack of reality than we do, even when they seem to involve psychological contradictions. If they were not felt as disturbingly artificial by the people of his own day, they are less likely to have worried Shakespeare. Parallels to the Mariana–Angelo episode cannot be drawn from earlier history, since it was not traditional, but rather the result of his own deliberate introduction of the *All's Well* theme into *Measure for Measure*. We have seen, however, in examining the former play, that the ruse practised by Helena was common in story, and that there is no evidence that it was conceived as humiliating, as Schücking feels it must have been. . . .

One more stone has been cast at Isabella – that it is 'a scandalous proceeding' for her to marry the Duke, as she seems about to do at the end of the play, since she is a novice in a nunnery. Before we consider this question, however, it may be well to look somewhat carefully at the Duke himself, and see what is to be said about his part in the story.

The great prominence of the Duke is, as we have already seen, one of Shakespeare's most important

additions to the plot. The sources give the ruler of the
state a part only at the end of the story; Shakespeare
makes him active throughout the play. Whatever short-
comings may be charged to the Duke are then, due to
Shakespeare alone.

The ruler of the degenerate city of Vienna is, I believe, to be regarded as a conventional and romantic
figure, whose actions are mainly determined by
theatrical exigencies and effectiveness; he is as it were,
a stage Duke, not a real person. In this respect he contrasts strikingly with Isabella and Angelo and Claudio
and Lucio, and the low-comedy people. Most of the
misunderstandings of his part in the play have been
due to failure to perceive this. Nothing shows more
vividly the conventional elements in Shakespeare's
technique than an analysis of the Duke's varied activi-
ties.

In the dramas written before *Measure for Measure,*
two agencies stand out prominently as representatives
of right and justice in straightening out complications
of plot: the State and the Church. The former is represented by the person in supreme lay authority – a
Duke in *The Comedy of Errors, The Two Gentlemen
of Verona, Twelfth Night, A Midsummer Night's
Dream* (Theseus as Duke of Athens), *The Merchant of
Venice, As You Like It* (the Banished Duke); the King
of France in *All's Well.* The latter is represented by
priest or friar – Friar Laurence in *Romeo and Juliet,*
Friar Francis in *Much Ado,* who suggest, respectively,
the stratagems by which the Veronese lovers are united,
and the honour of Hero vindicated. The law and
authority in these pieces is romantic law and authority;
it cannot be judged by strict legal ecclesiastical standards. The quibbles which are the undoing of Shylock
are as much a part of popular story as the sleeping
potion which sends Juliet to the tomb. Shakespeare
used dukes and friars when the peculiar powers and
opportunities afforded by their station would help his
narrative. He did not bother himself about the strict
legality or rationality of their actions. What they sug-

gest or decide has in his plays the binding force of constituted and final authority, and was so understood by
his audiences.

The Duke in *Measure for Measure* combines the
functions both of State and Church in his person. As
Duke, he is supreme ruler of Vienna, who returns at
the end to straighten out the tangles of the action, and
dispense justice to all. In his disguise as Friar, he represents the wisdom and adroitness of the Church, in
directing courses of action and advising stratagems so
that good may come out of evil. But the plots which he
sets in motion and the justice which he dispenses are
the stuff of story; they cannot be judged as if they were
historical occurrences. And the Duke's character cannot
be estimated on a rationalistic basis. If he really wished
to set matters right between Angelo, Isabella, Mariana,
Claudio, and the rest, he had a short and easy way of
doing it. He was in full possession of the facts; he could
have revealed himself, brought all before the bar of his
authority, freed the innocent and punished the guilty
in short order, and this would have saved Isabella and
Claudio much suffering. Such an arrangement would,
however, have been much less effective dramatically
than his continued disguise, his suggested ruses, the
prolongation of the suspense of the accused and the
false security of the villain. No, he knows what is expected of him as a stage Duke, and makes the most of
his part. Similarly, in *All's Well*, the King, assisted by
Diana, squeezes the last drop of theatrical effectiveness
out of the complications at the end of the play. Of
course, as Hart complains, the Duke's way of bringing
Angelo to justice is 'shifty', and not a straight prosecu-
tion. But it is just these shifts which keep the audience
alert and interested. Of course the Duke 'plunges into
a vortex of scheming and intrigue'; it is this which
makes the play. Of course, as Hazlitt says, 'he is more
absorbed in his own plots and gravity than anxious for
the welfare of the State'; of course he 'upsets all his
crafty schemes for setting up his tottering and infirm
authority by a general forgiveness and gaol-delivery all

round'. The audience were interested in the Duke's
reforms only in so far as these served the plot. They did
not care a straw about the triumph of his theories as a
reformer or the moral welfare of Vienna. What they
did wish was that the play should end, as a comedy
should, in a general atmosphere of happiness, even for
the sinful Lucio who had amused them by his drollery.
Of course the Duke lies when he tells Isabella that her
brother is dead (iv iii), in order to spur her on to vengeance, and in order, as he himself says, 'to make her
heavenly comforts of despair, when it is least expected',
that is, to restore her suddenly to happiness later on,
with dramatic effectiveness. Of course he lies when he
tells Claudio that as confessor to Angelo he knows that
Angelo's purpose is only to try Isabella's virtue; the
plot requires that Claudio should believe that he is
going to lose his life. It really does seem a little absurd
to accuse the Duke of 'transgressing against the confessional'. His statement that Angelo had confessed to him
appears to be only a ruse for the deception of Claudio.
Nowhere in the play does the Duke in disguise come
face to face with Angelo until the final scene; it would
appear that he was steering clear of him. Granted,
however, that Shakespeare meant us to understand
that he had actually, in his disguise, received Angelo in
the confessional, it seems highly unlikely that Angelo
would have confessed thus falsely. In any case, the
Duke, who knew Angelo's purposes, would not have
been deceived. But I do not think that Shakespeare
intended us to think that there had really been any
confession at all. The Duke, in his capacity as Friar,
was telling a falsehood to Claudio in order that the
ends of justice (and of effective drama) might be
served. He lies for a good purpose again and again; in
saying that he has come from the Pope (iii ii), in saying
that Angelo is holy and just (iv ii), and he even lies to
Isabella at the end in his habit as the Duke (v i 394 ff.).
The counsels of a stage friar are, however, *ipso facto*
holy and just, and to be obeyed without question.
Quiller-Couch, however, scornfully remarks, 'We are

all acquainted with the sort of woman who will commit herself to any deed without question, if it be
suggested by a priest', but we can find that sort of
woman – or man too, for that matter – in Hero, Juliet,
Romeo, Benedick, Beatrice, and Leonato.

The 'scandalous proceeding' of the approaching
union of the Duke and Isabella, a novice of the sisterhood of St Clare, must be judged in similar fashion. An
Elizabethan audience was not likely to be scandalized
by the heroine's leaving a convent and pleading with
the deputy for the life of her brother, and finally being
rewarded for her trials and virtue by marrying the
most distinguished man in the play, in the good old
story-book fashion. Small niceties of ecclesiastical in-
fringement were not shocking to Protestant England in
Shakespeare's day. But the play makes it perfectly clear
that Isabella had not as yet taken vows. Sister Francisca
says:

> It is a man's voice. Gentle Isabella,
> Turn you the key, and know his business of him.
> You may, I may not; *you are yet unsworn.*   (I iv)

Of course a Roman Catholic novice who has not yet
taken vows in the order may forsake the religious life,
and marry. It looks as if Shakespeare had deliberately
prepared for the marriage of Isabella to the Duke, by
making this point at the very beginning. It has been
noted that she does not formally assent to the Duke's
proposal in the closing lines of the play:

>   Dear Isabel,
> I have a motion much imports your good;
> Whereto if you'll a willing ear incline,
> What's mine is yours and what is yours is mine.

But I do not think that there is any doubt that Isabella
turns to him with a heavenly and yielding smile. And I
cannot see in the least why she should not. . . .

The essentially artificial character of the Duke may, as has already been suggested, be well illustrated by comparing him with the 'comic relief'. If, as is possible, Mistress Overdone, Pompey and Elbow were suggested by Lamia, Rosko and Gresco of Whetstone's play, they have been so transformed and made natural as to be scarcely recognizable, while a new and elaborate portrait, unlike any of the wooden figures in *Promos and Cassandra*, has been introduced, the impudent, dissolute, and engaging Lucio. Here we have striking studies of the riff-raff of the Southwark bank, the unsavoury yet amusing types of the Elizabethan brothels. They are unhampered in the play by incidents or characterization drawn from conventional story; they show us, in naked realism, the unlovely side of London life, etched deep with the penetrating acid of keen observation. But in spite of all their vices, they are likeable as well as human. To quote Raleigh's penetrating words they are 'live men, pleasant to Shakespeare'. Pompey is 'one of those humble, cheerful beings, willing to help in anything that is going forward, who are the mainstay of human affairs...., Froth is an amiable, feather-headed young gentleman – to dislike him would argue an ill nature, and a small one. Even Lucio has his uses; nor is it very plain that in his conversations with the Duke he forfeits Shakespeare's sympathy. He has a taste for scandal, but it is a mere luxury of idleness; though his tongue is loose, his heart is simply affectionate, and he is eager to help his friend. Lastly, to omit none of the figures who make up the background, Mistress Overdone pays a strict attention to business, and is carried to prison in due course of law.'

Beside men and women like these, full of vigorous life, the Duke, with his shifts and tricks, which strain plausibility to the breaking-point, seems a puppet, manufactured to meet the exigencies of dramatic construction. He is more important but quite as artificial as Oliver or the Usurping Duke in *As You Like It*, who are wicked as long as Shakespeare needs them so, and

are then, with a grotesque lack of probability, con-
verted, because it helps the plot to have them virtuous
at the end. We cannot analyse such characters psychologically. The Duke of Vienna, on account of his great
prominence in the play, has just enough plausibility of
characterization to make an audience accept him; he
has none to spare. Perhaps we may sum the whole
matter up by saying that Shakespeare drew the Duke as
he did because he needed him, and that he drew the
main protagonists and the low-comedy people as he did
because they interested him. Pompey and Mistress
Overdone and the rest, in particular, serve an important purpose, in their very detachment from the artificial details of plot; they serve to make us forget the
improbabilities which Shakespeare imported into the
play, improbabilities which revolve about the Duke
and his schemings; and they throw over the whole an
illusion of vivid and unforgettable reality.

I imagine that some readers will take issue with me
for regarding the Duke as an essentially artificial
figure, elaborated to meet the requirements of plot,
and as a study in characcer, of minor importance in
himself, or for the play. Critics have frequently regarded him as the mainspring of the action, and his
peculiar disposition as having profoundly influenced
the development of the plot. This I believe to be quite
the reverse of the truth.

Let us try to reconstruct the way in which the play
took shape. In the first place, Shakespeare took from his
sources the complete intrigue which forms the back-
bone of the plot, but introduced into it important new
elements of his own. In order to set in motion these
new elements, he hit upon the expedient of using the
Duke as a *deus ex machina*. Whetstone had brought
forward the King, whose function is to set right the
errors of the deputy, and who is a prototype of the
Duke, only in the Second Part of his play. Shakespeare,
with the utmost adroitness, introduced the Duke at the
very beginning, and then made him direct the action
throughout, in disguise as a friar. It thus became neces-

sary to make his withdrawal from power plausible. This Shakespeare did by depicting him as a man temperamentally unsuited to his high office, who 'cannot face the odious necessities of his position'. So the Duke's character was, in the actual writing of the play, determined by the plot; the plot did not spring from his character. By beginning the very first scene of his play with the Duke's retirement from office, Shakespeare indeed made it seem that this retirement was the direct cause of the events following; but we know that these events were already in the plot, and independent of the Duke's withdrawal from power.

We have no right to object to the remodelling of a play, no matter how this has taken place, if it results in a logical and consistent whole. But in *Measure for Measure* no such result has been attained. The art of the expert craftsman has only partially concealed the stages by which his structure has been erected. The picture of the Duke at the very beginning, his retirement, and the appointment of a deputy, are natural and plausible, but what follows is story-book business – Haroun al Raschid disguised, Substituted Bride, Severed Head, and the various mechanical tricks and turnings of a complicated *dénouement*. As soon as the Duke gets into action, the artificiality of his figure is evident. Moreover, his very activity ill accords with his retiring disposition, his desire to lay aside power, and delegate it to another. More than any fictitious character in Shakespeare except Iago, the Duke is the directing force in the intrigues of the plot. Yet, says Lucio, 'a shy fellow was the Duke', and recent criticism has taught us that such comments from minor characters report truth. In a word, then, Shakespeare has not succeeded in making the Duke both serviceable to the purposes of drama, and psychologically consistent. Not only in origin, but in the effect which he produces upon the spectators, he is entirely different from Angelo and Isabella and Claudio. Their experiences are transcripts of actual human life, and usually in accord with their characters. They are real people. The

Duke's part in the plot, excepting for his abdication, is little in accord with his disposition as sketched in the beginning, and little in accord with probability. He is essentially a puppet, cleverly painted and adroitly manipulated, but revealing, in the thinness of his colouring and in the artificiality of his movements, the wood and pasteboard of his composition.

Coleridge, in a familiar passage, wrote: 'The pardon and marriage of Angelo not merely baffles the strong, indignant claim of justice (for cruelty, with lust and damnable baseness, cannot be forgiven, because we cannot conceive them as being morally repented of), but it is likewise degrading to the character of woman.' Here are matters which deserve consideration. The 'strong, indignant claim of justice' extends, however, far beyond the pardon and marriage of Angelo; it concerns the whole solution of the action at the end, and the appropriateness of the title *Measure for Measure*. Analysis of the character of Angelo, and of the reasons why he does not get his just punishment, will form an admirable introduction to a discussion of the Duke, of how far the ends of justice are in general served by the decisions once more enthroned in power at the end of the play.

Let us begin at the beginning. Did Shakespeare mean Angelo to be regarded as a good, though narrow, man, suddenly gone wrong through an overmastering sexual temptation? Dr Furnivall said of Isabella, 'Her unhappy words, "Hark! how I'll bribe you," seem to have first brought out the evil in Angelo.' Or was Angelo a villain from the start, who deceived the Duke as to his real character? I do not imagine that there is any way of settling this point. It is even possible that Shakespeare had not made up his mind about the virtue of Angelo, any more than Thackeray had – in a different sense – about the virtue of Becky Sharp. But it seems more likely that Angelo is to be regarded as having been a smooth rascal, who had been successful in concealing his baseness. His cruel and unjust treatment of Mariana, which has sent that unhappy lady to languish in her moated grange, his readiness not only to put Isabella in her dreadful predicament in order to satisfy his lust, but also to break faith with her and to kill her brother, do not point to native virtue. True, the Duke puts confidence in him, raising him to power above the older and more temperate Escalus, but even if this be regarded as a trial of his character, as Blackstone suggested, it proves little. Some of the most conscienceless of Shakespeare's characters, Edmund, Goneril, Regan, Iago, seem so effectively to have concealed their wickedness that the virtuous people whom they destroy have no suspicion of their real baseness. True, Mariana pleads for Angelo's life, and even Isabella greatly as she has suffered, joins in urging that he be spared. But the complete repentance and forgiveness of the villain is a common dramatic convention, which Shakespeare found in Whetstone in this particular instance, and used frequently in other plays. A further piece of evidence seems to point to Angelo's native baseness; his flat refusal to temper justice with mercy, and spare Claudio, long before the dishonourable proposal is made to Isabella (II ii). One is reminded of Shylock and the trial scene by Angelo's stand, in this first interview with Isabella, upon the strict letter of the law, and the deaf ear which he turns to her eloquent appeal for mercy for her brother. Rigorous enforcement of the law is indeed no crime, but an audience would hardly see virtue in a man who insisted on sending a youth to death for a venial offence, in the face of moving appeals for mercy uttered by a beautiful heroine.

There can be no doubt, however, that as soon as Angelo has resolved to use his power to satisfy his passion, and at the same time to compass the death of Claudio, he must be regarded as a 'strong and fast'ned villain'. Against his double wickedness the Duke prepares a double stratagem: the substitution of Mariana, and the decapitation of Ragozine. Both of these ruses were, as we have noted, introduced into the play by

Shakespeare. The Duke says, at the end of the Third
Act,

> Craft against vice I must apply.
> …
> So disguise shall, by the disguised,
> Pay with falsehood false exacting.

This balancing of one trick against another gives point
to the title of the play. But the phrase 'Measure for
Measure' also means as Shakespeare has emphasized,
the balancing of the penalty which Angelo meted out
to Claudio for violation of chastity by a similar penalty
against Angelo himself for a fault which he is supposed
to have committed – 'An Angelo for Claudio, death for
death!'

The whole passage is so significant that it must be
quoted. The Duke says to Isabella,

> For this new-married man approaching here,
> Whose salt imagination yet hath wrong'd
> Your well-defended honour, you must pardon
> For Mariana's sake; but as he adjudg'd your
> 　　brother,—
> Being criminal, in double violation
> Of sacred chastity and of promise-breach
> Thereon dependent, – for your brother's life
> The very mercy of the law cries out
> Most audible, even from his proper tongue,
> 'An Angelo for Claudio, death for death!'
> Haste still pays haste, and leisure answers leisure;
> Like doth quit like, and *Measure* still *for Measure*.
> Then, Angelo, thy fault's thus manifested;
> Which, though thou wouldst deny, denies thee
> 　　vantage.
> We do condemn thee to the very block
> Where Claudio's stoop'd to death, and with like
> 　　haste.
> Away with him!　　　　　　　　(v i 405–21)

This has often been misunderstood and mispunctuated. Notice that lines 409–11 refer to Angelo's own misdemeanours, not to those of Claudio, who has been guilty of no promise-breaking. The Neilson text indicates this, but I emend the punctuation by ending the parenthesis in the middle, not at the end, of line 411, with the words 'Thereon dependent'. The sense of the passage is: Angelo's plot against the honour of Isabella may be pardoned, but not the breaking of his promise to spare the life of Claudio. Measure for Measure; the punishment must fit the crime: as Angelo condemned Claudio to the block, he must in like manner suffer on it himself. 'Measure' is sometimes 'used as a judicial term for dealing out justice' (Schmidt), as in III ii 256: 'He professes to have received no sinister measure from his judge.' The curious phrase 'leisure answers leisure' was probably influenced by desire for a rhyme to 'measure'.

Angelo has made full confession, and asked for death. It turns out, however, that Claudio has not been put to death, after all, and that Angelo has not succeeded in his plot against the honour of Isabella. Both of the women whom Angelo has wronged now plead for his life. What is the Duke to do? What does the 'strong, indignant claim of justice' require?

The whole point of the closing scene is that justice should be tempered with mercy. The mercy which Angelo had refused to Isabella is extended by the Duke in far greater measure, and under far stronger provocation. There is no stickling upon the letter of the law. Claudio is forgiven his venial offence. Even the wretched Barnadine, 'unfit to live or die', is pardoned.

> But, for those earthly faults, I quit them all;
> And pray thee take this *mercy* to provide
> For better times to come.

And Angelo is pardoned too. No doubt Shakespeare was influenced by the ending of Whetstone's play, in which Promos is not only forgiven, but restored to his governorship, but he took advantage of the conven-

tional solution of the plot to lift the whole into a
higher moral conception of justice than 'an eye for an
eye and tooth for a tooth'. The ending of the play,
then, really contradicts the title. Our modern feeling
may be that Angelo gets off altogether too lightly, but
the pardon of the repentant villain and his union to a
heroine was a commonplace in Elizabethan drama,
and would certainly have been readily accepted by a
contemporary audience. So Proteus, Oliver, Posthumus
and Bertram are 'dismissed to happiness', despite their
earlier cruelties. The claims of strict justice are secondary to those of stage entertainment. *Measure for
Measure* is not a tract on equity, any more than it is on
government; it is not an expression of Shakespeare's
convictions in regard to the administration of law, but
a story of human passion, sin and forgiveness.

In judging this situation, we are likely to be led
astray by failing to realize the difference between conceptions of justice in medieval and modern times. The
medieval attitude still persisted in the days of Elizabeth, especially in the minds of the common folk, and
in literature reflecting their views. The modern idea of
a progressive amelioration of the social body by far-
sighted legislation, and its application to particular
cases, was anticipated by the best minds of the Renaissance, but had by no means gained acceptance in the
days when Shakespeare wrote. A passage in a book by
the Dutch scholar Huizinga has an especial bearing
upon justice in *Measure for Measure*, though obviously
written to point no such application. 'Instead of le-
nient penalties, inflicted with hesitation, the Middle
Ages knew but the two extremes: the fullness of cruel
punishment, and mercy. When the condemned criminal is pardoned, the question whether he deserved it
for any special reason is hardly asked; for mercy has to
be gratuitous, like the mercy of God.' Altruistic and
advanced social philosophy like that of Coleridge,
then, is no touchstone for judging an Elizabethan play.

Shakespeare might, after the dark shadows of the
preceding intrigue, have ended *Measure for Measure*

as tragedy, had he so chosen, but he determined that it should close in the spirit of comedy. The transition from the heights of tragic experience to the cheerfulness of a happy ending is too abrupt for the taste of modern critics, who like a play to be psychologically consistent. Shakespeare, however, did not shrink from violating such consistency, and executing a deliberate *volte-face* at the end. This is bitter medicine for those who claim that Shakespeare's works will appear as perfect and well-rounded wholes, if we only have the wit to look at them in the right way. We may as well admit that Shakespeare's art oscillates between extreme psychological subtlety, and an equally extreme disregard of psychological truth, in the acceptance of stock narrative conventions. To attempt to explain away the Shakespearean happy ending seems to me a hopeless task.

The one thing upon which the Duke insists is the good old conventional English demand that the wronged maid be made a recognized wife by marriage. So Angelo weds Mariana, and Lucio, though pardoned other offences, has to marry his punk. Coleridge's objection that Angelo's marriage is 'degrading to the character of woman' is that of a nineteenth century philosopher, strong in moral judgements, and weak in knowledge of Elizabethan narrative and social conventions. The same miraculous processes which lead to the forgiveness of erring male characters, and their conversion to the paths of rectitude, also automatically make them perfect husbands. The audience in the Globe Theatre, we may be sure, did not worry their heads over the illogicalities of the situation. They knew that the raptures of reunion and the music of marriage bells were a prologue to the good old story-book ending, 'And so they lived happily ever after.'

SOURCE: *Shakespeare's Problem Comedies,* 1931 and 1969.

L. C. Knights

THE AMBIGUITY OF *MEASURE FOR MEASURE* (1942)

It is probably true to say that *Measure for Measure* is that play of Shakespeare's which has caused most readers the greatest sense of strain and mental discomfort. 'More labour than elegance' was Dr Johnson's way of expressing his sense of something forced in 'the grave scenes' (he found 'the light or comic part . . . very natural and pleasing') whilst to Coleridge the whole play was 'painful', and even, a few years later, 'hateful, though Shakespearean throughout'. The most obvious reason for this discomfort is to be found in the conflicting attitudes towards the main characters that seem to be forced upon us, and it is easy to list questions of personal conduct for which it is impossible to find a simple answer. (What, to take one example, are we to think of Isabella? Is she the embodiment of a chaste serenity, or is she, like Angelo, an illustration of the frosty lack of sympathy of a self-regarding puritanism?) Hazlitt's explanation of the painful impression created by the play, that 'our sympathies are repulsed and defeated in all directions', is, however, only part of the truth. It is not merely that the play is a comedy, so that the 'general system of cross-purposes between the feelings of the different characters and the sympathy of the reader' can be in part attributed to the needs of the plot – complication, suspense and a conventionally happy ending; the strain and conflict goes much deeper than that, being in fact embedded in the themes of which the characters are made the mouthpiece.

Like many other Elizabethan plays, *Measure for Measure* has an obvious relation to the old Moralities. It is too lively and dramatic – too Elizabethan – to be considered merely as a homiletic debate, but it turns, in its own way, on certain moral problems, the nature of which is indicated by the recurrent use of the words 'scope', 'liberty' and 'restraint'. What, Shakespeare seems to ask, is the relation between natural impulse and individual liberty on the one hand, and self-restraint and public law on the other?

The mainspring of the action is of course the sexual instinct: Claudio is condemned 'for getting Madam Julietta with child', Angelo discovers the force of suppressed impulse, and most of the lesser characters seem to have no other occupation and few other topics of conversation but sex. Angelo on the one hand and Mrs Overdone and her clients on the other represent the extremes of suppression and licence, and towards them Shakespeare's attitude is clear. The figure of Angelo, although a sketch rather than a developed character study, is the admitted success of the play. In few but firm lines we are made aware that his boasted self-control is not only a matter of conscious will ('What I will not, that I cannot do'), but of a will taut and strained. The Duke speaks of him as 'a man of stricture and firm abstinence', and the unfamiliarity of the word 'stricture' ensures that its derivation from *stringere*, to bind together or to strain, shall contribute to the meaning of the line. In his 'gravity' ('Wherein, let no man hear me, I take pride') there is an unpleasantly self-conscious element – summed up in Claudio's exclamation 'The prenzy Angelo!'[1] – which relates him to the objects of Shakespeare's irony in the sonnet about 'lilies that fester':

> Unmoved, cold, and to temptation slow:
> They rightly do inherit heaven's graces,
> And husband nature's riches from expense.
> They are the lords and owners of their faces,
> Others, but stewards of their excellence.

It is the unnaturalness and rigidity of his ideal that is insisted on. That it is unnatural is stressed not only by

Lucio – 'this ungenitured agent will unpeople the
province with continency; sparrows must not build in
his house-eaves because they are lecherous' – but by the
Duke:

>   Lord Angelo is precise;
> Stands at a guard with envy; scarce confesses
> That his blood flows, or that his appetite
> Is more to bread than stone.

Once the precarious balance is upset it is the despised
'blood' – an uncontrolled and unrelated sensual impulse – that runs away with him:

>   I have begun,
> And now I give my sensual race the rein:
> Fit thy consent to my sharp appetite. . . .

His lust, like his forced chastity, is felt as something
excessive, urgent and disproportionate in its demands:

> Why does my blood thus muster to my heart,
> Making both it unable for itself,
> And dispossessing all my other parts
> Of necessary fitness?

And the relation between the two extremes is further
emphasized by the gratuitous cruelty of his demands
on Isabella:

>   Redeem thy brother
> By yielding up thy body to my will,
> Or else he must not only die the death,
> But thy unkindness shall his death draw out
> To lingering sufferance;

for the savagery of this had been foreshadowed, before
his own temptation, not only in his peremptory harshness to Juliet (II ii), but in the sadism of his parting
words to Escalus, when the latter was about to try the
offenders from the suburbs: 'I'll take my leave . . .
Hoping you'll find good cause to whip them all.'

Lucio and his associates, on the other hand, follow their impulses without scruple or restraint. They have a natural vitality, expressing itself at times in a certain raciness of comment ('Heaven grant us its peace, but not the King of Hungary's'); and it is the 'fantastic' Lucio who urges the easily discouraged Isabella to further efforts to save her brother's life. 'Those pleasant persons' – as Hazlitt calls them – Lucio, Pompey and Froth, are often referred to as an example of Shakespeare's sympathy for scoundrels; but although we are not required to get up any moral steam about their vices, the artistic handling is cool and clear. The note of frothy triviality, struck in the first conversation between Lucio and 'two other like gentlemen' (i ii), is never absent from their talk for long. They sufficiently represent the 'scope' or 'liberty' that, it is postulated, has made 'Vienna' what it is.

Neither Angelo nor the traffickers in sex are the source of the sense of uneasiness that we are trying to track down. It is Claudio – who is scarcely a 'character' at all, and who stands between the two extremes – who seems to spring from feelings at war with themselves, and it is in considering the nature of his offence that one feels most perplexity. Soon after his first appearance, led by a gaoler, he is accosted by Lucio:

Lucio. Why, how now, Claudio? Whence comes this
    restraint?
Claudio. From too much liberty, my Lucio. Liberty,
    As surfeit is the father of much fast,
    So every scope by the immoderate use
    Turns to restraint. Our natures do pursue,
    Like rats that ravin down their proper bane,
    A thirsty evil, and when we drink we die.

Lucio. If I could speak so wisely under an arrest, I
    would send for certain of my creditors. And yet, to
    say the truth, I had as lief have the foppery of
    freedom as the mortality of imprisonment. What's
    thy offence, Claudio?

Claudio. What but to speak of would offend again.
Lucio. What, is it murder?
Claudio. No.
Lucio. Lechery?
Claudio. Call it so.

That Shakespeare was aware of an element of sententiousness in Claudio's words is shown by Lucio's brisk rejoinders. The emphasis has, too, an obvious dramatic function, for by suggesting that the offence was indeed grave it makes the penalty seem less fantastic; and in the theatre that is probably all one notices in the swift transition to more explicit exposition. But on coming back to the lines with fuller knowledge of what is involved it is impossible to avoid the impression of something odd and inappropriate. Apart from the fact that Claudio was 'contracted'[2] to Juliet, he does not seem to have 'surfeited', and he was certainly not a libertine: his 'entertainment' with Juliet was, we learn, 'most mutual' – they were in love with each other – a fact that is emphasized again later (II iii 24–8), when the Duke makes it a matter of special reproach to Juliet: 'Then was your sin of heavier kind than his.' And consider the simile by which Claudio is made to express feelings prompted, presumably, by his relations with the woman who – except for 'the denunciation ... of outward order' – is 'fast my wife': –

> Our natures do pursue,
> Like rats that ravin down their proper bane,
> A thirsty evil, and when we drink we die.

The illustrative comparison has, we notice, three stages: (i) rats 'ravin down' poison, (ii) which makes them thirsty, (iii) so they drink and – the poison taking effect – die. But the human parallel has, it seems only two stages: prompted by desire, men quench their 'thirsty evil' in the sexual act and – by the terms of the new proclamation – pay the penalty of death. The act of ravening down the bane or poison is thus left on our

hands, and the only way we can dispose of it is by
assuming that 'our natures' have no need to 'pursue'
their 'thirsty evils' for it is implanted in them by the
mere fact of being human. This of course is pedantry
and – you may say – irrelevant pedantry, for Shakespeare's similes do not usually demand a detailed,
point by point examination, and the confusion between desire (thirst) and that from which desire springs
does not lessen the general effect. The fact remains,
however, that there is some slight dislocation or confusion of feeling, comparable, it seems to me, to the
wider confusion of Sonnet 129, 'An expense of spirit in
a waste of shame ...' (for not even the excellent anal
ysis by Robert Graves and Laura Riding in their *Survey
of Modernist Poetry,* pp. 63–81, can make me feel that
the sonnet forms a coherent whole). And even if you
accept the simile as completely satisfactory, nothing
can prevent 'our natures' from receiving some share of
the animus conveyed by 'ravin', a word in any case
more appropriate to lust than to love, and so used by
Shakespeare in *Cymbeline*:

> The cloyed will –
> That satiate yet unsatisfied desire, that tub
> Both fill'd and running – ravening first the lamb
> Longs after the garbage.

The sentiments expressed here concerning what,
compared with Angelo's abstinence and Lucio's sexuality, looks like a natural relationship, are not the only
ones voiced in the course of the play. Shakespeare in
fact dramatizes various attitudes, and one would say
that our estimate of their relative validity depended on
our sense of the character embodying them were it not
that some of the characters are themselves either ambiguous or without much dramatic substance. Angelo's
unqualified contempt for Juliet –

> See you the fornicatress be remov'd:
> Let her have needful, but not lavish, means

– is sufficiently 'placed', as are Pompey's remarks about 'the merriest usury'; and Lucio, embodying a vulgar flippancy that blurs all distinctions, is obviously not disinterested when, pleading for 'a little more lenity to lechery', he complains of Angelo, 'What a ruthless thing is this in him, for the rebellion of a codpiece to take away the life of a man!' But we can feel no such certainty about the Duke or Isabella, who are sure enough of themselves: each of them is disposed to severity towards 'the sin' (II iv 28–36; III i 148) of Claudio and Juliet, and the Duke seems to regard it as an instance of the 'corruption' that boils and bubbles in the state: 'It is too general a vice, and severity must cure it' (III ii 103). To Escalus, who, so far as he is anything, is simply a wise counsellor, the 'fault' (II i 40) is venial; and the humane Provost describes Claudio as

> a young man
> More fit to do another such offence,
> Than die for this   (II iii 13–15)

Yet even in the Provost's sympathy there are overtones from a different range of feelings, and the excuse he finds for Claudio, 'He hath but as offended in a dream' (II ii 4), seems to echo once more the sonnet on lust:

> Made in pursuit and in possession so,
> Had, having, and in quest, to have extreme,
> A bliss in proof and prov'd a very woe,
> Before a joy propos'd behind a dream.

The play of course is only 'about' Claudio to the extent that he is the central figure of the plot; he is not consistently *created*, and he only lives in the intensity of his plea for life.[3] But I think it is the slight uncertainty of attitude in Shakespeare's handling of him that explains some part, at least, of the play's disturbing effect. Shakespeare, we know, had a deep sense of the human worth of tradition and traditional morality, but his plays do not rely on any accepted scheme of values. Their morality (if we call it that) springs from the unshrinking exploration of – the phrase is Marston's – 'what men were, and are,' and the standard is as we say loosely, nature itself. In the period immediately preceding the greatest plays – the period of *Measure for Measure, Troilus and Cressida, Hamlet* and perhaps some of the sonnets – analysis is not completely pure, and an emotional bias seems to blur some of the natural, positive values which in *Macbeth* or *Lear* are as vividly realized as the vision of evil.

II

The theme of liberty and restraint has, in *Measure for Measure,* another and more public aspect. The first full line of the play is, 'Of government the properties to unfold,' and the working out of the new severity of the law against licence leads to an examination of more general questions – the relations of law and 'justice', of individual freedom and social control, of governors and governed. Here again one finds not only divided sympathies but the pressure of feelings that fail to reach explicit recognition, as in the Duke's lines about the folly of keeping laws on the statute book but not enforcing them:

> We have strict statutes and most biting laws,
> The needful bits and curbs to headstrong weeds,
> Which for this fourteen years we have let slip;
> Even like an o'er grown lion in a cave,
> That goes not out to prey. Now, as fond fathers,
> Having bound up the threat'ning twigs of birch,
> Only to stick it in their children's sight
> For terror not to use, in time the rod
> Becomes more mock'd than fear'd; so our decrees,
> Dead to infliction, to themselves are dead,
> And liberty plucks justice by the nose;
> The baby beats the nurse, and quite athwart
> Goes all decorum.

What one first notices here is the crisp and lively de-

scription of the disorder resulting from official negligence; but behind this there are more complex feelings. If the offenders are 'weeds', they are also full of
natural energy, like the horse that needs the curb,[4]
whilst the concluding lines suggest mischief or childish
tantrums rather than deliberate wickedness. And if the
unenforced law is ludicrous – 'a scarecrow', as Angelo
says (II i 1) – the law and the lawmakers are not exactly
amiable. If the Duke's metaphors are given due weight
('biting', 'prey', 'rod', etc.) one begins to sympathize
with Lucio's feelings about 'the hideous law' (I iv 63),
especially when, a few lines later, the Duke is explicit
that to enforce the laws is, now, 'to strike and gall' the
people. It is, however, a postulate of the play that laws
are necessary; and although Shakespeare's deep – and
characteristically Elizabethan – sense of social *order* is
not expressed here with the same force as it is elsewhere, it is not, I feel, simply Angelo who thinks of the
law as 'all-building.' It is when this epithet is restored
to its context that the underlying dilemma of the play
becomes apparent: the full phrase is,

> the manacles
> Of the all-building law. (II iv 93–4)

Once more, Shakespeare presents various possible
attitudes and points of view. The perplexity of the
ordinary man confronted with the application of the
laws to a particular fellow human is expressed by
Escalus when, towards the end of Act II scene i he
reverts to Angelo's explicit instruction that Claudio
shall 'be executed by nine to-morrow morning':

Escalus. It grieves me for the death of Claudio;
    But there's no remedy.
Justice. Lord Angelo is severe.
Escalus.   It is but needful:
    Mercy is not itself, that oft looks so;
    Pardon is still the nurse of second woe.
    But yet, poor Claudio! There is no remedy.

Whilst laws are necessary, they may be enforced; yet
one's readiness to accept the logic of this is qualified by
various considerations already, in the same scene,
brought to our attention. Elbow, chosen constable by
his neighbours for seven years and a half, is not simply
a stock figure of fun: those who are concerned for the
validity of the law can hardly ignore the fact that its
instruments may be as foolish as he. 'Which is the wiser
here?' says Escalus, confronted with Elbow, Froth and
Pompey, 'Justice or Iniquity?' Again, how many escape
the law!

> Some run from brakes of vice and answer none,
>   And some condemned for a fault alone.

'Robes and furr'd gowns hide all,' as the mad king
says in *Lear*. More important still, those who make or
administer the laws may be as corrupt, at least in
thought, as those they sentence. This is what Escalus
urges on Angelo at the beginning of the scene, and the
exchange between them leads to the heart of the problem.

> *Escalus.* Let but your honour know,
>   Whom I believe to be most straight in virtue,
>   That, in the working of your own affections,
>   Had time coher'd with place or place with wish-
>   ing,
>   Or that the resolute acting of your blood
>   Could have attain'd the effect of your own pur-
>   pose,
>   Whether you had not, sometime in your life,
>   Err'd in this point which now you censure him,
>   And pull'd the law upon you.
> *Angelo.* 'Tis one thing to be tempted, Escalus,
>   Another thing to fall. I not deny,
>   The jury, passing on the prisoner's life,
>   May in the sworn twelve have a thief or two
>   Guiltier than him they try; what's open made to
>   justice,

That justice seizes: what know the laws
That thieves do pass on thieves?

Angelo, self-righteous and unsubtle, claims that the
law is impersonal: equating law with justice, he com-
placently overlooks the fact that justice had a moral
basis, and that morality is concerned with men's
thoughts and desires, not merely with their acts. When,
in the following scene (II ii), Isabella takes up this
theme –

How would you be
If He, which is the top of judgment, should
But judge you are you are?

– she is met with the same answer: 'It is the law, not I,
condemns your brother.' Given Angelo's premise, that
law *is* justice, his further contention, that any devia-
tion from strict law involves injustice to 'those ...
which a dismiss'd offence would after gall,' is unassail-
able. Isabella, when her plea for mercy fails, takes the
only course open to her and attacks the human motive
that sets the logical machine in motion,

Hooking both right and wrong to the appetite,
To follow as it draws.   (II iv 176–7)

Claudio has already made some bitter comments on
'the demi-god Authority,' And Isabella, in words that
remind us once more of *Lear*, now forces the personal,
as opposed to the purely formal, issue:

So you must be the first that gives this sentence,
And he, that suffers ...
Could great men thunder
As Jove himself does, Jove would ne'er be quiet,
For every pelting, petty officer
Would use this heaven for thunder; nothing but
    Thunder!

That, really, is as far as we get. That Angelo has to
reverse his former opinion and to tell himself,

> Thieves for their robbery have authority
> When judges steal themselves,

is not a full answer to the questions we have been
forced to ask; and it is significant that the last two acts,
showing obvious signs of haste, are little more than
drawing out and resolution of the plot. Angelo's temptation and fall finely enforces the need for self-knowledge and sympathy which seems to be the central
'moral' of the play,[5] and which certainly has a very
direct bearing on the problems of law and statecraft
involved in any attempt to produce order in an imperfect society. But the problems remain. Important in
any age, they had a particular urgency at a time when
established social forms were being undermined by
new forces, and Shakespeare – who in several plays had
already pondered 'the providence that's in a watchful
state' – was to return to them again with a developed
insight that makes most political thought look oddly
unsubstantial. The development was, of course, to be
in the direction indicated by *Measure for Measure* –
the continued reduction of abstract 'questions' to
terms of particular human motives and particular
human consequences, and the more and more explicit
recognition of complexities and contradictions that
appear as soon as one leaves the realm of the formal
and the abstract. But in this play the paradox of human
law – related on one side to justice and on the other to
expediency – is felt as confusion rather than as a
sharply focussed dilemma. The reader exclaims with
Claudio,

> Whether the tyranny be in his place,
> Or in his eminence that fills it up,
> I stagger in.[6]   (I ii 164–6)

I hope that no one, reaching the end of this examination, will feel that it would have been more appropriate if *Measure for Measure* had been written by Mr Shaw. The play itself – and this is a sign of its limitations – tends to force discussion in the direction of argument; but I certainly do not wish to imply that its admitted unsatisfactoriness is due to Shakespeare's failure to provide neat answers for Social Problems. Even when, later, he probes far more deeply the pre-occupations that have been touched on here, he offers no solutions. *Lear, Coriolanus, Antony and Cleopatra,* – each is a great work of clarification, in which there is the fullest recognition of conflicting 'truths'; in these plays, therefore, there is that element of paradox which seems inseparable from any work of supreme honesty. In *Measure for Measure* the process of clarification is incomplete, and one finds not paradox but genuine ambiguity.

SOURCE: *Scrutiny*, x 1942.

NOTES

1. 'Prenzy' – Burns's 'primsie'.
2. Elizabethan matrimonial law was a nasty tangle on this subject. The simplest explanation is that given by Pollock and Maitland, *A History of English Law*, II 383 ff. The curious may consult Henry Swinburne's *A Treatise of Spousals* (1686, but written *c.* 1600).
3. In scene (III i) which, it is worth noticing, reflects once more the conflict running through the play be-tween the claims of 'reason' on the one hand and of instinct and instinctive sympathy on the other. The Duke's speech, 'Reason thus with life...', is frigid and unconvincing because (except for three fine lines) it ignores the reality of emotion; Claudio's retort to the equally 'reasonable' Isabella, 'Ay, but to die, and go we know not where ...', though magnificent, is blindly in stinctive. There are only a few suggestions in this play of the more positive acceptance of death that we

find later.

4. Mr Empson, making this point, remarks, 'You may say that Shakespeare, though not the Duke, had both attitudes towards the wicked in mind, and would have preferred to call them "steeds". But this element in his judgment is sufficiently expressed by calling them *headstrong*; it is *Measure for Measure* to move from one attitude to the other' (*Seven Types of Ambiguity*, pp. 107–8).

5. Mr Wilson Knight's essay in *The Wheel of Fire* is headed, aptly, '*Measure for Measure* and the Gospels'.

6. 'His eminence,' – as one might say, 'his high and mightiness.'

Clifford Leech

THE 'MEANING' OF *MEASURE FOR MEASURE* (1950)

The nineteen-twenties, distrustful of 'enthusiasm', strove to see Shakespeare as above all the practical dramatist, led to the choice and the manipulation of his stories, to his manner of theatrical speech and character-presentation, by the stage-conditions of his time and the passing fashion of dramatic taste. This approach strengthened our understanding of Elizabethan stage-technique, and it was a useful corrective to the heavily romanticized Shakespeare of earlier years. But when the student of stage-conditions set up as the complete interpreter, the limitations of the approach were obvious enough. The poetic and the dramatic power were only foster-children of the industrious apprenticeship to the stage: the heart of the matter was not to be weighed in a Shakespeare laboratory.

The realization that the greatness of the poet lies, partly at least, in the scope of his mind has led in recent years to a close study of the ideas communicated through the plays. We now tend to see the histories as dramatic essays on a political theme, the final romances as embodiments of religious truth. Even the tragedies are dredged for underlying 'meanings'. But in one characteristic these searchers for theses do not differ from the stage-conditions men of a generation ago. They, too, emphasize the Elizabethanism of Shakespeare, and relate the significance of his plays to the general current of Elizabethan thought on political and religious themes. In the two tetralogies, we are told, Shakespeare speaks after the fashion of Halle and the Homilies; in the romances he is at one with the Christian attitude, adding – as G. Wilson Knight has it[1] –

his *Paradiso* to complete the structure of his collected works. And Miss Elizabeth M. Pope, in her article on 'The Renaissance Background of *Measure for Measure*,'[2] has set out to demonstrate that Shakespeare's handling of this dark comedy gives a thoughtful examination of the Christian views of justice and pardon. If we accept these interpretations unreservedly, we may see Shakespeare as the superb expositor of his age's thought, but perhaps we shall be giving both to the Shakespeare plays and to the Elizabethan age a a consistency of texture that they can hardly claim. Historically it was a time of important social transition, and the birth-pangs of the new order often induced doubt of old premise and new practice: the Homilies are of necessity orthodox, but we would do violence to *Tamburlaine* to interpret it exclusively in their light; Chapman's tragedies and Jonson's comedies are the products of independent minds, ever ready to scrutinize an accepted code; in *Troilus and Cressida* the traditional values of Hector and Ulysses are seen as unavailing in a world given over to disorder. If, then, we are to think of Shakespeare as the dramatic champion of the Tudor supremacy and the Anglican Church, we must recognize that this makes him, not the complete Elizabethan, but the sturdy partisan.

Yet it would appear particularly strange for Shakespeare's plays to be the embodiments of theses. In all matters of detail we find contradictions between one part of a play and another: the time-schemes are hardly ever consistently worked out; the manner of the dialogue may be rhetorical, intimate, sententious, euphuistic, compact, staccato, orotund, facetious, according to the particular demands of the individual scene; the statement of one passage may be at odds with others in the play, as with the differing accounts of Ophelia's death, the riddle of Macbeth's children, and Prospero's claim that he has raised men from the dead on his enchanted isle. Of course we can argue that contradictory time-schemes will fuse in the theatre, that the style in the best plays brings diversity into unity, and that incidental contradictions of statement will go unnoticed by an audience under a poet's spell. It remains significant that there are these discrepancies, for they may lead us to expect to find contradictory 'meanings' juxtaposed in the plays, to see the ending of *Macbeth* as simultaneously the destruction of a brave spirit and the reassertion of a political and moral order. In fact, when Shakespeare wrote *Macbeth*, he was thinking with part of his mind in the fashion of the Homilies, and at the same time he conveyed something of Seneca's concern with the individual's destiny, something of Euripides' cosmic challenge. For this reason, perhaps, *Macbeth* and the other tragedies leave us uneasy, in suspense. If we can, we shall escape from our uneasiness by disregarding certain parts of the dramatic statement, we shall claim *Macbeth* as first cousin either to *Gorboduc* or to *Jude the Obscure*, according as the fashion of the moment and our personal inclinations may lead us. But to escape in either direction is to do violence to the play.

In Miss Pope's account of *Measure for Measure* we have, I think, a corresponding simplification. Her relation of certain utterances in the play to Elizabethan statements of Christian doctrine does indubitably throw light on those utterances, and on the strands in the play's thought and feeling that they represent. But the total impression she leaves with us hardly coheres with the effect produced by the play in the theatre or when read as a whole. We are disturbed by it, not because its Christian doctrine is strict and uncompromising – as we may be disturbed by François Mauriac or Graham Greene – but because the very spokesmen for orthodoxy in the play repel us by their actions and the manner of their speech: they are not too hard for us, but rather too shifty, too complacent, too ignorant of their own selves, and for these failings they are nowhere explicitly reproved. That there is a Christian colouring in the play Miss Pope has securely demonstrated, particularly in the prayer of Isabella for Angelo's life and in the ultimate transcendence of

justice by mercy. But this Christian colouring is, I hope
to show, not more than intermittent in the play: it
wells up, as it were, from Shakespeare's unconscious
inheritance, and it does not determine the play's
characteristic effect.

We should note first of all that *Measure for Measure*
is not free from those incidental contradictions of
statement that are to be found in almost all of Shakespeare's plays. Dover Wilson has observed gross inconsistency in the time-references and has drawn attention
to the way in which Mistress Overdone in I ii first tells
Lucio and the others of Claudio's imprisonment and
immediately afterwards, in her talk with Pompey, displays ignorance of it.[3] A much more serious puzzle is
provided by the Duke's statement about Angelo in
different parts of the play. In I i the Duke is presumably serious in his profession of trust in Angelo. If he
were not, the appointment of Angelo would be inex-
cusable. Moreover, he professes that Angelo's higher
character is fully manifest:

> There is a kind of character in thy life,
> That to th' observer doth thy history
> Fully unfold;

and he adds that such merit should not go unused. Yet,
in his conversation with Friar Thomas, the Duke is by
no means so sure: part of his object in deserting his
post and turning spy is to find out whether Angelo is
all that he appears:

> Lord Angelo is precise;
> Stands at a guard with envy; scarce confesses.
> That his blood flows, or that his appetite
> Is more to bread than stone: hence shall we
>   see,
> If power change purpose, what our seemers be.
>   (I iii 50–4)

We will not stay to consider whether, in view of these
suspicions, the appointment of Angelo should have
been made. In III i, however, the Duke professes himself amazed at Angelo's fall from grace:

> but that frailty hath examples for his falling,
> I should wonder at Angelo;

and then, some forty lines later, tells Isabella of
Angelo's former relations with Mariana. We should in
particular note the Duke's assertion that Angelo, wishing to escape from his dowerless bride, pretended 'in
her discoveries of dishonour': his past conduct is, in
fact, here presented as so infamous that Isabella is
moved to cry:

> What corruption in this life, that it will let this
> man live!

Yet the Duke knew all this long before, we must assume. Not only, therefore, does Angelo's appointment
reflect on the Duke, but we must find Shakespeare
curiously engaged in deceiving his spectators: we have
been led to believe that Angelo was honest in his
puritanism, was convinced of his own strength against
temptation, was horrified when Isabella was used to
bait vice's hook. It is difficult to see how even a revision-
theory could explain these inconsistencies. Rather
it seems likely that, as so often, it was the immediate
situation that primarily engaged Shakespeare's attention.

If that is the case, however, should we expect to find
consistency of thought and feeling through the play?
Are we to try to reconcile the deeply Christian cry of
Isabella:

> Why, all the souls that were were forfeit once;
> And He that might the vantage best have took,
> Found out the remedy;   (II ii 73–5)

with the Duke's speech on death in III i? In this
connexion we should remember that, though Miss
Pope will not accept Roy Battenhouse's view of the
Duke as representing 'the Incarnate Lord', she does see
him as the good ruler, doing God's work and moving
through the play as 'an embodied Providence'.[4] Yet,
despite his Friar's gown, the Duke offers no hint of
Christian consolation: Claudio must welcome death
because there is no real joy to be found in life: he
denies even personality itself:

> Thou art not thyself;
> For thou exist'st on many a thousand grains
> That issue out of dust.

Man, he says, is not master of his own mind:

> Thou art not certain;
> For thy complexion shifts to strange effects,
> After the moon.

And there could hardly be a more dreadful or more
sober denunciation of human lovelessness than we are
offered here:

> Friend hast thou none;
> For thine own bowels, which do call thee sire,
> The mere effusion of thy proper loins,
> Do curse the gout, serpigo, and the rheum,
> For ending thee no sooner.

We can, of course, see the dramatic reason for this
speech. It provides the thesis to which Claudio's shrink-
ing from death is the antithesis. But cleaves too near
the bone to be regarded as a mere dramatic convenience. We have to recognize that the ideas in the speech
reverbertated in Shakespeare's own mind, that they
could co-exist with echoes of redemption and of a
human as well as divine forgiveness.

The Duke, ultimately the dispenser of pardon, has

something of Prospero's magisterial place and nature, is indeed at certain moments a morality-figure, a god out of the playwright's pigeon-hole. G. Wilson Knight assures us that 'Like Prospero, the Duke tends to assume proportions evidently divine',[5] while W. W. Lawrence argues that the Duke is but 'a stage Duke', a mere instrument in the play's economy.[6] Both these judgements, however, overlook the strong antipathy which the Duke has aroused in many readers during the past hundred years. The contrast between Wilson Knight's view and that, for example, of H. C. Hart[7] suggests an ambivalence in the character, a contradiction between its dramatic function and the human qualities implied by its words and actions. As F. P. Wilson was briefly shown, the character's morality-outline cannot be preserved in a play where other characters are as fully realized as Isabella, Angelo, Claudio and Lucio.[8]

Raleigh pointed out how the Duke plays at cat-and-mouse with Angelo in the last act,[9] and indeed his supreme indifference to human feeling is as persistent a note as any in the play. In II iii he catechizes Juliet, and in bidding her farewell casually breaks the news of Claudio's imminent execution:

> Your partner, as I hear, must die to-morrow,
> And I am going with instruction to him.
> Grace go with you! *Benedicite!*

We should note perhaps that as yet there is no hint that the Duke will interfere with the sentence: he has no criticism of Angelo's severity to make here, and in IV ii he insists that the sentence would be unjust only if Angelo fell short of the standards he is imposing on others. If, however, we are to assume that the Duke undergoes a 'conversion' which brings him to the exercise of mercy, we should be given some clear token of this in the play: as things stand, it appears as if the Duke pardons because he has not the strength to be severe and because he enjoys the contriving of a last-

minute rescue. He is indeed like Prospero in this, who
pretends sorrow for Alonso's loss of his son, and then
extracts a stage-manager's thrill from the sudden discovery that Ferdinand is safe. When Lucio refers to
'the old fantastical duke of dark corners', he gives us a
phrase that our memories will not let go: it comes, too,
most appropriately in IV iii, just after the Duke has
told us that he will proceed against Angelo 'By cold
gradation and well-balanced form' and has informed
Isabella that Claudio is dead. Of course, he gives us a
a reason for this behaviour: Isabella shall have
'heavenly comforts of despair, When it is least   expected', but this implies an odd principle of conduct,
which we should challenge even in 'an embodied Providence'. Indeed, it appears that there is nothing the
Duke can do directly. After he has spied on the interview between Isabella and her brother in III i, he tells
Claudio that Angelo has merely been testing Isabella's
virtue: one can see no reason for this beyond the
Duke's love of misleading his subjects. Having, moreover, hit upon the Mariana-plan, he still urges Claudio
to expect immediate death. We should note, too, that
he claims to know Angelo's mind by virtue of being
Angelo's confessor. One does not have to be deeply religious to be affronted by this piece of impertinence,
but later we find that the Duke takes a special delight
in the confessor's power which his disguise gives him:
in Angelo's case he doubtless lied, but in IV ii he is
prepared to shrive Barnardine immediately before
execution and in the last speech in the play he recom-
mends. Mariana to Angelo as one who has confessed to
him. We have reason to believe that the home of
Shakespeare's childhood was one in which the old religion was adhered to: [10] be that as it may, however, it
is difficult to believe that he could look with favour on
a man who deceived a condemned criminal with a
pretence of priestly power and who tricked Mariana
into giving him her confidence. [11]

But mystification is his ruling passion. He sends
'letters of strange tenour' to Angelo, hinting at his own

death or retreat into a monastery (iv ii); he gives
Angelo a sense of false security at the beginning of v i,
announcing:

> We have made inquiry of you; and we hear
> Such goodness of your justice, that our soul
> Cannot but yield you forth to public thanks,
> Forerunning more requital.

Then he orders Isabella to prison, calls Mariana 'thou
pernicious woman', and then, in his Friar's disguise,
tells them both that their cause is lost. Later he
laments with Isabella that he was not able to hinder
Claudio's death:

> O most kind maid!
> It was the swift celerity of his death,
> Which I did think with slower foot came on,
> That brain'd my purpose.

Apart from considerations of common decency and
kindness, we must assume at this point that Isabella is
a woman he loves. Later he pretends to discharge the
Provost for beheading Claudio, though here presumably only the standers-by were deceived.

It may be argued that we are taking the last act too
seriously, that here, as Raleigh put it, we have mere
plot, devised as a retreat, to save the name of
comedy.[12] Indeed, there is evidence that Shakespeare's mind was not working at full pressure in this
part of the play: Isabella tells Mariana in iv vi that
the Friar may 'speak against me on the adverse side':
this he does not do and we may assume that when
writing iv vi Shakespeare had not fully worked out the
conduct of the final scene. Nevertheless, the stage-man-
aging Duke of v i is of a piece with the man we have
seen eavesdropping and contriving throughout the play.
But now he forsakes his 'dark corners', focuses the light
on himself as Richard did at Coventry, gives pardon to
all, even to Escalus for being shocked at the Friar's

seeming impudence, and promises himself an added delight in further discourse of his adventures.

We should not forget in this last scene that the Duke is still outraged by the manner of Viennese life. Speaking as the Friar, he puts forward the same view as at the beginning of the play:

> My business in this state
> Made me a looker-on here in Vienna,
> Where I have seen corruption boil and bubble
> Till it o'er-run the stew: laws for all faults,
> But faults so countenanc'd, that the strong statutes
> Stand like the forfeits in a barber's shop,
> As much in mock as mark.   (v i 318–24)

Apart from his desire to spy on Angelo, his whole object in abandoning his ducal function was that the law should be exercised with greater rigour; yet at the end all are forgiven – except Lucio, whose punishment is grotesque rather than stern – and it would seem inequitable to discriminate between Barnardine and Mistress Overdone. But perhaps at the end, like the Duke himself, we forget Vienna and the governmental function: it may be that a *coup de théâtre* should not supply a legal precedent.

There is, moreover, something odd in the relations between the Duke and Lucio. Miss Pope, in exalting the Duke's ultimate dispensation of mercy, says that Lucio has to make amends 'to the girl he has wronged'.[13] This is a sententious way of putting it, for Shakespeare seems to take it much less seriously: in iii ii Mistress Overdone gives us the lady's name, and 'wronging' seems too romantic a term for Lucio's association with her. Our reaction to the Duke's punishment of the one man he could not forgive is compounded of amusement at Lucio's discomfiture and astonishment at the intensity of the Duke's spite. When Lucio protests against the sentence, the Duke's reply is 'Slandering a prince deserves it': this is a different matter from righting a wrong done to Mistress Kate Keepdown. Before that, I think, most readers and spectators have frankly enjoyed Lucio's baiting of the Friar. Not only do his words 'old fantastical duke of dark corners' bite shrewdly, but it is amusing to see how the Friar tries in vain to shake Lucio off when he is garrulous concerning the Duke's misdemeanours. Critics, searching for ethical formulations, are apt to forget that in the theatre the low life of Vienna and Lucio's persevering wit can arouse our sympathetic laughter.[14] And because we have earlier tended to side with Lucio against the Duke, we are amused when the Duke is petulant at Lucio's interruptions in the final scene. As for the judgement, we may remind ourselves as we hear it that, about this time, Shakespeare wrote in *Lear* of a judge and a condemned thief who might exchange places.

But much in this play seems to provide a comment on the administration of justice. The law's instruments include Abhorson, Elbow and, as a recruit from the stews, Pompey: their combined efforts take something away from the law's majesty. During Shakespeare's middle years he made much use of trial-scenes and other ceremonial unravellings. There is the Venetian court in *The Merchant of Venice*, the dismissal of Falstaff by the newly crowned Prince in 2 *Henry IV*, the King's putting of things to rights in *All's Well*, and the Duke's similar exercise of his function in this play. In each instance the sentence given can be justified; some clemency is allowed to mitigate the letter of the law; the way is cleared for the return of common conditions. And yet in every case our feeling is hardly of complete satisfaction. Shylock, Falstaff, Lucio arouse some resentment on their behalf, and we have little pleasure in the assertion of the law. It is frequently argued that we are too sensitive in our attitude to these victims of justice, and Miss Pope[15] suggests that Shakespeare's first audience would have been at least as well contented if Angelo, Lucio and Barnardine had been, like Shylock, punished severely. But perhaps the atti-

tude of the audience is not so necessary to an understanding of Shakespeare's purpose as his own attitude
must be, and it is in *Measure for Measure* that we are
given one of the clearest statements of his wide-reach-
ing sympathy: Isabella herself reminds us that

> the poor beetle, that we tread upon,
> In corporal sufferance finds a pang as great
> As when a giant dies.   (III i 79–81)

We may remember too that Barnardine, a convicted
malefactor, seems to be introduced into the play for the
sake of providing a substitute for Claudio's head: that
he is not executed and that Ragozine dies so conven-
iently would suggest that Shakespeare could feel the
horror of execution in the case of the common ruffian
as well as in that of the gentlemanly, merely imprud-
ent Claudio. It would be dangerous to base a judgement of Shakespeare's purpose on the assumption that
his feelings were less than ours.[16]

No more than the other plays incorporating 'trial-
scenes' is *Measure for Measure* to be interpreted as a
dramatic satire. It is indeed the overt purpose of the
play to demonstrate, as Miss Pope has suggested, a
governor's duty to practise mercy, to requite evil with
forgiveness or with the gentler forms of punishment.
Even the Duke's cat-and-mouse tricks with Claudio
and Angelo may be justified as the mitigated punishment for their wrongdoing. Miss Pope has judiciously
drawn attention to the Duke's soliloquy at the end of
Act III, where in gnomic octosyllabics he speaks with
chorus-like authority:[17] here, indeed, the morality
element in the play is uppermost, and Wilson Knight
has noted the resemblance of these lines in the theo-
phanic utterances of the last plays.[18] But, as so often
with Shakespeare, the play's 'meaning' is not to be
stated in the terms of a simple thesis: there are secondary as well as primary meanings to be taken into
account, and the secondary meanings may largely determine the play's impact. We can see 2 *Henry IV* as a

play with a morality-outline, with the Prince tempted by disorder and finally won over to the side of Royalty. At the same time, that play seems a dramatic essay on the theme of mutability, with sick fancies, the body's diseases, senile memories, and lamentations for a lost youth constituting its lines of structure. And we can see it, too, as part of the great historical design, of the chain of actions that led from Gloucester's murder to Bosworth Field. There is a satiric element as well, which appears uppermost when Prince John teaches us not to trust the word of a noble, and which is perhaps latent in Falstaff's rejection-scene.

It is this complexity of meaning that makes it possible for us to see and read these plays so often, that enables the theatrical producer to aim at a new 'interpretation'. We are tempted always to extract a meaning, and the undertaking may be profitable if it leads us to inquire into the bases of Elizabethan thought and does not limit our perception to those things in the play that are easy to fit in place. In *Measure for Measure* in particular we should be careful of imposing a pattern of Shakespeare's thought, for the silence of Isabella in the last hundred lines suggests either a corrupt text or a strange heedlessness of the author. But we should always be ready for the by-paths which Shakespeare's thoughts and feelings may take at any moment of a play. If we would penetrate into his state of mind during the composition of *Measure for Measure*, we should not, I think, overlook the name he gave to Claudio's young mistress[19] and the light thrown on Isabella's childhood when she cries that she would rather think her mother a strumpet than her father Claudio's begetter. Shakespeare cannot have forgotten an earlier Juliet when he used her name again, and the words of Isabella illuminate her cult of chastity. In our search for the play's 'meaning', we should not neglect these hints of a suppressed but deep sympathy with Juliet and of an almost clinically analytic approach to Isabella. In *Measure for Measure* we have a morality-framework, much incidental satire, a deep probing into the springs of action, a passionate sympathy with the unfortunate and the hard-pressed. Only if we concentrate our attention on one of these aspects will the play leave us content.

SOURCE: *Shakespeare Survey,* III, 1950.

NOTES

1. *The Crown of Life* (1947) p. 30.
2. *Shakespeare Survey,* II (1949) 66–82.
3. New Cambridge ed. (1922) pp. 99–100.
4. *Shakespeare Survey,* II 71.
5. See p. 99 above.
6. See p. 126 above.
7. Arden ed. (1905) pp. xxii–xxiii.
8. *Elizabethan and Jacobean* (1945) p. 118.
9. *Shakespeare* (English Men of Letters, 1939 ed) p. 158.
10. Cf. J. H. de Groot, *The Shakespeares and 'The Old Faith'* (1946).
11. Lawrence, p. 127 above, is at pains to convince us that the Duke did not confess Angelo, but he does not consider the implications of his exercise of priestly function with Mariana and (in intention) with Barnardine.
12. *Shakespeare,* p. 169.
13. *Shakespeare Survey,* II 80.
14. Raleigh, *Shakespeare,* p. 166, is here as so often an exception.
15. *Shakespeare Survey,* II 79.
16. Even with the trick of the substituted bed-fellow, we should not too readily argue that its frequency in earlier literature would make it acceptable to Shakespeare. It is noticeable that the Duke broaches the subject with some hesitation and seems to anticipate oppositon from Isabella. He has, indeed, to suggest that the end justifies a doubtful means: 'If you think well to carry this, as you may, the doubleness of the benefit defends the deceit from reproof. What think

you of it?' Isabella's quick assent is in sharp contrast to the Duke's laborious persuasions.

17. *Shakespeare Survey*, II 73.

18. See p. 99 above.

19. In Whetstone her name is Polina.

E. M. W. Tillyard

REALISM AND FOLK-LORE (1950)

Measure for Measure has been singularly apt to pro-
voke its critics to excess; and in the most different
manners. Earlier critics vented their excesses on two of
the main characters, Isabella and the Duke. Later
critics have, in reaction to the earlier, gone to two
different extremes. Some, in righteous and justified
defence of the play's heroine, have refused to see any
fault in the play at all; others, rightly recognising a
strong religious tone, have sought to give the whole
play an allegorical and religious explanation. This is
not to say that the above critics have not written well
of the play. Many of them have; but nearly all have
yoked their truths to strong and palpable errors. If I
now proceed to enumerate some of the errors, it does
not mean that I fail to recognise and pay tribute to the
truths.

I begin with an earlier type of criticism. To an age
whose typical mistake in criticism was to judge the
persons of Elizabethan plays by the standards of actual
life it is very natural that the Duke should be offensive.
He is an eavesdropper; he chose as his deputy a man
whom he knew to have behaved shabbily to his betrothed lady; and he displayed the utmost cruelty in
concealing from Isabella for longer than was strictly
necessary the news that her brother still lived. Certainly, as a real person, he is a most unsympathetic
character; and though we may feel wiser than the Vic-
torians and find no difficulty in the Duke as an allegorical figure or as a convenient stage machine, we can
understand Victorian resentment. With Isabella the
case is different. Here is a character who, in those parts
of the play where she really counts, will stand up to the

test of the most rigid realism; and yet how they hated
her! – this hard, smug, self-righteous virgin, preferring
her own precious chastity to the actual life of a far
more sympathetic person, her brother, and then, having got the utmost kick out of her militant virginity,
having it both ways by consenting to marry the Duke
at the end of the play. This actual error of interpretation no longer requires refutation. There is a fine
defence of Isabella in R. W. Chambers's British Aca-
demy Shakespeare Lecture for 1937, the *Jacobean
Shakespeare and 'Measure for Measure'*, while trouble,
not long before that date, over the royal succession had
revealed latent in the British public at large superstit-
ious feelings on the virtue of chastity that had their
bearing on the way Shakespeare's audience would have
taken Isabella's problem. Not that these happenings
were necessary to point to the truth; for the definitive
interpretation of Isabella's action was given by Walter
Scott when he prefixed quotations from *Measure for
Measure* to some of his culminating chapters in the
Heart of Midlothian. Before the twentieth chapter,
when Effie Deans in prison pleads with her sister Jeanie
to save her life, by swearing to do something which she
cannot know to be true, Scott set these lines:

> Sweet sister, let me live;
> What sin you do to save a brother's life,
> Nature dispenses with the deed so far,
> That it becomes a virtue.

Isabella and Jeanie Dean are, as characters, very
different women; yet Scott knew that he was here com-
peting with Shakespeare and that Jeanie's problem was
Isabella's problem. Jeanie's regard for truth was, like
Isabella's for chastity, a matter of fundamental principle, a condition of life's validity. And both regards
were equally redeemed from hypocrisy through their
holders being less reluctant to sacrifice their own lives
than to contribute by their ineluctable inaction to the
required sacrifice of the lives of their kin. Let anyone

who doubts how Shakespeare meant the principal episodes in *Measure for Measure* (and none of these occurs
after the first scene of Act Three) to be taken read or re-
read these culminating episodes of the *Heart of Midlothian*, including Jeanie's resolution to go to London
to obtain a royal pardon for her sister. Not only will he
learn how to take the first half of *Measure for Measure*
but he should note that in the play there is nothing to
correspond to Jeanie Deans's journey to London in the
novel.

So much generally for Isabella's nature and motives.
Why was it that many readers mistook them? Partly, I
think, because of an unfortunate habit of treating
Shakespeare's heroines as a repertory of ideal brides,
quite detached, poor things, from their native dramatic settings. If *you* were a young man, free to choose
a bride, would it be Miranda or Beatrice? Wasn't
Beatrice something of a risk? And wouldn't you really
be safer with Portia? Yes, perhaps, if your tastes were
high-brow enough. And so on, and so on. You will find
that a proportion of writing on Shakespeare's heroines
was conducted on those lines. Now Isabella comes off
very ill on such a criterion. The husbands of such
female saints or martyrs as were married have, as far as
I know, never been the object of much envy; the role of
martyr—consort is a hard one. And such would have
been that of Isabella's husband. And so the day-dream-
ing bride-pickers very naturally found her distasteful
and turned and rent her. And yet, in defending her, we
must not forget that in the play Isabella marries and in
so doing makes herself the more open to irrelevant
comparisons. Her enemies have at least that excuse for
their attacks; and her friends, like R. W. Chambers,
however well justified in defending her behaviour towards her brother, have erred in justifying the sum
total of her conduct.

This brings me to the other type of error, which is
roughly that of seeing nothing wrong with the play.
There are several ways of establishing it. One (and I
here think mainly of R. W Chambers) is to begin by

making hay of the mythical sorrows of Shakespeare and
of the mythical hypocrisy of Isabella and to go on to
prove that the high ethical standards set in the first
half are maintained and carried through in the second.
And the proof can be fascinating. Nothing could be
more ingenious and plausible than Chambers's notion
of Shakespeare's keeping Isabella ignorant of her
brother's survival and filled with justified fury at
Angelo's having done him to death, in order that her
powers of forgiveness might be tested to the uttermost
when she brings herself to join Mariana in pleading
for Angelo's life. And how much more creditable to
Shakespeare and pleasanter to most of us, to whom his
credit is very dear, if he did in fact keep Isabella in the
dark for so high and moral a motive and not merely to
pander to that appetite for ingenious plot-complica-
tions and improbable and strained moments of suspense which was one of the regrettable qualities of an
Elizabethan audience. Nothing, too, could help to
colour the last part of the play more happily than a
truly heartfelt and impressive repentance on the part
of Angelo. And, relying on the undoubted truth that
Angelo does profess himself very repentant, Chambers
does duly find Angelo's repentance very impressive.
The other way to find the play faultless is to cut out all
the Bradleian character-stuff from the start and to go
straight to ideas or allegory or symbols. There is much
thought and much orthodox piety in *Measure for
Measure*, and during the time when Shakespeare was
writing the Problem Plays he had the Morality form
rather prominently in his mind. That in some sort the
relation of justice and mercy is treated, that Angelo
may stand at one time for the letter of the law or for
the old law before Christian liberty and at another for
a Morality figure of False Seeming, that the Duke contains hints of heavenly Grace and that he embodies a
higher justice than mere legality, that Isabella is Mercy
as well as Chastity – all these matters may very likely
be concluded from the text and they may help us to

understand the play. But they are conclusions which are ineffective in just the same way in which Chambers's theories on Isabella's ignorance and Angelo's repentance are ineffective: they have little to do with the total play, however justifiable they may appear by these and those words or passages in abstraction. Now the doctrinal or allegorical significance of *Measure for Measure* culminates in the last long scene. And this scene does not succeed whether witnessed or read. Its main effect is that of labour. Shakespeare took trouble, he complicated enormously; he brought a vast amount of dramatic matter together. The actors know it is a big scene and they try to make it go. Perhaps their efforts just succeed; but then the success will be a tribute more to their efforts than to the scene itself. In the strain the supposed subtle reason for Isabella's ignorance or Claudio's survival goes unnoticed, while Angelo's repentance is a perfunctory affair amidst all the other crowded doings. Similarly, fresh from reading or seeing the play, how little aware we are of any allegorical motive. Even if the Duke stands for Providence he does not begin to interpose till after the first and incomparably the better half of the play. Claudio and Juliet may have been designed by their author to represent unregenerate mankind; yet Claudio at his first appearance is in a highly chastened and penitent frame of mind, well on the road to salvation: as when he says,

> The words of heaven: on whom it will, it will;
> On whom it will not, so. Yet still 'tis just.

Claudio is paraphrasing scripture, namely St Paul I's words in Romans ix: 'Therefore hath he mercy on whom he will have mercy, and whom he will he hardeneth'. But though he may class himself among the hardened sinners on account of his misdeed, there is no hardness left in him now. And quite apart from whether Claudio can, from his words, represent the unregenerate *homo* of the Moralities, he does in fact show himself

to us first and foremost as a most unfortunate young
man, deeply to be pitied.

The simple and ineluctable fact is that the tone in
the first half of the play is frankly, acutely human and
quite hostile to the tone of allegory or symbol. And,
however much the tone changes in the second half,
nothing in the world can make an allegorical interpretation poetically valid throughout.

Recent critics, in their anxiety to correct old errors,
have in fact gone too far in the other direction and
ignored one of the prime facts from which those old
errors had their origin: namely that the play is not of a
piece but changes its nature half-way through. It was
partly through their correct perception of something
being wrong that some earlier critics felt justified in
making the Isabella of the first half of the play the
scapegoat of the play's imperfections.

The above inconsistency has long been noted, but
since of late it has been so strongly denied, I had better
assert it once more, and if possible not quite in the old
terms. Briefly, the inconsistency is the most serious and
complete possible, being one of literary style. Up to III i
151, when the Duke enters to interrupt the passionate
conversation between Claudio and Isabella on the conflicting claims of his life and her chastity, the play is
predominantly poetical, the poetry being, it is true, set
off by passages of animated prose. And the poetry is of
that kind of which Shakespeare is the great master, the
kind that seems extremely close to the business of
living, to the problem of how to function as a human
being. One character after another is pictured in a
difficult, a critical, position, and yet one which all of us
can imagine ourselves to share; and the poetry answers
magnificently to this penetrating sense of human inti-
macy. Up to the above point the Duke, far from being
guide and controller, has been a mere conventional
piece of dramatic convenience for creating the setting
for the human conflicts. Beyond that he is just an on-
looker. And, as pointed out above, any symbolic poten-
tialities the characters may possess are obscured by the

tumult of passions their minds present to us. From the
Duke's entry at III i 151 to the end of the play there is
little poetry of any kind and scarcely any of the kind
described above. There is a passage of beautiful verse
spoken by the Provost, Claudio, and the Duke in the
prison, IV ii 66 ff. Take these lines from it:

> *Prov.*   It is a bitter deputy.
> *Duke.* Not so, not so: his life is parallel'd
>   Even with the stroke and line of his great justice.
>   He doth with holy abstinence subdue
>   That in himself which he spurs on his power
>   To qualify in others. Were he meal'd with that
>   Which he corrects, then were he tyrannous;
>   But this being so, he's just.

In their way these lines cannot be bettered but they do
not touch the great things in the early part of the play;
their accent is altogether more subdued. Again, the
episode of Mariana and Isabella pleading to the Duke
for Angelo's life, in the last scene of all, does rise somewhat as poetry. But this exceptional passage counts for
little in the prevailing tone of lowered poetical tension. Where in the first half the most intense writing
was poetical, in the second half it is comic or at least
prosaic. While the elaborate last scene, as I have
already pointed out, for all its poetical pretensions is
either a dramatic failure or at best a Pyrrhic victory, it
is the comedy of Lucio and the Duke, of Pompey learning the mystery of the executioner from Abhorson, of
Barnardine (for Shakespeare somehow contrives to
keep his gruesomeness this side the comic) that makes
the second half of the play possible to present on the
stage with any success at all. And the vehicle of this
comedy is prose, which, excellent though it is, cannot
be held consistent with the high poetry of the first half.
Another evident sign of tension relaxed in the second
half of the play is the increased use of rhyme. Not that
it occurs in such long stretches as in *All's Well*; but
there are many short passages, like this soliloquy of the

Duke after hearing Lucio's scandalous remarks on his character in III ii:

> No might nor greatness in mortality
> Can censure 'scape; back-wounding calumny
> The whitest virtue strikes. What king so strong
> Can tie the gall up in the sland'rous tongue?

or the couplet containing the title of the play:

> Haste still pays haste, and leisure answers leisure;
> Like doth quite like, and Measure still for Measure.

Here an antique quaintness excuses the lack of poetic intensity. Most characteristic of this quality in the last half of the play are the Duke's octosyllabic couplets at the end of III ii:

> He who the sword of heaven will bear
> Should be as holy as severe:
> Pattern in himself to know,
> Grace to stand, and virtue go;
> More nor less to others paying
> Than by self-offences weighing –

and the rest. Far from being spurious, the Duke's couplets in their antique stiffness and formality agree with the whole trend of the play's second half in relaxing the poetical tension and preparing for a more abstract form of drama.

A similar inconsistency extends to some of the characters. From being a minor character in the first half, with no influence on the way human motives are presented, the Duke becomes the dominant character in the second half and the one through whose mind human motives are judged. In the first half of the play we are in the very thick of action, where different human beings have their own special and different problems and are concerned with how to settle them. Mistress Overdone's problem of what's to be done now all the houses of resort in the suburbs are to be pulled down stands on its own feet quite separate from Claudio's problem of what's to be done now he has been arrested. We are in fact too close to them both to be able to distance them into a single perspective or a common unifying colour. Reality is too urgent to allow of reflection. In the second half the Duke is in charge. He has his plans, and, knowing they will come to fruition, we can watch their workings. Reflection has encroached on reality. W. W. Lawrence wrote a fine chapter on *Measure for Measure*, in which he points to the Duke's multifarious functions. The Duke's part derives both from the old folk-motive of the sovereign in disguise mixing with his people and from the conventional stage-character of the plot-promoting priest. He combines the functions of church and state. In his disguise he 'represents the wisdom and adroitness of the Church in directing courses of action and advising stratagems so that good may come out of evil'. He is also the supreme ruler of Vienna who at the end 'straightens out the tangles of the action and dispenses justice to all'. He is also a stage figure, highly important for manipulating the action and contrasted strikingly with the realistic characters. Admitting most truly that 'Shakespeare's art oscillates between extreme psychological subtlety and an equally extreme disregard of psychological truth, in the acceptance of stock narrative conventions', Lawrence may imply that the Duke does succeed in uniting these extremes. If so, I can only disagree, because Lawrence's description of the Duke applies only faintly to the first half of the play.

Nowhere does the change in the Duke's position show so strikingly as in Isabella. There is no more independent character in Shakespeare than the Isabella of the first half of the play: and independent in two senses. The essence of her disposition is decision and the acute sense of her own independent and inviolate personality; while her own particular problem of how to act is presented with all that differentation which I attributed to the problems of Claudio and Mistress

Overdone. At the beginning of the third act, when she
has learnt Angelo's full villainy, her nature is working
at the very height of its accustomed freedom. She enters
almost choked with bitter fury at Angelo, in the mood
for martyrdom and feeling that Claudio's mere life is a
trifle before the mighty issues of right and wrong. Her
scorn of Claudio's weakness is dramatically definitive
and perfect. To his pathetic pleas, 'Sweet sister, let me
live', etc., the lines Scott prefixed to the twentieth
chapter of the *Heart of Midlothian*, comes, as it must,
her own, spontaneous retort from the depth of her
being,

> O you beast,
> O faithless coward, O dishonest wretch!
> Wilt thou be made a man out of my vice?
> Is't not a kind of incest to take life
> From thine own sister's shame? What should I
>   think?
> Heaven shield my mother play'd my father fair,
> For such a warped slip of wilderness
> Ne'er issued from his blood. Take my defiance,
> Die, perish! Might but my bending down
> Reprieve thee from thy fate, it should proceed.
> I'll pray a thousand prayers for thy death,
> No word to save thee.

That is the true Isabella, and whether or not we like
that kind of woman is beside the point. But immediately after her speech, at line 152, the Duke takes
charge and she proceeds to exchange her native ferocity for the hushed and submissive tones of a well-
trained confidential secretary. To the Duke's inquiry
of how she will content Angelo and save her brother
she replies in coolly rhetorical prose:

> I am now going to resolve him: I had rather my
> brother die by the law than my son should be unlaw-
> fully born. But, O, how much is the good duke de-
> ceived in Angelo! If ever he return and I can speak

to him, I will open my lips in vain or discover his
government.

But such coolness is warm compared with her tame
acquiescence in the Duke's plan for her to pretend to
yield to Angelo and then to substitute Mariana:

> The image of it gives me content already, and I trust
> it will grow to a most prosperous perfection.

To argue, as has been argued, that the plan, by Elizabethan standards, was very honourable and sensible
and that of course Isabella would have accepted it
gladly is to substitute the criterion of ordinary practical common sense for that of the drama. You could just
as well seek to compromise the fictional validity of
Jeanie Deans's journey to London by proving that the
initial practical difficulties of such a journey at such a
date rendered the undertaking highly improbable. In
Scott's novel Jeanie Deans does travel to London, and,
though Scott had better have shorn her journey of
many of its improbable and romantic complications, it
is a consistent Jeanie Deans who takes the journey, and
her action in taking the journey and in pleading with
the Queen is significant. Isabella, on the contrary, has
been bereft of significant action, she has nothing to do
corresponding to Jeanie's journey, and she has turned
into a mere tool of the Duke. In the last scene she does
indeed bear some part in the action; but her freedom
of utterance is so hampered by misunderstanding and
mystification that she never speaks with her full voice:
she is not, dramatically, the same Isabella. That the
Duke is in this way impressive, that he creates a certain
moral atmosphere, serious and yet tolerant, in the
second half of the play need not be denied; yet that
atmosphere can ill bear comparison with that of the
early part of the play. To this fact Lucio is the chief
witness. He is now the livest figure and the one who
does most to keep the play from quite falling apart, and
he almost eludes the Duke's control. He is as it were

a minor Saturnian deity who has somehow survived into the iron age of Jupiter; and a constant reminder that the Saturnian age was the better of the two.

The fact of the play's inconsistency, then, seems to me undoubted: the reason for it must be conjectural, yet conjectural within not excessive bounds of probability. I believe it may be found through considering Shakespeare's originals.

The plot of *Measure for Measure* goes back to one or both versions of a similar story by George Whetstone. The earlier is a play in two parts called *Promos and Cassandra* and published in 1578, the later a short narrative called the *Rare History of Promos and Cassandra* and included in his story-collection called the *Heptameron of Civil Discourses*, 1582. Behind both versions is a story of Cinthio. I think Shakespeare was indebted to both versions. He certainly must have known the play, for this contains, as the narrative does not, scenes of low life that correspond to similar scenes in *Measure for Measure*. There is also the incident (*Promos and Cassandra*, Part 2, v 5) when Polina (=Juliet), though wronged by Promos (=Angelo) through the death of her plighted lover Andrugio (=Claudio), joins Cassandra (=Isabella, but in this version of the story married ultimately to Promos) in praying God to relieve Promos. It is not found in the narrative and it seems to be behind the incident in *Measure for Measure* of Isabella joining Mariana to plead for Angelo although he has done her brother Claudio to death. But the way Shakespeare deals with the theme of the principles of justice is nearer the narrative. There is a lot about justice in Whetstone's play, including disquisitions on the true meaning of what Shakespeare called measure for measure. But there is more about the wickedness of bribery in the government and the need for the magistrate to be a pattern of virtue. It is in the narrative that the theme of what true justice is predominates. That Shakespeare was drawn to that theme, and possibly in the first stages of roughing out his plot, may be conjectured.

But there were things in Whetstone's play that kindled his imagination more warmly than the theory of justice, whether derived from narrative or drama. Whetstone's best scene (and even so it is a very poor affair) is Part 1 III 4 where Cassandra debates with her brother Andrugio and with herself whether she will let him die or whether she will yield her honour to Promos. Like Isabella she would gladly die in place of her brother and she thinks death in itself a lesser evil than loss of honour. But Andrugio points out that Promos might after all end by marrying her and then all might be well. And Cassandra is so impressed by this argument that she decides to save her brother. However feeble the scene, it does present to the reader or the re-caster certain simple and basic human passions and conflicts: Promos's dilemma between justice and lust; Andrugio's instinct to save his life at almost any cost; Cassandra's dilemma between the desires to save her brother's life and to save her honour. The human interest and the dramatic possibilities of these passions and conflicts kindled Shakespeare's imagination and he proceeded in the first half of *Measure for Measure* to give his version of them.

But in so doing he altered Whetstone in one very important matter; he made his heroine resist the appeal of her brother to save his life. In accordance with this change he turns his heroine into a much more decided and uncompromising person. In Whetstone the chief dramatic interest is the heroine's divided mind, her struggle with herself: Shakespeare's heroine has a whole mind and has no struggle with herself: all her struggles are outside, with her brother and her would-be seducer. It looks as if Shakespeare had been carried away by his conception of Isabella without realising the dramatic difficulties it involved. Whetstone's Cassandra, however inferior in execution to Shakespeare's Isabella, was through her very weakness a more flexible dramatic character. Her mind, divided once, can be divided again and provide interesting dramatic situations. After Promos has enjoyed her, he

decides nevertheless to have Andrugio killed, because
to spare him would be to show partiality in the eyes of
the world. Actually Andrugio is spared and set free by
his jailors, but neither Promos nor Cassandra knows
this. Hearing of Andrugio's supposed death, Cassandra
would like to take her own life. But, then, she reflects,
Andrugio will lack an avenger; and her mind is divided between the desires for death and for revenge.
The first part of the play ends with Cassandra's resolve
to take her life only after having appealed to the King
for vengeance. Yet a third struggle occurs when the
King, hearing of Promos's crimes, has him married to
Cassandra, and then orders his death. As Andrugio
predicted, marriage puts everything right between
Promos and Cassandra; and Cassandra is now divided
between loyalty to a dead brother and loyalty to a new,
living, husband. The second loyalty prevails. Little as
Whetstone made of the play's dramatic possibilities, he
did at least allow those possibilities to permeate the
whole story consistently. Shakespeare by altering the
plot and by re-creating his heroine, however superb the
immediate result, could only ruin the play as a whole.
Not having been violated, Isabella has no call to medi-
tate suicide. Not having become Angelo's wife, she has
no reason to recommend him to mercy as well as to
justice. Her one possible line of action was to appeal
outright to the Duke; and that would be to sabotage
most of the substance of the last half of the play. With
significant action denied to Isabella, Shakespeare must
have seen that to carry the play through in the spirit in
which he began it was impossible; and after III i 151 he
threw in his hand.

Whether in the second half Shakespeare reverted to
an original plan from which he had played truant, or
whether he began to improvise when he found himself
stuck, we shall never know. But conjecture may be
easier when we recognise the large differences in the
material from which he derived the two portions of his
play. That we can do so is largely due to W. W. Lawrence. Lawrence distinguishes two kinds of material in

Measure for Measure. The central episode of a sister having to decide whether to save her brother's life at the expense of her honour may go back to a historical incident and anyhow is related to real life and not to folk-lore. Similarly the setting in the low life of a city, not found before Whetstone, is realistic and not traditional or magical. But Shakespeare grafted onto the realistic material of Whetstone two themes that belong to the world of the fairy-tale: first, the disguised King mingling with and observing his own people, and second, the secret substitution of the real bride in the husband's bed. At first sight the case seems to be much that of *All's Well.* There we have a highly realistic setting and array of characters, to which are attached the folk-themes of the person who by healing a king obtains a boon, of the setting of certain seemingly impossible tasks, and of the substitute bride. But actually the cases are very different and suggest that the plays were differently put together. In *All's Well* realism and folk-lore are blended from beginning to end; in *Measure for Measure* realism admits no folk-lore for half of the play, while all the folk-lore occurs in the second half. The same is true of allegory. The notions of Helena standing in some way for an emissary of heaven and of Bertram as a Morality figure drawn on one side by his mother and bride to good and on the other by Parolles to evil, faint in themselves, are yet spread throughout the play. Corresponding notions of the Duke as Heavenly Justice, or Isabella as Mercy, and so forth, though in themselves more evident and stronger than their parallels in *All's Well,* are quite absent from the first part of the play and appear quite suddenly in the second. It looks therefore as if *All's Well,* however deficient in execution, was conceived and executed consistently and with no change of mind, but as if the two types of material from which *Measure for Measure* was drawn betoken two different types of execution, and an abrupt change from one to the other. Exactly what happened in Shakespeare's mind we shall never know.

He may or may not have meant initially to write a play
on the great themes of justice, mercy, and forgiveness. If
he did, he seems to have changed his mind and sought
above all to give his own version of the human poten-
tialities of Whetstone's theme. Self-defeated half-way,
through the turn he gave that theme, he may have
reverted to his original, more abstract intentions, to
help him out. More likely, to my thinking, he sought
help from the methods and the incidents of the play,
written shortly before and still in temper akin to his
present self, *All's Well that Ends Well*.

It is, incidentally, because the folk-material is so
differently spaced and blended in the two plays that
the theme of the substitute bride is quite seemly in
All's Well and is somehow rather shocking in *Measure
for Measure*. In *All's Well* we have been habituated to
the improbable, the conventional, and the antique: in
Measure for Measure the change to these from the
more lifelike human passions is too violent; and it is
here a case not of a modern prudery unaware of Elizabethan preconceptions but of an artistic breach of in-
ternal harmony.

But I am loth to end on matters mainly conjectural,
and I will revert to the first half of *Measure for Measure* and pay my tribute to a quality in it that has not
quite had its due. Full justice can never be done to
what Shakespeare really achieved here, on account of
the imperfections of our only text, that of the First
Folio. For instance, scene II iv, when Angelo tempts
Isabella to buy Claudio's life by her virtue, is terribly
obscure in places and simply cannot be read with un-
impeded pleasure. But in spite of textual impediments
it has been recognised that the prevailing style matches
that of *Hamlet* and possibly of *Othello*. This comment
of Claudio on Angelo and his new official zeal has
surely the accent of *Hamlet*:

> And the new deputy now for the Duke –
> Whether it be the fault and glimpse of newness,
> Or whether that the body public be

> A horse whereon the governor doth ride,
> Who, newly in the seat, that it may know
> He can command, lets it straight feel the spur;
> Whether the tyranny be in his place
> Or in his eminence that fills it up,
> I stagger in – but this new governor
> Awakes me all the enrolled penalties
> Which have like unscour'd armour hung by the
>   wall
> So long that nineteen zodiacs have gone round
> And none of them been worn; and, for a name,
> Now puts the drowsy and neglected act
> Freshly on me.
>
>   (I ii 161–75)

The power of the verse in the early part of *Measure for Measure* has indeed been allowed. Less notice has been taken of the extreme subtlety of characterisation. I will illustrate this from scene II ii, where Isabella, seconded by Lucio, first pleads with Angelo for her brother's life. It is a scene whose power is obvious and has been generally admitted. Close reading is necessary to bring out the accompanying subtlety with which all the movements of Isabella's mind are presented. At first Shakespeare risks failure by asserting psychological truth almost at the expense of dramatic probability. Isabella begins her attack on Angelo with a crudity and a lack of strategy which on a first impact are staggering:

> There is a vice that most I do abhor
> And most desire should meet the blow of justice;
> For which I would not plead but that I must;
> For which I must not plead but that I am
> At war 'twixt will and will not.

Yet this crudity is absolutely natural. Claudio's arrest could not, from Isabella's point of view, have been timed worse. Young, ardent, neophytic, she has bent all her strength to embrace an other-worldly ideal. And in

the very act of embracement she is called on to plead in
mitigation of that which is most abhorrent to her. Her
crude self-explanation is psychologically inevitable.
And what is so brilliant in the rest of the scene is the
way in which she gradually discards the drawing-in of
herself into cloistral concentration and reaches out
again to a worldly observation she has newly re-
nounced. And that observation includes a bitter anger
that this mere man, this Angelo, this precisian, should
be able to decide her brother's fate.

At first she is helpless and is for giving over at the
first rebuff:

> O just but severe law!
> I had a brother then. Heaven keep your honour!

But Lucio intervenes and urges her to a fresh attack.
The best she can do now is to recall and utter some
current commonplaces about mercy and about the
judge being no better than the accused. But her accent
is, surely, still formal and cool:

> Well, believe this,
> No ceremony that to great ones 'longs,
> Not the king's crown, nor the deputed sword,
> The marshal's truncheon, nor the judge's robe,
> Become them with one half so good a grace
> As mercy does.

But something, whether an unconscious clash of wills
or a secret sense of Angelo's being stirred by her own
self, prompts Isabella to be personal and she goes on:

> If he had been as you and you as he
> You would have slipt like him; but he like you
> Would not have been so stern.

And when Angelo tells her to be gone, at once her
personal opposition stiffens, and, no longer the awe-
some wielder of the law and God's deputy, he becomes

in her eyes mere man and as deeply in need of God's
mercy as any sinner. Her renewed plea for mercy is
now impassioned, and when he tells her that Claudio
must die to-morrow he arouses the whole stretch of her
mind. Her concern for Claudio is cruelly sharpened
and prompts her to the kind of humour that lies next
to the tragic:

> He's not prepared for death. Even for our kitchens
> We kill the fowl of season. Shall we serve heaven
> With less respect than we do minister
> To our gross selves?

Angelo still resists but feels called on to defend his
action at greater length. His cold pompousness infuri-
ates her and calls forth her culminating and classic
denunciation of human pride. But first by her bitter
emphasis on the personal pronouns she makes it plain
that her attack on pride is far from being on an abstract and impersonal sin:

> So *you* must be the first that gives this sentence,
> And *he*, that suffers.

And we do Shakespeare's art less than justice if, absorbed in the detachable splendour of the lines that
follow, we forget the personal application.

> O, it is excellent
> To have a giant's strength; but it is tyrannous
> To use it like a giant. Could great men thunder
> As Jove himself does, Jove would ne'er be quiet;
> For every pelting, petty officer
> Would use his heaven for thunder, nothing but
>   thunder.
> Merciful heaven,
> Thou rather with thy sharp and sulphurous bolt
> Splits the unwedgeable and gnarled oak
> Than the soft myrtle. But man, proud man,
> Drest in a little brief authority,

> Most ignorant of what he's most assur'd,
> His glassy essence, like an angry ape
> Plays such fantastic tricks before high heaven
> As makes the angels weep; who, with our spleens
> Would all themselves laugh mortal.

Such eloquence cannot lack effect. Lucio (and we may assume Isabella too) sees that some change is taking place in Angelo. There is one kind of irony in Isabella's and a very different kind in Lucio's, who must have prided himself on his connoisseurship of the tokens of lust, being quite deceived as to the nature of that change. Isabella, now confident of victory, speaks less vehemently, and Lucio, anxious lest too much of the same thing may spoil the victory, signals for them to go at once, when Angelo says he will see Isabella again to-morrow.

The whole scene, and especially Isabella's speech on pride, illustrates the truth that in the drama the most powerful general effect comes by way of absorption into the immediate dramatic business, just as writers in general are most likely to speak to all ages when most sensitive to the spiritual climate of their own. Here, at any rate, problem play or no problem play, Shakespeare is at the height of his strength.

SOURCE: *Shakespeare's Problem Plays*, 1950.

William Empson

SENSE IN *MEASURE FOR MEASURE*
(1951)

There are only about ten uses of the word in the play,
But I think almost all of them carry forward a puzzle
which is essential to its thought. It is not denied that
the word then covered (1) 'sensuality' and (2) 'sensibility', and I maintain that it also covered (3) 'sensibleness', though in a less direct way, through the ideas of
'a truth-giving feeling' and 'a reasonable meaning'.
Clearly the equations between these three could carry
very relevant ironies, though the effect is not so much a
covert assertion as something best translated into questions. Are Puritans hard? (Is not-one not-two?) Are
they liable to have crazy outbreaks? (Is not-one not-
three?) Is mere justice enough? (Is three two?) To be
sure, these questions look very unlike the flat false
identity of one idea with another, but I think the state
of the word then made them easier to impose. It seems
to have been neither analysed nor taken as simple; it
points directly into the situation where it is used, im-
plying a background of ideas which can be applied to
the situation, but somehow as if the word itself did not
name them; it is a shorthand term, rather than a solid
word in which two of the meanings can be equated.
And yet, as the play works itself out, there is a sort of
examination of the word as a whole, of all that it covers
in the cases where it can be used rightly; or rather an
examination of sanity itself, which is seen crumbling
and dissolving in the soliloquies of Angelo.

No doubt, in any case, the play is not fully satisfactory, and it has been argued that the suggestions of
extra meaning are merely the result of Shakespeare
doing the best he can with a bad plot. Mr R. W.
Chambers, in *Man's Unconquerable Mind*, seemed to

feel that the Bard had been unfairly insulted by modernistic persons, and urged truly enough that he made the plot less disagreeable than he found it. But no one, I take it, maintains that Shakespeare set out to write an attack on virginity (or for that matter on James I, if he is the Duke). The rebuttal does not come close enough to the idea in question; nor, I think, does Mr Dover Wilson's gallant and romantic defence of Prince Hal, or Dr Tillyard's patient and illuminating collection of evidence that the scheme of the Shakespeare History plays was drawn from a pompous contemporary myth made up to flatter the Tudors (a thing which he seems to admire more than it deserves). Nobody has denied that the Histories build up the Tudors, or that Prince Hal was meant to be a popular success. What has occasionally crossed the minds of critics, for quite a long time now, is to wonder what Shakespeare thought about it, and whether he cannot sometimes be found grumbling to himself about the plots that he was using, in a way that the audience was not expected to notice. No doubt this puts the contrast rather too strongly. I think a certain double attitude to Prince Hal is meant to be made public; indeed the idea that he could not be both a reliable friend and a popular hero is a very straightforward 'moral', even if not a prominent one. But in any case the question how many of the audience noticed the two levels of meaning does not seem to me crucial. As the evidence about the Elizabethan mind piles up, we are tacitly asked to believe that Shakespeare could not possibly have disagreed with it, or have dared to show that he disagreed. I think he was a more self-indulgent kind of man than that, as well as not such a stupid one. Of course the plot had to be something that would go down, but when he came to write the thing (pretty fast) the characters had to say what he could imagine for them. *Measure for Measure* is I think one of the most striking cases where the feelings in his words jib at a wholehearted acceptance of the story, without being planned as a secret meaning for the wiser few or even marking a clear-cut opinion in the author. Perhaps I am making too much fuss about adopting this common-place point of view, but the idea seems to have been much blown upon lately by historical-minded critics, and yet I cannot see that they have brought any evidence against it.

However, the recent drift of various British critics towards royalism is mild compared to that of various American ones towards behaviourism, which happens to go in the same direction. At least I imagine that that cult, so powerful in linguistics, is the ultimate reason why so many American critics of Shakespeare claim that their work is 'objective'. If we give *objective* its full claims, to 'wonder what Shakespeare thought about it' becomes a disgraceful self-indulgence; a critic should limit himself to rigid proofs, like the scientist that he is. That is, in effect, he should talk about the author as one of a type, not as an individual acquaintance; to a certain extent this really gets done, and it seems clear to me that the method produces superficial criticism. No doubt the timidity of the thing saves a critic from the more flamboyant errors of the last century; and you may reasonably say that we cannot make Shakespeare into a personal acquaintance. But it is enough to refute the behaviourist, on this issue, if he admits that we can make *anybody* into a personal acquaintance; that we can ever get any 'insight' into another person's feelings. One of the things a critic has normally claimed to do is to show this sort of insight about authors; there is nothing that I can see in the theory of behaviourism, only in its 'atmosphere', to get this forbidden; and if a critic insists that he has no such insight, it seems to me, he is only saying in an unnecessarily pompous manner (and sometimes quite falsely) that he is unfit to do his work.

I shall assume then, in the old-fashioned way, that the first thing to consider about *Measure for Measure* is why Shakespeare was interested in the story; because this interest is what will cause any drag there may be against the obvious theatrical values of the characters.

We are to imagine him coming across it in the Italian, perhaps translated offhand, of Cinthio's collection of 1565, which he was already using for the plot of *Othello*, and then looking up Whetstone's dramatisation of it (1578) for some extra tips. It was a clumsy plot, needing a good deal of tinkering, but it would carry a part of what was on his mind. This was very complex. There was a strand of loathing for sexuality in any form, partly no doubt as an intellectual agreement with the Puritans, but one that he recognises as a diseased frame of mind; and contrasting with this a loathing for the cruelty which this line of feeling produced in Puritans, above all for the claim that to indulge the cruelty satisfies justice. The contrast was one with many ramifications, and my own guess is that he saw the wicked deputy as one of the Cold People of Sonnet 94, the lilies that fester and smell worse than weeds; he christened him Angel; after that he found the plot interesting. He was not in the mood to write comedies, and the old real situation of the Sonnets, however irrelevant, was a source of energy. The first speech describing Angelo is a series of reminiscences from the Sonnets, and after that he develops on his own. I think that a use of *sense* in Sonnet 35 helps to show why the word became a crux of the play.

> No more be griev'd at that which thou hast done,
> Roses have thorns, and silver fountains mud,
> Clouds and eclipses stain both Moon and sun,
> And loathsome canker lives in sweetest bud.
> All men make faults, and I even in this,
> Authorising thy trespass with compare,
> Myself corrupting salving thy amiss,
> Excusing their sins more than their sins are:
> For to thy sensual fault I bring in sense,
> Thy adverse party is thy Advocate,
> And gainst myself a lawful plea commence,
> Such civil war is in my love and hate,
> > That I an accessary needs must be,
> > To that sweet thief which sourly robs from me.

'I bring in reason, arguments to justify it' or 'I bring in
feelings about it, feel it more important than it really
was (and therefore excuse it more than it needs)' or 'I
bring extra sensuality to it; I enjoy thinking about it
and making arguments to defend it, so that my sensuality sympathises with yours'. Sensuality is the predicate, I think. In any case the subtle confusion of the
word is used for a mood of fretted and exhausting casuistry; the corruption of the best makes it the worst;
charity is good, but has strange and shameful roots; the
idea of a lawsuit about such matters is itself shameful,
and indeed more corrupt than the natural evil. If he
associated the word with this passage it would carry
most of the atmosphere of *Measure for Measure*.

The first use of the word in the play is by the gay
Lucio, when he goes to Isabella at her nunnery to tell
her about the pregnancy and ask her to beg for her
brother's life. (To avoid obscurity I shall summarise
the plot here and there in brackets. Angelo, left in
command of the dukedom, has revived an old law
imposing death for sex outside marriage, and this falls
on Claudio though he is already betrothed and prepared to marry.) It is hard to get clear about Elizabethan politeness, but I take it Lucio is a bit muddled
though still casual. He wants to respect her high-
mindedness, but he has to treat the scandal as trivial to
induce her to help, so he falls into a verbose style which
the bitter woman thinks is mocking her virtue.

> *A man whose blood*
> *Is very snow-broth: one who never feels*
> *The wanton stings and motions of the sense;*
> *But doth rebate, and blunt his natural edge*
> *With profits of the mind; Study, and fast*
> *   ... hath pick'd out an act,*
> *Under whose heavy sense your brother's life*
> *Falls into forfeit: he arrests him on it....*

                                        (I iv 57)

'Profits of the mind' with its Puritan commercialism

makes an effort to get the nun's point of view, but 'blunt your natural edge' is a phrase he would more naturally use (say) of making yourself stupid by heavy drinking. He clearly feels, though he cannot say out-right, that Angelo's habits have cost him his 'common sense'. However we must guard against taking this as part of his intended meaning for *sense*; the meaning 'sensuality' is very unequivocal. Indeed one might say that this clear-cut use of the word is put first in the play to thrust the meaning 'sensuality' on our attention and make us treat it as the dominant one. Yet the word acts as a sort of euphemism, and this suggestion is sup-ported by the jauntiness of Lucio's whole tone. The form implies that sensuality is only one of the normal functions of the senses, and the rest of the speech im-plies that to neglect them is to become *blunted, heavy* (cruel) and so forth. Lucio does not want to annoy Isabella by saying this plainly, even by the relative plainness of a covert assertion; but it can hang about in his mind, and there is evidence that it does so when *sense* crops up again as the 'meaning' or 'intention' of the heavy Act. This sort of thing needs to be distin-guished from asserting an equation, and indeed is prior to it. If you say that I am ascribing magical powers to Shakespeare in making him put all this into the speech of Lucio, the answer is that the word was hanging about in Shakespeare's mind in the same way.

The next use is an aside of Angelo when first fasci-nated by Isabella (he will bargain to give her her brother's life in exchange for her body).

> She speaks and 'tis
> Such sense, that my sense breeds with it. Fare you
>   well.   (II ii 143)

Pope emended *breeds* to 'bleeds', making him express pity only, which is quite off the point. It shows I think how obscure the Shakespearean structure of meaning in the word had become to the Augustans; because the meaning 'sensuality' is obviously wanted here, if you can feel that it is linguistically possible. Angelo's first use of the word is 'wise or reasonable meaning', and then the meaning 'sensuality', which Lucio has made dominant for this stage of the play, pokes itself forward and is gratified by the second use of the word as a pun. Even in the second use I am not sure that 'sensuality' can be called the chief meaning of the word; the suggestion of *breeds* is rather that both the 'meanings in his mind' and his 'sense-data' have sensuality growing inside them – added to them, so to speak, as an Implication. So I think one could class both uses as equations of Type I, with sensuality acting as a dominant; however it is quite enough to feel that the word is given two simple meanings one after another. Presumably the capital letter when the word is repeated merely means that the actor should emphasize it to bring out the pun.

In real life it seems rather unlikely that this pun would occur to Angelo. It occurred to Shakespeare, and was wanted; to Lucio it could occur spontaneously, with a cheerful feeling that sensuality goes with sensibleness; but to Angelo the combination of meanings in the word can only appear as a hideous accident. The only touching side of Angelo is that he is genuinely astonished by his desires. (It is taken for granted that he could not make love to her in the ordinary way, though there is nothing to prevent him.) Yet the real irony, apart from the verbal accident, is that her coldness, even her rationality, is what has excited him; the two things are patently connected as in the word, though not in his system of ideas. Possibly with his usual injustice he feels that what she has just said ('if *you* remember a natural guiltiness') is already a loose way of talking. It is curious in any case to remember the decision of the N.E.D. that the meaning 'good judgement' for *sense* does not appear till the later half of the century; this passage is not using it alone, but gets all the effect of it.

In the next use, after the interview is over, Angelo is

not thinking of the word as a pun, and indeed the
possible connections have become so elaborate that the
meanings are hard to tie down.

> *What's this? What's this? is this her fault or mine?*
> *The Tempter or the Tempted, who sins most?*
> *Not she: nor doth she tempt: but it is I*
> *That, lying by the violet in the Sun,*
> *Do as the Carrion does, not as the flower,*
> *Corrupt with virtuous season. Can it be,*
> *That Modesty may more betray our sense*
> *Than woman's lightness?...*   (II ii 163)

The Arden editions' note says, very properly, that *sense*
here means 'sensuality, desire'; that of course is the
most prominent idea in Angelo's mind. But the recent
punning may easily be recalled, and the immediately
preceding metaphor is not obvious. In any case, why is
our sensuality betrayed by being excited and released?
We may be betrayed, but why it? To be sure, the
modest woman may make the sensuality show itself,
betray its presence; but if you adopt this rather
strained meaning for the phrase the word need not
mean 'sensuality' uniquely. What is betrayed is perhaps our general tendency, our 'gist or drift'. Or again
she may trick our sensuality into wrong actions, but
this implies that our sensuality is normally present and
usually good; it is nearer to Lucio's attitude than to
Angelo's. Nor does this attitude feel the meanings of
the word to be sharply opposed. Indeed I am begging a
question when I translate one of the meanings as 'sen
suality', because that tends to imply that the sexual
desire in question is of an evil kind, whereas *sense* in
itself does not have to add this Emotion. In the play it
seems to be added insistently, not only by Angelo but
by the presence of Isabella at the first use of the word;
but perhaps Angelo is trying to exorcise this Emotion
by the picture of the violet. There is a parallel confusion to that of *sense*, I think, in *season*; indeed part of
the strength of a ready-made puzzle like that of *sense* is

that it can impose itself as pattern on neighbouring
words. The Arden note gives 'benign influence of sum-
mer' for *virtuous season* – the warmth rots the carrion
but makes the flower sweet. This idea is certainly
present and gives a tidy metaphor. But it would make
Isabella the sun, whereas she is clearly the modest
violet, which he is lying by. If the sun is the natural
strength which causes sexual desire, that itself can be
good, the metaphor will imply. But if the violet is giving the *season*, the idea seems to be the smell of it, like
'*seasoning*' in food, pepper for instance. Unlike the
public and clear sunlight, this brings in ideas of pri-
vacy and of exciting the senses. He is no longer sure
what the natural process can be, to which he contrasts
himself, and has gone far towards accepting the confusion of meanings as a single and 'profound' one, as in
Type IV. I hope I have also shown that 'sensuality' can
still be regarded as a dominant, appearing only in the
predicate as for Type I; and of course the passage is
fully intelligible if you take 'sensuality' as the only
meaning of the word. In general I have not worried
about the possible use of a deliberate ambiguity of
equation structure, but when a character is actually
puzzling about a word it is not surprising that the
author should leave one open.

The next use of the word is in his second interview
with Isabella.

ANG. *Nay, but hear me,*
    Your sense pursues not mine; either you are
        ignorant,
    Or seem so craftily; and that's not good.

(II iv 73)

The pathetic or disgusting assumption of superior
morality, in this rebuke to her for not understanding
the bargain, finds an echo in the stock pun. Her meaning does not follow his, and also her desires do not start
running when his do – that's not good; a girl ought to
be docile. The Folio punctuation implies that ignor-

ance would be bad as well as craft. 'Now I give my
sensual race the rein,' he says soon after (II iv 160); he is
the only person in the play to use the adjective, and it
is felt to go with a split in the meanings of *sense*, which
should be harmoniously combined. In 'your sense pursues not mine' the immediate context very definitely
imposes 'interpretation' ('the sense you put on my
words') as the chief meaning, indeed to suppose it
means 'sensuality' is a satire on Angelo; but by this
time it is so strong a dominant meaning that it arises
easily.

There is a long pause before the next use of the
word; Angelo has now settled down into crime, and
can combine the meanings harmoniously enough in a
way of his own.

> *He should have lived*
> *Save that his riotous youth with dangerous sense*
> *Might in the times to come have ta'en revenge*
> *By so receiving a dishonour'd life*
> *With ransome of such shame.*   (IV iv 8)

It is still with superior morality that he looks back on
the most repulsive of his supposed actions. (Claudio
begged Isabella to pay the price of his life, and she
wished him dead for it. The Duke arranged that
Angelo had Mariana instead, but no man in an Elizabethan play can tell one woman from another in the
dark, and Angelo believes that he has killed Claudio
after taking the price for saving him.) The *danger* of
keeping the bargain and letting Claudio live would be
that he would feel too deeply about it; *sense* covers
'sensibility' here. But the reason why he is sure to have
a keen sense of honour is that he is *riotous*, he is 'sensual', for that either shows that you have strong feelings or develops them. In either case Angelo despises
him for it; he is himself one of the cold people. The
idea 'meaning, purpose' is still possible in the word, but
it is unimportant beside this startling irony.

There is no need to make these interpretations rigid,

especially in so fluid a word. The simple view of the
uses by Angelo is that he always means 'sensuality'
when in soliloquy and always pretends to mean something else when talking to other people. But this corresponds to the view of him as a hypocrite and villain
all through; if you take the character as capable of
struggle and development you need to suppose that his
language carries the marks of it. At first he felt it as
abnormal that the dominant meaning should emerge
at all. In this example one does not need to invoke the
idea of a 'dominant meaning', because Angelo is explicit enough to make the immediate context impose
both the meanings required; *riotous* gives 'sensuality'
and *dangerous* (to Angelo) gives 'sensibility'. *Riotous* is
said first; to be sure, it is further away than *dangerous,*
But it would be rather absurd to call this a less immediate context. I think 'sensuality' is the idea that
comes first in his mind, and acts as chief meaning of the
word; if you had to choose only one meaning, what the
logic of the passage requires is 'sensibility', but it is
regarded as a consequence. This is the order of the
terms in the equation; the idea is 'sensuality entails
sensibility'. He seems indeed to have moved the idea
'sensuality' from being an intrusive dominant to being
what he considers the head meaning of the word. He
has no more to say with it, and does not use it again;
the main force of its irony now turns against Isabella,
and 'sensuality', till now so prominent, becomes only a
solemn paradox making a darkness in the background.

> DUKE. *Away with her; poor soul*
> *She speaks this in th'infirmity of sense.*   (v i 47)

(Isabella is appealing against Angelo to the Duke at
the gates of the city.) The use is simple enough, but the
Duke is teasing Angelo, and a double meaning would
be in order. He could hint at such ideas as 'in the
disorder of strong feeling – she has much to make her
excited' or 'in the weakness of mere reason and truth,
which are inherently feeble beside the public monsters

of hypocrisy and law'. I think it is possible that the voice of Shakespeare behind him is preparing an irony of another kind. The Duke is still toying with the word a few lines later:

> By mine honesty,
> If she be mad, as I believe no other,
> Her madness hath the oddest frame of sense,
> Such a dependency of thing on thing,
> As ere I heard in madness.   (v i 59)

If she has reason it is of a queer kind, not common sense but the obscure wisdom that Shakespeare expected in clowns and the half-mad. It is true that she would put an odd construction on *sense* (give it an odd *frame*); she is too other-worldly to use it in the common way. There is no pressure behind the passage, but I think it adds to the cumulative effect. Then Mariana has a use, important because free from irony; and her rhetoric (it is like that of Troilus) gives the word a fine chance to spread the peacock tail of its meanings. She has the shame of begging in public to be married to Angelo, who deserted her because she lost her money.

> Noble Prince,
> As there comes light from heaven, and words from
>   breath,
> As there is sense in truth, and truth in virtue,
> I am affianced this man's wife, as strongly
> As words could make up vows: And my good Lord,
> But Tuesday night last gone, in's garden house,
> He knew me as a wife.   (v i 223)

There is meaning in a true statement; there is purpose in making one; it is wise to tell the truth frankly. But the series goes from *sense* to *virtue*, and this tends to call out another part of the word's range. The kind of truth that is in virtue seems rather to be constancy or correspondence to natural law. Desire or passion, sensuality or sensibility, may make her constant; and she

can decently assert them both in public; to be constant
is to have the common sense of our normal feelings.
The meanings are not merely compatible but undi-
vided here; this is what the whole word is meant to
do.

The next and final use raises a question about what
Shakespeare himself thought of the play. Isabella still
believes that Angelo had murdered her brother, and
Mariana begs her for his life.

> MARI. *Sweet Isabell, take my part:*
>   *Lend me your knees, and all my life to come,*
>   *I'll lend you all my life to do you service.*
> DUKE. *Against all sense you do importune her:*
>   *Should she kneel down, in mercy of this fact,*
>   *Her Brother's ghost, his paved bed would break,*
>   *And take her hence in horror.*   (v i 433)

In the Duke's earlier plotting with Isabella, the chief
impulse he appeals to in her is the desire to be re-
venged on Angelo, not to save her brother; indeed in
her first revulsion when he begs for his life she says ' 'tis
best that thou diest quickly'. Almost at the end of the
play, the Duke tells her that he could have saved her
brother but acted with 'slower foot', apparently because he wanted some more fun with his plot; but after
all Claudio is better dead: 'That life is better life, past
fearing death, Than one that lives to fear. Make it
your comfort, So happy is your brother.' 'I do, my lord,'
is the brisk and hearty answer. Here, by the way, we
find Bradley's principle, that the characters are better
dead, in full command of the stage; Angelo in his turn
'craves death more willingly than mercy'. But Isabella
does not apply it to Angelo. We are given a further test
of the quality of her feeling, in the appeal of Mariana
for his life. She does react with the mercy enjoined by
her religion, and this is certainly meant to be to her
credit, but she attains this height by an impulse of
personal vanity so repulsive as to surprise even Dr
Johnson.

> *I partly think,*
> *A due sincerity govern'd his deeds*
> *Till he did look on me.*   (v i 448)

She knows the history of Mariana, who is appealing for Angelo's life beside her; in fact the Duke has told her that when Mariana lost most of her marriage portion Angelo 'swallowed his vows whole, pretending in her discoveries of dishonour'. Afterwards, when Isabella's brother is presented to her still alive, she does not speak to him at all; no doubt the plot gave no room for a long speech, but the Bard is not as tongue-tied as all that if he can think of anything for a character to say. The apologists have objected that flippant modern critics merely do not understand the old reverence for virginity if they dwell on such points. But it is impossible to suppose all these details are accidental; they are not even clumsy; they are pointed. It seems to me the only working theory to suppose that Shakespeare could not quite stomach the old reverence either.

And on this view the final use of *sense* can carry a good deal of meaning, though if you suppose the Duke meant all of it he is not likely to have married her afterwards. 'Against all reason' – 'all normal decent feeling' – 'all depth or delicacy of feeling'; whatever kind of *sense* is meant here, she lacks it. For a moment, in the elaborate and teasing balance of the play, Shakespeare turns even against mercy, or at least against the abstract rule of mercy from which she acts. She is too otherworldly to feel the thing like a sane person; she is not sensual enough, the word might argue, to have tolerable human feelings.

This is certainly not what the Duke thinks; here as always, however savagely he tests her, he finds her ideally right. If he means any irony in the word, apart from the general triumph in knowing better than his audience which he is enjoying in all these uses of *sense*, it is that she is altogether above 'sense', above the whole view of life which even a good use of the suggestions of the word would imply. Miss M. C Bradbrook,

in an essay on the play (*Review of English Studies*, XVII
385), has maintained that the Duke did not expect
Isabel to forgive Angelo, but accepts her superior wisdom when 'her justice recognises the one grain of good
in him'. I am not sure how much a verbal analysis can
prove, and I would think this view wrong without one,
but surely those who support it must find it less plausible when they notice that this use of the word is the
last of a series of uses by the Duke in this scene, and
that the previous ones (whatever else they mean) have
all carried secret boasts of superior knowledge. It does
not seem to me that there was any subtle unconscious-
ness about the matter; I think Shakespeare felt he was
'polishing off' the series of puns on *sense* by this very
dramatic final use of it. But if he meant to kick away
his key word at the end, it seems to me, he could not
manage to do it. This is not to say that he took the
same cheery view of the affair as Lucio; the play re-
peatedly tells us that Lucio took venereal disease for
granted, and I think this practical argument gave the
basic emotional drive in favour of purity. Claudio ends
the old story with a brave and generous action, giving
himself up in the expectation of death to save the life
of Angelo, now married to his sister; Shakespeare
would not allow him so much dignity, and altered the
plot. This seems good evidence that he found the behaviour of Claudio disgusting. But he could not convince himself, it seems to me, even that the Duke was
agreeable, let alone that Isabella was. The pomposity
of the man he probably found natural, but the touchi-
ness, the confidence in error, the self-indulgence of his
incessant lying, must I think always have been absurd.

Various critics during this century have tried to
show that Shakespeare in his heart disliked his pompous old men, Prospero for example, and merely as-
sumed that the audience would put up with them
sufficiently to make the mechanics of the play tolerable.
On the other hand Mr Wilson Knight, who is high-
minded and warmhearted in a rather Victorian manner, tends to make these old men into practically un-

diluted symbols of heavenly virtue. The Duke raises
this problem particularly sharply, and I should not
agree that the problem is for some logical reason inherently unreal ('if we dig into the picture we only go
through the canvas'); surely any producer has to make
up his mind about it. Mr Wilson Knight considers
that:

> The Duke's ethic is born of his knowledge of good
> and evil potential in himself. And his remembrance
> of his own evil, which is crucial to his ethic, is kept
> alive by Lucio's chattering of his supposed vices at
> his side. Lucio causes the Duke to distrust the ideal
> of purity in Isabella by continually suggesting that
> such an ideal is a form of insincerity. Iago causes
> Othello to distrust his ideal of purity by suggesting
> its impurity; the two triangles may thus be shown to
> bear a close resemblance to each other.

I think this parallel is a searching one, but I do not see
that the text gives us any encouragement (apart from
one very obscure piece of doggerel closing the third act,
in which the unreal style lets the Duke act as a sort of
chorus) for ascribing to the Duke an idea about ethics
which is simply the playwright's. Mr Wilson Knight
seems to regard as important evidence the Duke's remarks about not liking to stage himself before the
people's eyes (the idea comes in twice, but he stages
himself very elaborately at the end of the play). The
same feelings had been expressed by James I, to the
annoyance of the public, and the audience might well
notice the resemblance; this is an argument against
supposing that the Duke was frankly ridiculed in performance, because it might be dangerous, but Shakespeare could not assume that everybody would interpret the foibles of James as a proof of a high and selfless
view of ethics. In any case, the higher you pitch the
ethics of the Duke, the more surprising you must find
his behaviour.

It seems hard not to regard him as a comic character.

Indeed the play gives us a sufficiently memorable
phrase to sum him up; he is 'the old fantastical Duke of
Dark Corners'. In the fourth scene the Friar points out
that, if the Duke defends the revival of the old law by
Angelo, he should have revived it himself; that would
have been more impressive. The Duke replies:

> *I do fear, too dreadful:*
> *Sith 'twas my fault to give the people scope*
> *'Twould be my tyranny to strike and gall them*
> *For what I bid them do.... Therefore indeed, my*
>   *father,*
> *I have on Angelo imposed the office*
> *Who may, in the ambush of my name, strike home*
> *And yet my nature never in the sight*
> *To do it slander.*

To be sure, he seems to be lying as usual; we heard him
specifically tell Angelo. 'Your scope is as mine own, So
to enforce or qualify the laws As to your soul seems
good'; and he goes on to tell the Friar that he is testing
Angelo. But surely on the stage this excuse is too
prominent to be forgotten, and the combination of
vanity and cowardice cannot be intended for praise. It
does have a note of puritanical self-examination, as Mr
Knight would claim, but I would not call that enough
to give it a high spiritual ethic. No doubt it could be
carried off by grandeur of manner; but when the Duke
buzzes from Claudio to Isabella, all agog, and busily
telling lies to both, I do not see how the author can be
banking on the simpleminded respect of the audience
for great persons. The subtlety of his justice has been
praised, and indeed there is a curious passage where he
claims that all his prisoners are either executed or released. But he is asking why Barnardine had been kept
in jail seven years; the excuse of the provost is that 'his
friends still wrought reprieves for him' while there was
no proof adequate to kill him on. What the Duke urges
Mariana to do ('He is your husband on a pre-contract;
To bring you thus together is no sin') can only be dis-

tinguished, if at all, by a technicality from what
Claudio is to be killed for doing ('she is fast my wife
Save that we do the denunciation lack Of outward
order; this we came not to, Only for propagation of a
dower'); and the Duke apparently approves of the law
which would kill Claudio, at least he tells the Friar
that he does, at considerable length. Incidentally this
law would also have killed Shakespeare, whose first
child was born soon after marriage; his distaste for lust
at the time of writing did not (I take it) carry him so
far as to make him agree with the Duke here.

But perhaps all this is picking holes. What makes the
Duke ridiculous on the stage is the fuss he makes about
the backbiting of Lucio, that is, precisely what makes
Mr Knight think him so high and pure. The Duke of
course is in disguise when Lucio tells him these things,
and he answers by boasting about himself, in a phrase
which seems an obvious dramatic irony, 'let him but be
testimonied in his own bringing forth, and he shall
appear to the envious a scholar, a statesman and a
soldier'. He anxiously questions Escalus in the hope
of hearing something better, and continues to drag the
subject up when we are thinking about the plot. The
soliloquy 'Oh place and greatness' (IV i 60), while Isabella is trying to induce Mariana to play her part, is so
much out of key that at first we think he is talking
about Angelo. In the final scene, the mutual petty
accusations of Lucio and the Duke, working up to 'yet
here's one in place I cannot pardon', are good farce
and nothing else. No doubt there was a casualness and
good-humour about the Elizabethan stage, so that the
great man could be laughed at for a bit and resume
greatness when required; but this is only to say that
there was room for Shakespeare to put in mixed feelings of his own.

But it is true, I think, that there is an agreeable side
of the Duke; it becomes dramatically prominent on the
occasions when he is proved absurdly wrong. He is
certain (IV ii) that Angelo will be sending a pardon for
Claudio to the prison (thinking he has enjoyed Isa-

bella); and he keeps boasting to the provost of his superior knowledge. When the letter is opened it orders an earlier execution under cover of night. The Duke immediately starts plotting again, apparently unperturbed, but the fact that he could not imagine the depth of evil that he is playing with does, I think, operate on us as somehow to his credit. From then on his tricks seem less offensive; the claim to divine foreknowledge has been broken. Also by this time it has become clear that nothing less than the fantastic behaviour of the Duke could have kept the play from being a tragedy. The whole force of the case against Angelo is that, in the ordinary way, he would have been completely safe; he is a symbol of justice itself, as Escalus points out (III ii, end); he can only be imagined as vulnerable if he is handled by very strange means. In the same way the Duke's final test of Isabella, that she must forgive Angelo still believing he killed her brother treacherously, is a result of his general expectation of mercy; the fact that she agrees to it for bad reasons is not one that he is likely to realise. One might even find it pathetic that the intended nun should say 'I partly think A due sincerity governed his deeds Till he did look on me'. Her new sensual vanity seems meant to imply a partial awakening of her senses after the battering she has gone through; and her decision to marry the Duke is perhaps not so grossly out of character as critics have supposed.

What is really offensive about the Duke is the other side of this quality which can be found agreeable; it is offensive, I mean, that he should treat his subjects as puppets for the fun of making them twitch. But here, I suppose, the Character is saved by the Plot. It seems a peculiarly brutal flippancy that he should not only trick Isabella about Claudio unnecessarily but take pains to thrust the imagined death of Claudio upon his mind. His moral claims about it –

> *But I will keep her ignorant of her good*
> *To make her heavenly comforts of despair*

– do not seem to me tolerable even on Bradley's principle; he is playing at being God. But there is a question here of the mechanics of working on an audience; we forgive him for it because Isabella turns out not to care a rap about Claudio, and we wanted to know whether she would. The reasons why it seems all right, if you followed them up, would lead to quite a different view of the story.

And yet I think the play is a whole in spite of this chasm in one's view of the two good characters; even if Shakespeare was only grumbling to himself about them, an audience could share his feelings without ruining the performance. The Duke's flippancy about justice corresponds to a deeper and more desperate feeling in the author, elaborated throughout the action and insisted upon in the title, that the whole business of public justice is fatuous and hideous, whether compared to the mercy of Christ or the humanity of private life. There is an echo of the same idea when Pompey shifts over comfortably from a bawd to a hangman. Mr Wilson Knight was quite right to feel that there is a subtle ethic in the play somewhere, and that it is mixed up with Christianity. But I think there is a balancing idea to this, one that accounts for the unpleasantness of the two good characters. It is perhaps simply the idea that one must not act on these absolutes prematurely. Even granting that the conditions of life are inherently repulsive, a man makes himself actually more repulsive by acting on this truth; you cannot get outside the world and above justice, and a ruler who sets out to do this (except under very peculiar circumstances, by luck) is merely bad at his job. And the same ambivalence clings to the divine Isabella. In a way, indeed, I think this is a complete and successful work of the master, but the way is a very odd one, because it amounts to pretending to write a romantic comedy and in fact keeping the audience's teeth slightly but increasingly on edge. And on this view, I should claim, the performance with the word *sense* is made to echo the thought of the play very fully up to the end.

In all this I have taken the text for granted, but the case for revision made out by the New Cambridge editors is I think stronger here than for any other play, and I need to consider whether that alters the case. The theory is that the play was cut down for a court performance before James I on 24 December 1604, when the two passages flattering his distaste for crowds, and a passage referring to a court masque, were added; that the original text was lost; that the court play was collected from the actor's parts and padded by another hand to the public stage length soon after November 1606. The padding was done by adding jokes for Lucio, also sententious rhymed couplets, and by turning some of Shakespeare's verse into longwinded prose. I doubt whether this makes much difference. All the references to *sense* are unaffected. Certainly the changes tend to make the Duke more ridiculous; the farce of his relations with Lucio is now largely due to the reviser, and the irrelevant self-regard of the 'Oh place and greatness' speech (IV i 59) is explained because the reviser took it out of the speech at III ii 178, where it is relevant, and used it to hide a join in the text. The phrase by Lucio about 'the old fantastical duke of dark corners' is added by the reviser. But if the Duke had originally been the half-divine figure described by Mr Wilson Knight it seems unlikely that this despised hack would have presumed to alter him so far; it is one thing to add to the jokes which had been found popular, and quite another to reverse the intention of a playwright who was still a leading member of the company. For that matter, the reviser is supposed to have added the doggerel lines at the end of III ii, spoken by the Duke, which are the strongest evidence for Mr Wilson Knight's theory of his high and subtle ethic. If we are to believe in this hack, it looks as if he was trying to keep the balance of the original conception, and not so very coarsely either. Indeed I think one might push the argument the other way; a special version was needed for the court performance in front of James, making the Duke much less funny, and afterwards some new jokes against the Duke could be written in on the lines of the original intention.

The editors also produce a reason for the silence of Isabella when reunited to her brother; she was originally reconciled to him by his mistress Juliet, and then the part of Juliet was doubled with Mariana, so all this had to be cut. I should have thought that some of Isabella's reply could easily be salvaged, and the play only wants three handsome women (anybody could take Mistress Overdone) – the same as *King Lear*. In any case, it seems hard to guess what she could have said that would greatly alter our impression of her, and the same doubt might perhaps occur to the author. But, even if we accept the whole theory of revision, I do not think it much affects the interpretation of the 'key word'.

We should now be able to look back and deal with the attitude of R. W. Chambers, which is by no means his alone. A variety of recent critics (young rather than old) have emphasized the strength of the Christian symbolism in the play, and treated it as a Morality Play about the dialectic of Justice and Mercy, ending in an atonement won through love. On this view the Duke is implicitly compared to God, who goes among his people and judges each case on its individual merits; he is the king of love wooing the human heart, and the symbolism is worked out in detail. I think this is in the text all right; and for that matter it would be foolish to suppose that a pro-Christian play on this theme would have to be 'reactionary'; any attempt to apply the anarchic mercy of Christ to the actual processes of government must be a pretty revolutionary affair. But I think the play simply did not work out like that; Shakespeare undertook to use this traditional theme, and found he did not like his saints when he had got them. It is thus an interesting example, by the way, of how wrong an 'analytical' critic can be when he industriously digs out a 'symbolism', even one that is really there.

However, it might be objected that this theory is
untenable unless it is taken very far, further than I
should want to go. The ostensible Christianity in the
play is very strong (the whole speech about 'Be absolute
for death' is powerfully in the Duke's favour; Claudio
himself does not question the justice of his punishment
for 'too much liberty'). Therefore, it may be said, any
irony against it in the play must also have been strong,
if it were to be effectually present at all. We must,
therefore, suppose a situation in the playhouse like
Verrall's interpretation of Euripides; people must
have quarrelled on the way out. Now, of course, we are
extremely ignorant about Shakespeare's audience, but
I do not believe that this happened either; for one
thing, it was just what the censorship system was designed to prevent. Nor, by the way, do I think that the
word 'justice' needs a thorough going treatment here,
analysing it into different conceptions of justice which
are to conflict in the minds of the audience and form
ironical equations in the word. I think that the audience would consider a death penalty for the fault of
Claudio quite patently *un*-just, so that no subtlety
about different sorts of justice need become prominent.
On this question of public opinion, and on Shakespeare's probable opinion, Mr Hotson's *I, William
Shakespeare* gives a useful light; the very reputable
man who became overseer of Shakespeare's will made
an arrangement similar to Claudio's for the same
reason, and finally regularized his marriage, when the
families agreed about the money affairs, just before
Measure for Measure was probably written. No doubt,
within the circle, there would be a touch of sardonic
fun about this retrospect, but nobody, it seems obvious,
was seriously entertaining the idea that he ought to
have been killed for it. Claudio himself accepts guilt,
and the sex-horror of the play requires him to; but he
is drawn as a weak character; the manly thing to say
would have been all men are sinners but that not all
sins deserve death from the law. The religious politics
of the thing are after all very clear; they are intention-

ally confused by the presence of nuns and friars, but Geneva was the only place where a law like this was conceivable. The more we make Shakespeare sympathetic to the old religion and the sanctity of virginity, the less likely we make him to have approved the Duke's law. And, on the other side of the *via media*, the audience would not be at all shocked by a suggestion that nunneries make for a narrowness of human feeling. It seems to me, therefore, that the ironies against the good characters would only strike the audience (or rather the kind of spectator who might have made trouble) as a balanced Anglican position, not put forward more obtrusively than the theatre was allowed to do. I don't mean that this is what Shakespeare felt about it; I am only concerned to show that my interpretation of the play is not wildly far from what a contemporary audience could be expected to recognise or endure.

As to the view that the gallants joking about syphilis are intolerably flat and crude, and therefore must have been put in by a hack reviser, I think the point needs to be made that they were exactly what Shakespeare wanted, whether he bothered to write them himself or not. The jokes are trench humour, not made out of insensitivity to a common mortal danger but to keep up strength, and jokes of this sort usually seem bad to an outsider. Indeed, the whole development of Puritanism can be viewed as a consequence of the introduction of syphilis (usually dated around the beginning of the sixteenth century). The point I think is important for the play because it gives a certain practical basis for the conflict between justice and mercy, which otherwise appears as a mere flat contradiction. One can interpret the Duke as saying 'There's too much syphilis in this town', and trying to find a way to reduce it without getting personally unpopular; on this view Claudio is obviously innocent because unlikely to spread disease. I must agree that this practical view of the case seems to be very remote from everyone's mind. But then the question whether the Duke proposes to continue enforcing his law is simply dropped; on any view, the questions that the play raises are not answered. It moves over, as the keyword does, from a consideration of 'sensuality' to a consideration of 'sanity', and then the action is forced round to a happy ending.

The idea of such a word as a 'compacted doctrine' hardly applies here; the equations can be made to give a variety of minor doctrines, but it is not clear how well they fit together. Indeed, whether they can be fitted together is treated as a problem, part of the play as a whole, and yet the word itself is used easily and with conviction. It seems to me another case of the incomplete double symbol, like the dog in *Timon of Athens*. And the word which can be treated like this, as one would expect, is in an unstable condition, because it is getting too hard to use. Metaphors about dogs can be complicated without getting in anyone's way, but a word like *sense* needs to be tolerably handy; and before the century was over it had settled down into a simpler form.

But though the change seems natural it may be more mixed up with politics, and therefore less inevitable, than this account would imply. Indeed, to call the later structure of *sense* the 'Restoration' one, already suggests that it was part of the reaction against Puritanism. Even this play which turns on the word, in spite of its apparent fantasy, is full of a brooding sense of what would happen if Puritans came to power, as they did in the next generation. One might argue, in fact, that these Jacobean uses of the word are already a weapon against the Puritans, which the Civil War only hardened and sharpened. And yet there seems no doubt that this would be going too far. The poor little word was too busy to be so much of a partisan; neither side had a monopoly of it. Indeed, if one can trust the earliest references in the N.E.D., what I am calling the Restoration use of it did not appear till around the death of Charles II; it was eventually produced by the Restoration settlement, but was definitely not produced by the Civil War. I wish I had more decisive evidence, particularly about the Commonwealth uses. But the broad point seems clear; the word was made to echo controversial questions that were both subtle and pressing, and Shakespeare had a keen nose for this kind of quality in a word; but it was not made to come down on one side of the fence till considerably after his time.

SOURCE: *The Structure of Complex Words,* 1951.

David L. Stevenson

DESIGN AND STRUCTURE IN
MEASURE FOR MEASURE (1956)

I should describe this early Jacobean comedy which
Shakespeare extracted from Whetstone's rather pedest-
rian drama of the crude sexual involvements of Promos
and Cassandra, as a brilliant intellectual tour de force
on the familiar Renaissance theme of the 'monstrous
ransom'.[1] It is constructed as I see it, somewhat after
the fashion of a Donne poem, made up of a series of
intricately interrelated moral ironies and reversals,
held together by the win themes of mercy and justice,
and resolved by a final balancing out of paradox. Its
comic and structural affinities are certainly far less with
Shakespear's own Elizabethan romantic comedies and
love-game comedies than with Jonson's satiric comedies
(as has been painstakingly demonstrated by O. J.
Campbell, in *Shakespeare's Satire*, 1943). Indeed, as
Miss M. C. Bradbrook has remarked, 'it is one of the
few of Shakespear's writings of which he [i.c. Jonson]
might wholeheartedly have approved'.[2]

The characteristic effect of *Measure for Measure* I
take to be that which Eliot has described generally for
Jonsonian comedy, where 'the immediate appeal ... is
to the mind'. That is, in *Measure for Measure*, the
force and impact on the audience comes not from its
unconscious involvement in the emotions and the des-
tinies of the individual characters of the comedy
where, in Eliot's phrase, 'swarms of inarticulate feelings are aroused'.[3] Rather the effect comes from a perception by the audience of the contrasting and balancing roles of the individual characters, and the attitudes
they stand for, in the completed design of the whole
play.

In such a comedy as *Measure for Measure*, the nor-

mal, tragic results of the actions and decisions of the
chief characters are suspended in favor of irony and
paradox. The characters, here, are deliberately simpli-
fied and made less interesting in themselves (as in
Hamlet for instance, or Falstaff) than interesting for
the ways in which the attitudes they embody fit in with
those of other characters, or balance out in the total
scheme of the play. One notes that Isabella and Angelo
are given exciting dramatic rhetoric in their great debate over mercy versus justice of Act ii. But the lines
are rather exciting in themselves than as the illustration of any dramatically created and characteristic
speaking voice of either person. Indeed, one of the
apparent difficulties of the play, I think, is that critics
have tried (and failed) to extract from *Measure for
Measure* an Isabella or an Angelo who would yield to
the kind of analysis accorded a Hamlet, an Iago, an
Othello. But the characters of *Measure for Measure*
resist analysis in isolation from the play where they are
viable in complementary relationship to each other.

The primary, given condition which permits one to
define *Measure for Measure* as an intellectual rather
than as a romantic comedy is that the audience is
forced to play the role of omniscient outsider and
observer. The dramatic device to assure the audience
this role is to place an outsider in the play itself: the
detached, rather aloof Duke of Vienna who observes,
controls, and comments on the actions of the other
characters. And in this comedy, where the skillfulness
of the complex design of action and character is the
whole play, the Duke acts as spokesman for the audience, is its articulate representative in the play. As F.
R. Leavis has put it, the Duke's 'attitude, nothing
could be plainer, *is* meant to be ours – his total attitude, which is the total attitude of the play'.[4]

Thus, one notes, it is the Duke who initiates the
business of the play, In the opening scene, in which his
challenge to Angelo, and his arbitrary departure from
Vienna, create what one might call the intellectual-
moral experiment which *is* the play. He sets the boun-

daries of the experiment by which Angelo, hitherto
virtuous in name only, must translate his theoretical
rectitude into action as absolute ruler of Vienna, and
under the twin obligations of justice and mercy (or
'mortality and mercy' as the Duke phrases it, I i 44).
Moreover it is the Duke who suspends the results of
Angelo's decisions to seduce Isabella and to behead
Claudio. By this dramatic stratagem, the moral problems created by Angelo remain theoretical and the
audience is made aware that it will not be involved in
tragedy, where no one is allowed to suffer the results of
his own folly. The audience, thereby, is permitted to
examine the moral decisions and conflicts of the
characters in a sardonic detachment equal to that of
the Duke. Finally, the Duke who sententiously sum-
marizes the themes of the play at key moments (e.g. III
ii 241 ff. and 283 ff.), anticipates Prospero in his control
of the long last scene of Act V. He is in full view of the
audience, and he stands for the audience as arbiter,
bringing about a final balancing and equalizing of
justice and mercy, and voicing the ironic results of the
experiment with which he opened the play.

In the thematic structure of *Measure for Measure*,
Claudio and Juliet are placed by Shakespeare at dead
center, and are not themselves subjected to the sardonic reversals of the play, but are the causal agents of
such irony in others. Unlike the Duke, they are relatively passive, the objects of others' discourse and
others' decisions. In the given condition of the play,
whereby Juliet is with child by Claudio before a marriage has taken place, they are revealed as transgressors
of the strict letter of the law, not from viciousness but
from natural, warm human instinct. In their predicament, they neither defend nor reject their actions.
They speak the neutral philosophy of average sensual
humanity. Thus Claudio jests wryly to Lucio, 'Our
natures do pursue.../ A thirsty evil, and when we
drink, we die' (I ii 137). And he ascribes his arrest for
lechery to ill luck:

> But it chances
> The stealth of our most mutual entertainment
> With character too gross is writ on Juliet. . . .
>   (I ii 165)

And Juliet, who has almost no other voice in the play,
in her confession to the Duke makes a very simple,
morally colorless evaluation of her own behavior:

> I do repent me, as it is an evil
> And take the shame with joy.   (II iii 35)

In keeping with the intended schematic nature of
the play, Shakespeare shows the predicament of
Claudio and Juliet as wholly sympathized with, or defended, by all other major voices in the comedy except
those of Isabella and Angelo, in order, no doubt, to
heighten the didactic and censorious reactions of these
two senators of virtue. Thus Escalus gives a common
sense appraisal of the affair in his logical protest to
Angelo against his severity. Angelo himself, Escalus
suggests – with anticipatory irony, preparing the audience for the Duke's measured retaliation – would be in
the same predicament as Claudio, 'Had time coher'd
with place, or place with wishing' (II i 11). On a slightly
lower level of action, it is the Provost who remarks of
Claudio that 'He hath but as offended in a dream' (II ii
4), and protests to the disguised Duke that Claudio is

> More fit to do another such offence,
> Than die for this.   (II iii 14)

And Lucio, the witty spokesman for the point of view
of the professional adepts in vice, Mistress Overdone
and her man Pompey, makes the play's classic evaluation of Claudio's difficulties in the remark to the Duke,
'Why, what a ruthless thing is this in him, for the rebellion of a codpiece to take away the life of a man!' (III ii
123).

It is curious to note, also, in the conscious design of

this comedy, the existence of a number of mocking and parallel repetitions of the central predicament around which all the reversals of the play are made to turn and swirl. The main repetition, of course, is that between Angelo and Mariana, in the second half of the play, with which the Duke deliberately involves Isabella, to make her the instrumental agent and Angelo the victim. He also arranges with great nicety to make Angelo's predicament an exact duplicate of the situation for which he had condemned Claudio: Mariana and Angelo had exchanged a troth-plight; they had not married because of a delay in a dowry; the Duke even suggests that after the assignation Mariana, like Juliet, may be with child (III i 248 ff.).

At a still lower, more boisterous level, Lucio and his mistress Kate Keepdown, whom he has promised to marry, and who has borne his child, are a further teasing of the central situation. They are referred to twice (III ii and IV iii) before the final scene in which Lucio is ordered to marry his Kate, and then to be whipped and hanged. Finally, Elbow's outraged cry, in response to Pompey's assertion that Elbow's wife is a respected woman, and was respected with him before he married her, deliberately extends the parallel with Claudio and Juliet to gross parody: 'I respected with her before I was married to her? . . . Prove this, thou wicked Hannibal, or I'll have mine action of battery on thee' (II i 188).

Claudio and Juliet are central to the play as the paired and parodied representatives of a kind of norm of sensual behavior. In so schematic a comedy as *Measure for Measure*, however, it is the actions and the decisions of Angelo and Isabella which are the main ones of the comedy. And as characters, they are paired and balanced representatives of elements in human nature far more complicated than those dramatized by Claudio and Juliet. Angelo, ostensibly, and by his rhetoric in the first half of the play, is the public advocate of the first of the two extremes of civil power announced by the Duke: mortal justice. Isabella, ostens-

ibly, and likewise by her rhetoric in the first half of the
play, speaks for the second of the two, for grace or
mercy, the complementary opposite of iron justice.
These central figures are also carefully paired in that
Angelo, by the Duke's opening statement, is an announced exemplar of a sternly puritanical masculine
honor and virtue, and Isabella, by her opening identification as a novice of the order of Saint Clare, is an
announced exemplar of chastity in women.

In addition, in order to heighten the audience's
sense of the linked relationship of these two in the
structure of *Measure for Measure*, both Angelo and
Isabella, on their first appearance in the play, make
public boast of the virtues with which they are to be
identified. Angelo, having been cited by Escalus as the
only man in Vienna worthy to exercise ducal power,
selfrighteously demands:

> Now, good my lord,
> Let there be some more test made of my metal,
> Before so noble and so great a figure
> Be stamp'd upon it.   (I i 47)

Isabella's first words in the play, interlocking her role
with that of Angelo, are a contentious quibbling that
the order of Saint Clare does not have strict enough
rules. 'And have you nuns no farther privileges,' she
asks. And to the reply 'Are not these large enough,'
Isabella complains:

> Yes truly: I speak not as desiring more
> But rather wishing a more strict restraint
> Upon the sisterhood, the votarists of Saint Clare.
>   (I iv 1 ff.)

Quite unlike the protagonists in Shakespeare's romantic comedies, Angelo and Isabella exist in *Measure for
Measure* to demonstrate the ironies in which they are
involved, and their ironic modes of being are a given
element in the dramatic strategy of this intellectual

comedy. We do not know why Isabella has decided to renounce the world, nor what has caused Angelo to be an austere puritan. There are no 'objective correlatives' for their actions in the play, and none are demanded.

Angelo's ironic mode of being in the comedy flows rather patently from his initial, too easy commitment to honor and justice, and we follow with our minds, not our emotions, his reversals which are constantly, almost too carefully, balanced against those which flow from Isabella's too easy commitment to chastity and mercy. The basic reversal, or paradox, in Angelo's existence in the play is the obvious one that in proposing that Isabella meet him at an assignation as the price of her brother's life, Angelo reveals himself to be infinitely more depraved as a man and as an administrator of justice than Claudio whom he has condemned for a mere genial slip of nature. Angelo then extends the dimension of his vicious lack of all sense of justice by his ordering the instant beheading of Claudio after the consummation of the supposed assignation with Isabella.

It is curious to note the sheer quantity of dramatic incident which the play heaps up to intensify Angelo's reversal into perfidy. Before his own lust has been aroused by Isabella, Angelo has been warned by Escalus that he may find himself as human as Claudio (II i 4 ff.). And Angelo at once heightens the impact on the audience of his own fall, by the shocking lack of self-knowledge in his sneering reply:

> When I, that censure him, do so offend,
> Let mine own judgment pattern out my death
> And nothing come in partial.   (II i 29)

In the great debate scene of Act II, Isabella repeats Escalus' arguments twice to Angelo:

> If he had been as you, and you as he,
> You would have slipp'd like him;   (II ii 64)

and

> Go to your bosom;
> Knock there, and ask your heart what it doth know
> That's like my brother's fault.   (II ii 136)

It is another of the insistent ironies of the play that it is precisely this argument of Isabella's that first brings self-knowledge to Angelo, and quickens his lust for her.

After the climactic third act, Angelo continues to exist by a still further elaboration of irony which takes its meaning from his initial identification with honor and justice. The Duke's original charge to Angelo had included the request that he take his private virtue into the open market and verify it in action:

> Thyself and thy belongings
> Are not thine own so proper, as to waste
> Thyself upon they virtues, they on thee.
> . . . for if our virtues
> Did not go forth of us, 'twere all alike
> As if we had them not.   (I i 29)

And at the inception of Angelo's long and protracted exposure, in Act v, the Duke reminds the audience of this original charge in the high mockery of the Duke's exclamation that he had heard 'such goodness' of Angelo's justice that he cannot keep it hidden in his own bosom. He must give it the public display all such virtue merits:

> . . . it deserves, with characters of brass,
> A forted residence 'gainst the tooth of time
> And razure of oblivion.   (V i 11)

But the dramatic moment of heaviest retaliatory mocking of the Angelo of Act i is reached when he is forced by the Duke to judge the veracity of Isabella's and Mariana's charges against him. In so doing, he is explicitly forced to judge himself, and implicitly, one notes, to re-judge the actions of Claudio and Juliet. Escalus' premonitory caution to him has returned to undo him.

The final twist, whereby Angelo is brought back onto a livable relationship with humanity comes as a result of his own self-judgment. When Angelo, the many-faced dissembler, at last stands revealed to *himself*, naked in his perfidy, he pleads his own immediate death, and against Isabella's cries for mercy:

> I am sorry that such sorrow I procure;
> And so deep sticks it in my penitent heart
> That I crave death more willingly than mercy:
> 'Tis my deserving, and I do entreat it.   (v i 475)

The justice which Angelo had first insisted upon, was improperly directed against a too easy, too passive target in Claudio; but at long last, it is properly, if paradoxically, directed against himself. He has identified himself for the audience with real evil, and really deserves the iron of justice.

The title of this comedy of ideas gives the clue, I think, to the ultimate irony that Isabella, who is the causal agent of self-knowledge in Angelo as well as the causal agent in Angelo's public exposure, finally pleads for mercy for her own victim. It is a plea based on Isabella's insight that Angelo's slip was instinctual, and the obverse of his puritanism:

> ... I partly think
> A due sincerity govern'd his deeds
> Till he did look on me....   (v i 446)

The title of the play, then, as emphasized by Isabella's plea, suggests an ultimately necessary 'measure' or moderation in human affairs, and not merely that one be judged as one judges. And the Duke, pardoning Angelo, emphasizes, as Leavis has noted, that the

'point of the play depends upon Angelo's not being a
certified criminal-type, capable of a wickedness that
marks him off from you and me'.[5]

The events which flow from Angelo's initial commitment to a dramatically untenable honor and justice
are easily followed. Those which flow from Isabella's
equally schematic commitment to chastity and to
mercy, apparently, are not. But the difficulties for contemporary Shakespearean scholars, it seems to me,
spring not from the play itself but from their own curiously perverse criticism which has almost totally obscured her role as complementary to that of Angelo.
And the elemental difficulty, at least for most of our
contemporary critics, has remained the proper interpretation of the first scene of Act III, the climactic scene
in which Isabella excoriates her brother at his suggestion that she accept the assignation with Angelo to save
his life.

What are the conventional views of Isabella in this
scene? One school of commentators, given voice in our
time by Hardin Craig, feels that Shakespeare deliberately created Isabella as an examplar of chastity in
women as she nobly rejects her brother. Moreover, she
is even somewhat contaminated by her mere *existence*
in *Measure for Measure*, and is wholly extractable
from the play for observation and discussion, a kind of
literary monument to virtuous womanhood. The theo-
logical-allegorical school, as represented by Battenhouse, restates and qualifies this view of her so that she
acts to save the other characters in the play from their
depravity. She becomes a 'holy Isabella, like Christ in
the wilderness' who 'at once discerns that a laying
down of her life in obedience to the will of this Devil
[Angelo] is not the allowable answer to the problem
posed by the fact of human sin'.[6] (Is she really this
philosophical?) From such a perspective of her role in
Measure for Measure, the great moment of the play is
her triumphant recovery from temptation (when was
she ever tempted, one asks!), voiced in the words:
'More than our brother is our chastity' (II iv 186).

Other critics, beginning with Johnson in the eighteenth century, one notes, have considered Isabella to be something less exalted, not because of her refusal of Angelo (which is guaranteed by her identification with a religious order), but because of her attack on her brother. Johnson remarks that there is 'something harsh, and something forced and far-fetched'[7] in her declamation to Claudio, wishing him death. Quiller-Couch, in our time, finds that Isabella is 'something rancid in her chastity'.[8] Wylie Sypher has described her as 'the prurient Isabella';[9] Edith Sitwell lets her go as 'the unconscious hypocrite';[10] and Mark Van Doren concludes, rather too acidly perhaps, that 'we do not see her in her goodness; we only hear her talking like a termagant against those who doubt it'.[11]

Without attempting to weigh, here, whether a Jacobean audience generally, or the first English Stuart in particular, would be as apt to regard Isabella as a Christ-like figure as would Professor Battenhouse, I want to introduce briefly one other problem in interpretation which Isabella's rejection of her brother has created. Does Shakespeare produce in Isabella, through a gross failure in his art, a character whose actions and attitudes in the climactic Act III are inconsistent either with our moral sense or with a developing dramatic pattern? The critics who have argued this theory (e.g. Tillyard and O. J. Campbell), feel that Isabella involves the audience with her destiny in the first three acts, only to be let go as a character, interesting in her own right, after the first scene of Act III. Thereafter, in the Mariana episode, and finally in being paired off with the Duke, she seems to these critics, though variously stated by them, to be caught up and submerged in the working out of the plot of *Measure for Measure* to a conventionally-happy conclusion.

Since I cannot agree with Battenhouse that Isabella is 'holy' in her ferocity toward her brother, nor with Quiller-Couch that she is morally offensive, I proceed to my own answers both to the problem of our proper

attitude toward Isabella's insistent virtue, and to the
question as to whether the play breaks in two after the
climactic third act. As far as our attitude toward Isabella's virtue is concerned, I note that in an intellectu-
alized comedy as careful in equilibrium as this one,
where the audience is permitted only a limited identification with individual characters, neither Isabella
nor the audience can be allowed to succumb to the
emotional violence which her surrender to Angelo
would evoke. The play would at once lose its intentionally, and intensely, theoretical nature, its rigidly
schematic measure for measure. Isabella, in her actions,
must be held subordinate to the over-all dramatic
equation, where there are to be no casualties, where
the results of Angelo's dissembling in the Duke's moral
experiment are to be suspended. She must remain to
the end a foil for Angelo, and not his victim.

Her early identification with a sisterhood[12] is foisted
upon Isabella for the very purpose of creating a character who will not be able to surrender her chastity on
Angelo's unlawful terms. She is the intentional representative of an absolute sexual virtue in her actions
and decisions up to the end of Act III, in part to act as
contrast to the more casual morality of Claudio and
Juliet. She also embodies an extreme Pauline attitude
toward sex, to the end of scene i of Act III, in a larger
world which includes, among other voices, that of
Lucio and that of Angelo. This is the point in Shakespeare's making her a novice and not just a lady of
Vienna: as one interested in joining a religious order
she creates a neat balance of attitudes in the structure
of the comedy. She is surely not intended to live in the
play as Shakespeare's personal eulogy of chastity any
more than Angelo's early severity is intended as Shakespeare's eulogy of puritanism. Indeed, an Isabella who
surrendered to an Angelo would be as violently impro-
able as a Cressida who refused to surrender to her
Troilus. In either case, the main balance of the play
would be broken.

But I do think that Isabella, like Angelo, is equally

intended by Shakespeare to be subjected to the discipline of the title: *Measure for Measure*. She is a kind of obverse of Angelo, in which the ironies of attitude and decision by which she exists in the play are complementary to those of her opposite. Just as Angelo turns out to be infinitely more depraved than the lovers he condemns, so too the 'ensky'd and sainted' Isabella is revealed to be totally merciless in her reviling of her brother for whose life she has so arduously pleaded mercy. And to keep the reversals in *Measure for Measure* which flow from this pair of rhetoricians in complete equilibrium, the play is allowed to come to an end only at the moment of exact equivalence between Isabella and Angelo. It ends only when Isabella has really become the thing she had argued for her brother in Act II, that is, merciful ('against all sense' as the Duke points out); and Angelo has really become the first he had argued for in the great debate of Act II, absolutely just.

As with Angelo, so with Isabella, the basic contradictions which make up her character in the play are the results of her initial public proclamation of her virtue, and her subsequent public pronouncements on mercy. As far as her chastity is concerned, it is important to note the series of contradictions with which Isabella is involved after her first declaration that she could wish 'a more strict restraint' upon the nuns of the order of Saint Clare. Lucio at once juxtaposes her self-righteousness against the cynicism of a less austere world in his taunt, 'Hail, virgin, if you be' (I iv 16). Then Lucio persuades her to plead with Angelo for her brother, but *not* in the role of an unsexed anchorite who, when sworn, must not speak with men but in the presence of her prioress. He asks her, rather, to teach Angelo, 'a man whose blood is very snow broth' (I iv 57), the meaning of a woman's power:

> Go to Lord Angelo
> And let him learn to know, when maidens sue,
> Men give like gods.   (I iv 79)

But we have already been warned of the woman in
Isabella (just as we are early warned of the man lurking
behind the puritan Angelo) by Claudio's description of
her to Lucio:

> ... in her youth
> There is a prone and speechless dialect,
> Such as move men.   (I ii 193)

And William Empson has remarked of Claudio's
words: 'This is the stainless Isabel, being spoken of by
her respectful brother ... "speechlesse" will not give
away whether she is shy or sly, and "dialect" has aban-
doned the effort.'[13] It is Lucio, moreover, in the debate
between Isabella and Angelo, who keeps making demands upon the woman in her, urging her to 'kneel
down before him, hang upon his gown'. It is Lucio who
cautions her that she is too cold:

> ... if you should need a pin
> You could not with more tame a tongue desire it.
>   (II ii 45)

(And I remark, parenthetically, that in her line 'might
but my bending down / Reprieve thee' (III i 142), Isabella seems to remember Lucio's pin as the standard by
which she evaluates her brother's life.)

The obvious, if deliberately ironic, result of her
wooing Angelo for her brother's life with all her
powers as a woman is what we should expect in a
comedy of ideas: Angelo's own aroused desire for this
woman in her, which he voices in sharp and unmistakable challenge,

> ... Be that you are,
> That is, a woman; if you be more, you're none.
>   (II iv 135)

Isabella, herself, belatedly recognizes that the actual
role she had played with Angelo was not that of novice

at all, but that of a woman. It is this recognition, late in the play, which vindicates her request for his life:

> Look, if it please you, on this man condemn'd
> As if my brother liv'd. I partly think
> A due sincerity govern'd his deeds,
> Till he did look on me.   (v i 445)

It is, finally, not the novice Isabella for whose 'lovely sake' the Duke offers marriage. It is for the woman who emerges from her to conduct the Mariana episode, the woman who in Act III puts on the 'destin'd livery' of secular femininity. (Equally, it is the man who emerges from the 'prenzie' Angelo whom the Duke is able to forgive.)

As far as Isabella's initial misunderstanding of the real nature of mercy is concerned, it is important to note that we hear her voice only as a series of declamations in her pleading for Claudio. We hear it as a series of skillful rhetorical manœuvres pitted against, but not actually winning the argument against, Angelo's own very skillful defense of the justice of the law. Where her brother's life is concerned, moreover, Isabella remains somewhat aloof, almost a disinterested commentator to Angelo on the conflicting claims of justice and mercy in her brother's case, 'At war 'twixt will and will not' (II ii 33). She becomes somewhat more passionately involved, and argues at her most brilliant, against what Claudio had called 'the demi-god Authority' (I ii 129). But this occurs only after she has personally felt the sting of Angelo's contemptuous, arrogant dismissal of her person:

> Be satisfied:
> Your brother dies tomorrow: be content.
>   (II ii 104)

When she finally becomes vehemently involved with Angelo, be it noted, it is not over her brother's life at all. It is a fury which commences only when Angelo

proposes that she who had defended, in her own words,
Claudio's 'natural guiltiness' so well, herself become
what she had defended and surrender her own virginity to him to save her brother's life. At this point in Act
II, the saintly Isabella, perhaps somewhat unlike Christ
in the wilderness, turns what Tillyard has called her
'native ferocity' loose on Angelo and attempts, unsuc-
cessfully, to snatch a pardon for Claudio by blackmail:

> Sign me a present pardon for my brother,
> Or with an outstretch'd throat I'll tell the world
>   aloud
> What man thou art.   (II iv 153)

I think the violence of this chaste and merciful
Isabella's response to Angelo is made by Shakespeare as
intentionally derisive as is the lustful response of
Angelo to her. It is the dramatic nature of this pair, at
the active center of *Measure for Measure*, to be inconsistent and contradictory in their virtue in order to
create the ironies and reversals of which the comedy is
made. Indeed, if we need proof of the meaning of the
debate with Angelo in Act II, it lies in our detached
spectator's sardonic comment on this scene, the Duke's
heavily understated description to Claudio of the violent encounter between Isabella and Angelo which the
audience has just witnessed:

> She, having the truth of honour in her, hath made
> him [Angelo] that gracious denial which he is most
> glad to receive.   (III i 164)

The Isabella that we know cannot make the gracious
denial that a less publicly virtuous Isabella might have
made.

After the Duke's double-edged comment on this
pair, we need not conjure up any special Jacobean attitude toward chastity to understand the play's intention in Isabella's ferocity toward her brother. If her
rejection of Claudio in a white heat of rage seems to

need further elucidation, however, I suggest first of all that the whole play up to this point has prepared us for it by Isabella's initial self-righteousness. We are prepared for the anger of her denial by the *temper* of her previous rejection of Angelo's offer. And I think we should be prepared for the irony of her total lack of mercy toward her brother's love of life, his fear of death, by our own sense of the need for this hardness, here, to prepare for the contrast of the final yielding to mercy by Isabella. Moreover, we would be totally unprepared, I think, for a display of tender solicitude on the part of Isabella toward Claudio, for any 'gracious denial' of him in the Duke's damning phrase. We have difficulty conjuring up such a picture of her. It would be a devastating violation of the whole tenor of the play.

One last element needs to be noticed in Act III scene i: the teasing quality of Isabella's informing her brother of Angelo's offer. Isabella is very brisk in the opening of this scene, in which she is to inform her brother that there is no hope for a reprieve, remarking to the Provost that 'her business is a word or two with Claudio'. In addressing her brother, a man condemned to the block, and resigned to his fate, her first words carry a kind of taunt:

> Lord Angelo, having affairs to heaven,
> Intends you for his swift ambassador.

> (III i 55)

Claudio, indeed, is actually forced into his great, dramatic outcry on the fear of death, not by the 'truth of honour' in her, that she has been put in an intolerable position, but by her teasingly repeated suspicion that if she were to tell Claudio how he might be saved (but she won't!), he would not be enough of a man to die for her. She plays a grim game with a man facing the axe, hinting, hesitating, but not quite telling, how he may escape death. It is she who actually maneuvers him from his mood of resignation to the point where he will be forced to ask her to accept Angelo's offer.

And the sudden appearance of the merciless Isabella at
this juncture, crying to Claudio

> Mercy to thee would prove itself a bawd:
> 'Tis best that thou diest quickly   (III i 148)

is the second of the two climactic ironies of *Measure for
Measure*. The merciless pleader for mercy is neatly
poised in paradox against the lustful puritan.

   Measure for Measure pivots on these two reversals in
its paired champions of virtue. Indeed, the turning of
Isabella on Claudio is the turning of the whole play on
itself so that real justice and real mercy may eventually
win out. Does the play collapse with Isabella's reviling
of her brother, as it has been argued? Or does the play
move into theological allegory here? Neither, I think.
'There has been so great a fever on goodness,' the Duke
tells Escalus, 'that the dissolution of it must cure it' (III
ii 241). What Tillyard describes as Isabella's 'hushed
and submissive tones' to the Duke ('Let me hear you
speak farther. I have the spirit to do anything that
appears not foul in the truth of my spirit'), it seems to
me are rather the intended and dramatically effective
beginning of the dissolution of her overweening 'goodness', the beginning of her redemption into actual,
livable goodness. Her subsequent role as a kind of
pander in the Mariana episode, contradicts the absolute chastity to which she had first committed herself,
no doubt, as she permits Angelo to show her the way to
the assignation 'twice o'er'. But it represents her first
surrender to a more measured, less absolute, mercy,
whereby she can come to plead for Angelo in the end,
and can thus be finally aware of her own humanity.

   Measure for Measure, then, I consider a very great
comedy despite its dogmatically hostile critics, and despite its eagerly theological analysts who find it a
simple matter to name 'its lesson driven home'.[14]
Surely, however, it has no more easily definable meaning than has *Hamlet*. One can demonstrate its inherent

design, but its 'meaning' is, as always in art, impossible to extract into a neat phrase from its complex structure of conflicting attitudes and feelings. The play has illustrated merciless chastity and merciless justice in action, and has shown the possibility of their mitigation. But we have certainly not witnessed a narrow homily on mercy, I think. The various and shifting points of view toward the passive 'natural guiltiness' of humanity at the center of the play have been dramatized, as is usual in Shakespeare, rather than evaluated. We have not been called upon to judge Claudio's slip, nor Lucio's. We have not been asked to evaluate Isabella's chastity any more than we have been called upon to evaluate that of Elbow's wife.

As in reading one of Donne's most intellectual, teasing and subtle poems, so in reading or in seeing *Measure for Measure*: we find that with its design completed, the perimeter of our awareness of important things we already half knew about human potentiality for good and evil has been perceptibly extended. The meaning of *Measure for Measure* resides, however, not in a scholar's notes on history or on theology, but in our capacity to respond to the amplitude of the play's dramatic design of irony and paradox, its demonstration of the enormous range of human response, as focussed and caught between justice and mercy.

Source: *English Literary History*, XXIII iv, 1956.

NOTES

1. Mary Lascelles invents the phrase in *Shakespeare's 'Measure for Measure'* (London, 1953).
2. 'Authority, Truth, and Justice in *Measure for Measure*,' *RES* XVII (1941) 399
3. 'Ben Jonson', in *Elizabethan Essays* (London, 1934) p. 67.
4. 'The Greatness of *Measure for Measure*', in *The*

Importance of Scrutiny, ed. Eric Bentley (New York, 1948) p. 154.

5. Ibid., p 161

6. Battenhouse, PMLA LXI (1946) p. 1046

7. *The Plays of William Shakespare* (London, 1765) I 321.

8. *Measure for Measure,* ed. Sir Arthur Quiller-Couch and John Dover Wilson (Cambridge, 1922) p. xxx.

9. 'Shakespeare as Casuist: *Measure for Measure',* *Sewanee Review,* LXVIII ii (1950) 273.

10. *A Poet's Notebook* (Boston, 1950) p. 128.

11. *Shakespeare* (New York, 1939) p. 221.

12. In his identifying Isabella as a novice of a religious order, and in his pairing her off with the Duke, Shakespeare seems to have remembered the character Lucia Bella of Whetstone's *An Heptameron of Civill Discourses* (London, 1582). Whetstone's Lucia Bella 'who in the beginning of Christmasse, was determyned to have beene a vestall Nunne' (Sig. Z$_2$), and who had defended the single life in the debates, is won over to an acceptance of marriage after the seventh day's entertainment.

13. *Seven Types of Ambiguity,* 3rd ed. (London, 1953) p. 202.

14. See p. 94 above.

JUSTICE AND KING JAMES IN
MEASURE FOR MEASURE (1963)

In his views on Justice Shakespeare is by no means an isolated figure in his own day, but has most humanist writers, from Sir Thomas Elyot to Bacon and King James, behind him. A thesis directly opposite to this is advanced by E. T. Sehrt in the work previously cited. He argues that Shakespeare's view of the relation of Justice and Mercy is essentially at odds with the prevailing view of his own day, whether Puritan or humanist. For while the Puritans turned to the Old Testament conception of Justice, with its insistence on severe and rigorous punishment and the humanists pleaded for equity and clemency, Shakespeare returned to the medieval conception of Mercy as abrogating rather than mitigating punishment. This conception, almost unique in Shakespeare's day, he finds expressed in Portia's and Isabel's mercy-speeches. It stems from Shakespeare's increasing sense of man's weakness and his dependence on God's grace. I have no space to dispute at length the validity of this thesis, which is argued cogently, learnedly, and throughout an entire book. I would merely make two points, as far as it affects *Measure for Measure*. First, had Shakespeare's concern in this play really been to stress man's need for a mercy which does not 'shake hands with her sister Justice', but which abrogates rather than mitigates it, it seems more than unlikely that he would have introduced into the same play the Duke's insistence on the evils to which his past failure to punish offenders has given rise, or have made the wise and kindly Escalus declare, 'Mercy is not itself that oft looks so; / Pardon is still the nurse of second woe' (II i 269–70). Secondly, the fact that Isabel, in her plea for her brother's life, talks of mercy and *not*, like her counterparts in Cinthio and Whetstone, of equity, seems to me not, as Professor Sehrt claims, to be an expression of the mature Shakespeare's Christian outlook, his sense of man's frailty and his need for absolute pardon, but rather to stem from his wish, for reasons discussed above, to make Isabel consider the sentence just, and therefore not to be disputed on the grounds of equity.[1] But though she talks of mercy and not of equity, I do not think that she speaks of a mercy that takes the place of justice, but rather, like Portia, of a mercy that seasons and mitigates it. (In the final pardon extended by the Duke to Angelo and to Barnardine such an abrogation of Justice by Mercy no doubt is found. But we are surely to see this neither, with some commentators, as an expression of the play's teachings on the relation of Mercy and Justice, nor, with others, as a sign that the Duke has learnt nothing and has lapsed again into his old habit of excessive clemency, but rather as an amnesty, which allows the play to end as happily as Shakespeare could contrive.[2])

I come now to my final point about the Duke in *Measure for Measure*. In 1799 the Scottish Antiquarian George Chalmers wrote: 'The commentators seem not to have remarked, that the character of *the Duke*, is a very accurate delineation of that of King James, which Shakespeare appears to have caught, with great felicity, and to have sketched, with much truth.' And he added, 'Knowing that King James's writings; his *Basilikon Doron*; his *True Law of Free Monarchies*; and other treatises; had been, emulously, republished in 1603, by the London booksellers, in many editions, Shakespeare could not fitly give a closer parody.'[3] This claim, though echoed by Charles Knight,[4] received little attention until it was taken up and developed at great length by the German scholar Louis Albrecht in his study of the play published in 1914. Albrecht maintained that *Measure for Measure* was written as an act of homage to the King upon his accession to the throne of England, that James's tract on 'the properties of government', the *Basilikon Doron* (written *c*. 1598), constitutes one of the chief sources of the play, that the Duke was intended to be recognized as an idealized portrait of James, and that the whole play was written, from first to last, with an eye upon the King's special interests and predilections.[5] This thesis, too, was largely ignored by commentators, or referred to only to be curtly dismissed. Quite recently an American scholar, David L. Stevenson, unaware, apparently, of the existence of both Chalmers's and Albrecht's discussions, has put forward a very similar thesis, declaring that *Measure for Measure* 'is a play in which the political element bears the conscious and unmistakable imprint of the predilections of James I himself as Shakespeare and his London audience were aware of them in the first flush of the post-Elizabethan era'; that the poet 'deliberately sketched in Duke Vincentio a character whose behaviour as a ruler would be attractive to James (and therefore to a Jacobean audience) because it followed patterns which the King had publicly advocated'; and that 'Shakespeare, we may infer, was as anxiously (if more subtly) courting James I with *Measure for Measure* as was a Bilson, for example, in his flattering repetition of James's opinions in his "Coronation Sermon", or as was a Barlow in his flattering portrait of James's role in the Hampton Court Conference'. Quoting many of the same parallels between *Measure for Measure* and the *Basilikon Doron* as Albrecht, Stevenson comes to much the same conclusion: 'One is forced to think that Shakespeare carefully mined the *Basilikon Doron* in order to be able to dramatize the intellectual interests of his new patron in his comedy.'[6]

In discussing the validity of these theses it will be usful to distinguish between two quite separate though related claims: (1) that *Measure for Measure* was deliberately made to turn upon themes which were of special interest to James, whether this was done in order to pay homage to the King, as Albrecht claims, or to court his favour by flattery, as Stevenson maintains,

or to exploit the current public interest in the theory
of government which was inspired by the accession of
James, as Miss Pope suggests;[7] and (2) that the Duke is
drawn as an image of James, whether this is to be regarded as an idealized image, as Albrecht and Stevenson contend, or as 'a very accurate delineation', as
Chalmers asserts.

The first of these claims seems to me to have a great
deal of plausibility (among the three I would favour
Albrecht's hypothesis of the play's principal *raison
d'être*, which, of course, does not exclude Miss Pope's).
And it is much strengthened by the analogous case of
Macbeth, where again Shakespeare seems deliberately
to have written a play on themes that were of special
interest to the King and on which the latter had published erudite works (indeed, it could be said that the
Basilikon Doron is to *Measure for Measure* what it and
the *Daemonology* together are to *Macbeth*). That
Shakespeare had read the *Basilikon Doron* before writing *Measure for Measure* is inherently probable. It was
unquestionably the Book-of-the-Year in 1603, when it
went through one Scottish and two English editions.
'This book,' wrote Francis Bacon, 'falling into every
man's hand, filled the whole realm as with a good per-
fume or incense before the King's coming in....'[8] But
though many of the views on Justice and Good Rule in
the *Basilikon Doron* find fairly exact parallels in
Shakespeare's play, these are of too commonplace a
nature to prove indebtedness in the absence of close
verbal echoes. (As a typical instance of this tantalizing
relationship compare the Duke's

> Thyself and thy belongings
> Are not thine own so proper as to waste
> Thyself upon thy virtues, they on thee.
> Heaven doth with us as we with torches do,
> Not light them for themselves; for if our virtues
> Did not go forth of us, 'Twere all alike
> As if we had them not.

(I i 29–36)

with the following passage from the *Basilikon Doron*:
'For it is not ynough that ye haue and retaine (as
prisoners) within your selfe neuer so many good qualities and vertues, except ye employ them, and set them
on worke, for the weale of them that are committed to
your charge: *Virtutis enim laus omnis in actione con-
sistit.*[9])

As for the second claim – that the Duke is drawn as
an image of James – I think both Albrecht *and* Chalmers are right: that it is an idealized image, made up
of the qualities in a ruler which James in his writings
had particularly praised; and that it is yet sufficiently
particularized, and endowed with traits peculiar to the
King, to enable Shakespeare's audience and James
himself to recognize the likeness. Several of these idio-
syncrasies, such as the Duke's dislike of the people's
'loud applause and Aves vehement' (I i 71), his fond-
ness for mystifying his subjects and playing cat-and-
mouse with them, his description of himself, 'let him be
but testimonied in his own bringings-forth, and he
shall appear to the envious a scholar, a statesman, and
a soldier' (III ii 133–5), in that significant order[10]
(compare also the order of his words to Lucio at the
end of the play, 'You, sirrah, that knew me for a fool, a
coward, / One all of luxury, an ass, a madman!' What
smarts most is Lucio's denial of his sagacity) – all these
when taken together seem to me too uniquely characteristic of James to be dismissed as mere accidental
likenesses. Even the one trait in the Duke which does
not accord with the presentation of him as a model
ruler, his failure to enforce the laws with sufficient
severity, fits James, who in the *Basilikon Doron* confesses to have been over-lax in punishing offenders at
the beginning of his reign, and to have reaped only
disorder.[11]

What further supports the hypothesis that the Duke
is deliberately drawn as an image of James is the fact
that it may help to explain the presence in the play of
at least two somewhat puzzling passages. One is the
Duke's denunciation of 'newfangledness', which seems

curiously isolated, not linking up with any of the satiric preoccupations of the rest of the play. To Escalus's question, 'What news abroad i' th' world?', the Duke replies, 'none, but that there is so great a fever on goodness that the dissolution of it must cure it. Novelty is only in request; and it is as dangerous to be aged in any kind of course as it is to be inconstant in any undertaking.[12] (III ii 208–11). But James was much given to denouncing newfangledness. In the *Basilikon Doron*, for instance, Shakespeare would have read: 'But vnto one fault is all the common people of this kingdome subiect, as well burgh as land; which is, to iudge and speake rashly of their Prince, setting the Common-weale vpon foure props, as wee call it; euer wearying of the present estate, and desirous of nouelties.'[13] The other puzzling passage is the Duke's words upon first hearing of Barnardine: 'How came it that the absent Duke had not either deliver'd him to his liberty or executed him? I have heard it was ever his manner to do so' (IV ii 124–6). This *penchant* for the two extremes of free pardon and immediate execution, surprising in a model ruler, may, perhaps, be explained as an illusion to an action by James upon first coming into England (25 April 1603) which caused much comment: at Newark he had a cutpurse, taken in the act, hanged at once without trial, while at the same time he commanded all the prisoners in the Castle to be set free.[14]

Lastly, the hypothesis helps to explain the sentence initially imposed upon Lucio by the Duke (v i 505 ff.). Its extreme harshness (whipping and hanging) comes as a shock, epecially through its juxtaposition with the free pardon which Angelo has just received. It becomes much more comprehensible in the light of James's notorious sensitiveness to slander, which led to the passing of a Scottish Act of Parliament in 1585 that made slander of the King a treasonable offence, punishable with death. Several people were, in fact, executed under this act, one in 1596 for calling James 'ane bastarde'.[15]

It seems to me, then, that the view that in the Duke Shakespeare drew an image of James, partly as he was, partly as he would like to have been or was then thought to be, is supported by too much evidence to be dismissed. And it may help to account for another fact often remarked upon by critics: the shadowiness of the Duke, compared to the other main *dramatis personae*. For, paradoxically, dramatic characters become less 'real' the more they are modelled on living persons and the less they are conceived wholly in the poet's imagination.[16]

An acceptance of the belief (which I share with Albrecht and Stevenson) that *Measure for Measure* deliberately turns upon themes which were of special interest to James, and that the views on Justice and Good Rule which it expresses are closely similar to those found in the political writings of the King, in no way compels one to see the play less as an expression of Shakespeare's most personal and sincerely held convictions. For, as I have said, Shakespeare's own views on these matters seem to have been in close accord with those of the King and other humanist writers of his day. I do not find anything peculiarly Christian in these views. James's own references in support of them are to ancient, pre-Christian writers, such as Aristotle, Cicero, and Seneca. They are views held by humane and enlightened men in all ages.

Indeed, the claim, which has been reiterated so much in recent years, that *Measure for Measure* expresses a specifically Christian ethos seems to me without foundation.

SOURCE: *The Problem Plays of Shakespeare*, 1963

NOTES

1. [Editor's note.] Schanzer has agreed that Isabel remains ignorant of the fact that her brother and Juliet are (legally) 'married'.

2. Though I have taken issue with its main thesis, Professor Sehrt's book contains much that is valuable and from which I have profited, including an exemplary discussion of the sources of *Measure for Measure*.

3. *A Supplemental Apology for the Believers in the Shakespeare-Papers* (1799) pp. 404–5.

4. *Studies of Shakespeare* (1849) p. 319.

5. Albrecht's thesis, like so many of the doctoral kind, suffers from being pushed too far (e.g. when he argues that Isabel represents an idealized image of James's wife, Queen Anne, even the most sympathetic must cry a halt), and from his failure to discriminate between important and trivial or between persuasive and wholly unpersuasive points of resemblance.

6. 'The Role of James I in Shakespeare's *Measure for Measure*', *ELH* XXVI (1959) 188, 189, 207, 196.

7. *Shakespeare Survey* II (1949) p. 70.

8. *Works*, ed. Spedding (1878) VI 278–9.

9. *Basilikon Doron*, p. 30. Both Albrecht and Stevenson compare the two passages.

10. This has also been pointed out by Albrecht. An additional point, which I have not seen made by anyone, is the use of the word 'bringings-forth'. For what can the Duke's 'bringings-forth' that bear testimony to his scholarship refer to except publications, or, less plausibly, public disputations, on learned matters? In either case, few people in the audience could have failed to be reminded of James.

11. p. 20.

12. I have adopted the emendation, first proposed by Staunton, of F's 'constant' to 'inconstant', which seems to me imperative. For the Duke to be saying that the danger of constancy is equal to its virtue is much too tame for the satiric context.

13. p. 27. The parallel has been pointed out by Albrecht.

14. See *A Jacobean Journal*, ed. G. B. Harrison (1941) p. 15. Stevenson oddly refers to this incident – without relating it to the passage in the play – as an example of how 'James had actually put theory into action' (*ELH*

XXVI 202). To me it seems rather an example of the notorious lack of accord between James's precepts and his practice.

15. See Craigie's note in his edition of the *Basilikon Doron* (1950) II 208.

16. It is, of course, true that the Duke's shadowiness is partly – but not, I think, entirely – due to his functions in the play.

SELECT BIBLIOGRAPHY

EDITIONS OF 'MEASURE FOR MEASURE' WITH USEFUL INTRO-
DUCTION AND NOTES

The New Cambridge edition, ed. Sir Arthur Quiller-
Couch and J. Dover Wilson (1922 and 1950).
Signet Classics edition, ed. S. Nagarajan (New York,
1964).
The New Arden edition, ed. J. W. Lever (Methuen,
1965).
The New Penguin edition, ed. J. M. Nosworthy (1969).

BOOKS ON 'MEASURE FOR MEASURE'

Mary Lascelles, *Shakespeare's 'Measure for Measure'*
(1953)
Comment on this very valuable book is made in
the Introduction. (footnote to p. 31.)
David L. Stevenson, *The Achievement of Shakespeare's
'Measure for Measure'* (Cornell University, 1968).
A full development of the point of view sketched
out in Stevenson's article reproduced in this
collection. Comment on this point of view is made
in the Introduction.

BOOKS CONTAINING CHAPTERS ON 'MEASURE TO MEASURE'

E. K. Chambers, *Shakespeare: A Survey* (1925; Pelican
Books, 1964). Chambers sees the play as an expression of Shakespeare's 'loss of faith,' at this
period of his development. Though Chambers's
biographical approach has gone out of fashion
for good reasons, he is always worth reading.

R. W. Chambers, *Man's Unconquerable Mind* (1939). Chambers' spirited defence of the play has had considerable influence. It makes some useful observations, but as a whole it proceeds rhetorically rather than analytically. In particular it depends too much on assertions of what Shakespeare *intends* us to feel, rather than a proper consideration of what we *do* feel.

F. R. Leavis, *The Common Pursuit* (1952). Leavis's article on *Measure for Measure* first appeared in *Scrutiny*, x (1942), in answer to the one by L. C. Knights reprinted in this volume. It is discussed in the Introduction. Dr Leavis would not grant permission for its inclusion in this collection.

E. E. Stoll, *From Shakespeare to Joyce* (1946). Stoll's excellent chapter on *Measure for Measure* is omitted from this collection only in order to keep a proper balance among various points of view.

Donald A. Stauffer, *Shakespeare's World of Images* (1949). A moderate and tactful application of the idea of the Duke as a semi-divine figure. Stauffer feels that Shakespeare's concerns in the play are essentially moral concerns, but that they do not translate into fully credible drama.

Harold C. Goddard, *The Meaning of Shakespeare*, II (1951). Goddard's two volumes on Shakespeare deserve more attention than they have received. His chapter on *Measure for Measure* is typical in revealing the wisdom of the critic as well as that of the play.

Arthur Sewell, *Character and Society in Shakespeare* (1951). Contains some sound observations, particularly on the character of Angelo.

D. A. Traversi, *An Approach to Shakespeare* (1957). The bulk and detail of Traversi's studies of Shakespeare make him a figure to be reckoned with. He proceeds by close analysis, on the assumption that every word and phrase is there to serve a moral purpose. The personality and experience of the *critic* are never brought into the picture. The more the method is expanded, the more mechanical it seems, and the resulting studies make somewhat exhausting reading.

A. P. Rossiter, *Angel with Horns,* ed. Graham Storey (1961). Rossiter's posthumously published lecture on the play contains a number of refreshing and sensible observations. He is particularly good on the character of Isabella.

Peter Ure, *Shakespeare's Problem Plays* (1961). Ure's pamphlet on these plays contains a useful introduction to *Measure for Measure.*

Ernest Schanzer, *The Problem Plays of Shakespeare* (1963). Only a small part of Schanzer's long chapter on *Measure for Measure* is reprinted in this collection. The whole chapter is worthy of attention.

ARTICLES ON 'MEASURE FOR MEASURE'

M. C. Bradbrook, 'Authority, Truth and Justice in *Measure for Measure,' Modern Language Review* (1946).

Elizabeth M. Pope, 'The Renaissance Background of *Measure for Measure,' Shakespeare Survey* II (1949).

R. M. Smith, 'Interpretations of *Measure for Measure,' Shakespeare Quarterly* (1950).

Nevill Coghill, 'Comic Form in *Measure for Measure,' Shakespeare Survey* VIII (1955).

Sydney Musgrove, 'Some composite Scenes in *Measure for Measure,' Shakespeare Quarterly* (1964).

NOTES ON CONTRIBUTORS

RICHARD DAVID: Secretary to the Syndics, Cambridge University Press, since 1963. His publications include *The Janns of Poets*, the Arden Edition of *Love's Labour's Lost*, and articles on the production of Shakespeare's plays in *Shakespeare Survey* and other periodicals.

WILLIAM EMPSON: distinguished English poet and critic. Author of *Seven Types of Ambiguity*, *Some Versions of Pastoral*, *The Structure of Complex Words*, etc. Professor of English at Sheffield University.

HAROLD HOBSON: theatre critic for the London *Sunday Times*.

G. WILSON KNIGHT: one of the most prolific and influential Shakesperian critics of this century. Emeritus Professor of English Literature in the University of Leeds. His books on Shakespeare include *The Wheel of Fire*, *The Crown of Life* and *The Imperial Theme*.

L. C. KNIGHTS: one of the original *Scrutiny* group. Formerly Winterstoke Professor of English in the University of Bristol. Now King Edward VII Professor of English at Cambridge. Author of *Drama and Society in the Age of Jonson*, *Explorations*, *Some Shakespearean Themes*, etc.

W. W. LAWRENCE: retired from his Professorship at Columbia University, New York, in 1936, and died in 1958. His books include *Beowulf and the Epic Tradition* and *Chaucer and the Canterbury Tales*. His *Shakespeare's Problem Comedies* was recently reissued by Penguin Books.

CLIFFORD LEECH: since 1964 Professor and Chairman of the English Department, University College, Toronto. Has written a great deal on the drama, from Elizabethan and Jacobean to O'Neill.

W. W. ROBSON. Fellow of Lincoln College, Oxford. Well known as an essayist and reviewer. In 1968 published a collection of poems, *The Signs Among Us*.

ERNEST SCHANZER: educated in Austria, England and Canada. Has lectured at the universities of Toronto and Liverpool.

DAVID L. STEVENSON: Professor of English at Hunter College (New York) and a frequent writer on Shakespeare and related topics.

E. M. W. TILLYARD: Master of Jesus College, Cambridge, 1945–59, and a leading scholar in both Shakespeare and Milton studies. His books include *Shakespeare's History Plays*, *The Elizabethan World Picture*, and *The Epic Strain in The English Novel*. He died in 1962.

INDEX

The italicised page references indicate the main treatment of the characters and subjects.